"Offshore cruising in an open boat can be hard, cold, wet, lonely and occasionally miserable, but it is exhilarating too. To take an open dinghy across a hundred miles of sea, taking weather as it comes; to know that you have only yourself and your mate to rely on in an emergency; to see the beauty of dawn creep across the ever restless and dangerous ocean; to make a safe landfall—is wonderful and all of these things develop a self-reliance that is missing from the modern, mechanical, safety-conscious civilised world."

Frank Dye, *Ocean Crossing Wayfarer,* 1977

BLOKES UP NORTH

by
KEV OLIVER & TONY LANCASHIRE

*Through the Heart of the
Northwest Passage
by Sail and Oar*

With a Foreword by SIR ROBIN KNOX-JOHNSTON

Published by
Lodestar Books
71 Boveney Road, London, SE23 3NL, United Kingdom

lodestarbooks.com

Copyright © Kev Oliver and Tony Lancashire 2014
Foreword copyright © Sir Robin Knox-Johnston 2014

All rights reserved.

A CIP catalogue record for this book
is available from the British Library

ISBN 978-1-907206-24-5

Typeset by Lodestar Books in Equity

Printed in Spain by Graphy Cems, Navarra

All papers used by Lodestar Books
are sourced responsibly

The authors' royalties have been assigned to the
Royal Marines Charitable Trust Fund
which exists to provide a better quality of life
to serving and retired Royal Marines and their families.
rmctf.org.uk

For our mothers,

Sheila Oliver (1936-1986)
and
Sandra Lancashire

CONTENTS

	Foreword by Sir Robin Knox-Johnston	9
	The Route	12-13
I	DREAMS TO REALITY	15
II	MACKENZIE AND TUK	43
III	OPEN WATER IN AN OPEN BOAT	67
IV	TRAPPED IN THE FREEZER	90
V	VISITORS ON THE DEW LINE	124
VI	FRANKLIN, AMUNDSEN AND GJOA	154
VII	INTERLUDE	182
VIII	HEADING NORTH	191
IX	POLAR HIGHS AND POLAR BEARS	203
X	JOURNEYS, NOT DESTINATIONS	223
	The Boat	234
	Kit List & Stowage Plan	236
	Further Reading	237
	Acknowledgements	238

FOREWORD

When we at Clipper Ventures were asked to help to sponsor the expedition by Kevin Oliver and Tony Lancashire, we looked long and hard. Plenty of such applications come in to us but this one was different. In the first place it was from Royal Marines, and I have always admired the Corps. Secondly, this expedition was to try something extremely difficult, perhaps not possible, but if we always flinched from attempting the difficult things in life then humans would never have progressed. Thirdly, we are living in an increasingly risk-averse society, but risk is what makes the adrenalin flow, brings spice into our lives and shows others that risks are part of living. Far from being discouraged it should be supported.

From the expedition of Martin Frobisher in 1576, European explorers have searched for a sea route to China around the north of the American continent. Expedition after expedition failed, the toll in lives being very heavy, the most famous being that of Captain Franklin in 1848 when the entire crew of the two vessels perished through starvation and the cold. The Canadian North-West Passage, the ice-filled gap between the bare north coast of Canada and its off-lying islands and the Arctic ice cap, proved to be impassable until the beginning of the 20th century. But then the voyage was completed in specially built, strengthened vessels, with shelter and protection from the freezing waters and icy, biting winds. Ice is as hard as floating rock. You navigate through it with great caution as one lapse in concentration, one bang instead of a brush against an ice flow, can lead to the boat being holed and sinking.

Despite the passage of a few large, well found and specially built vessels in recent years, as global warming has reduced the ice thickness, the route from the

Atlantic to the Pacific oceans via the North-West Passage has yet to become a regular route for trade. The depth of the ice may have diminished but the quantity is still there, and it is only possible to navigate through for about four months in each year.

It is into this remote, partially explored region that two Britons decided to venture in a ridiculously small 17-foot open boat. The Royal Marines are a Corps that actively seeks testing adventure, it is part of their nature, but despite Arctic warfare training, this was going to call upon all their resources of stamina and self-reliance and push them to their limits.

This was a voyage that needed to be made and a story that had to be told.

RKJ

Publisher's Note

This book is written by Kev Oliver and Tony Lancashire, each in his own 'voice,' giving two perpectives on events and on their personal interactions during the voyage described. To indicate the current writer we have placed a discreet inital in the left-hand margin where the 'voice' changes.

Waiting out the northerlies at Tasmania Island →

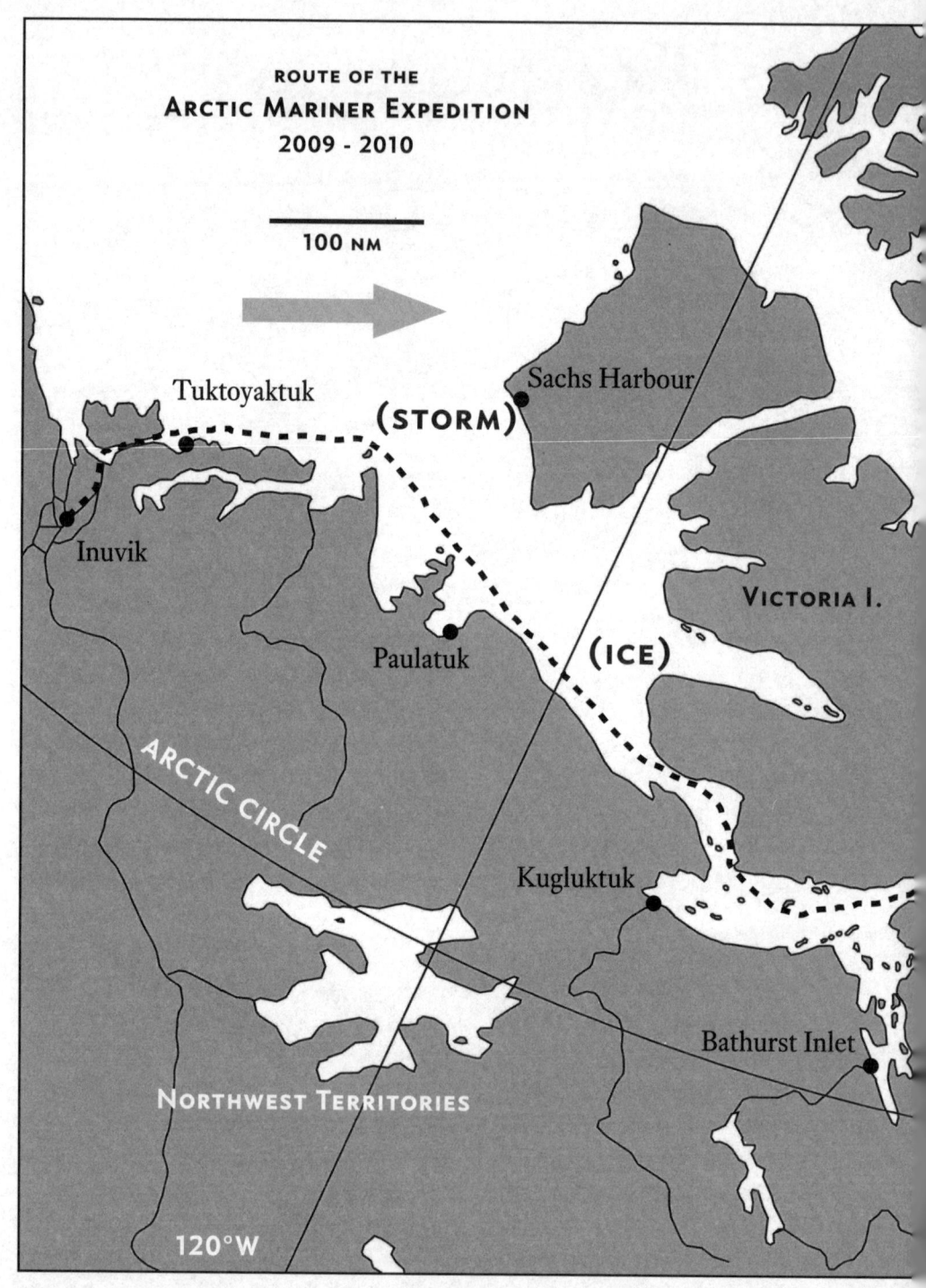

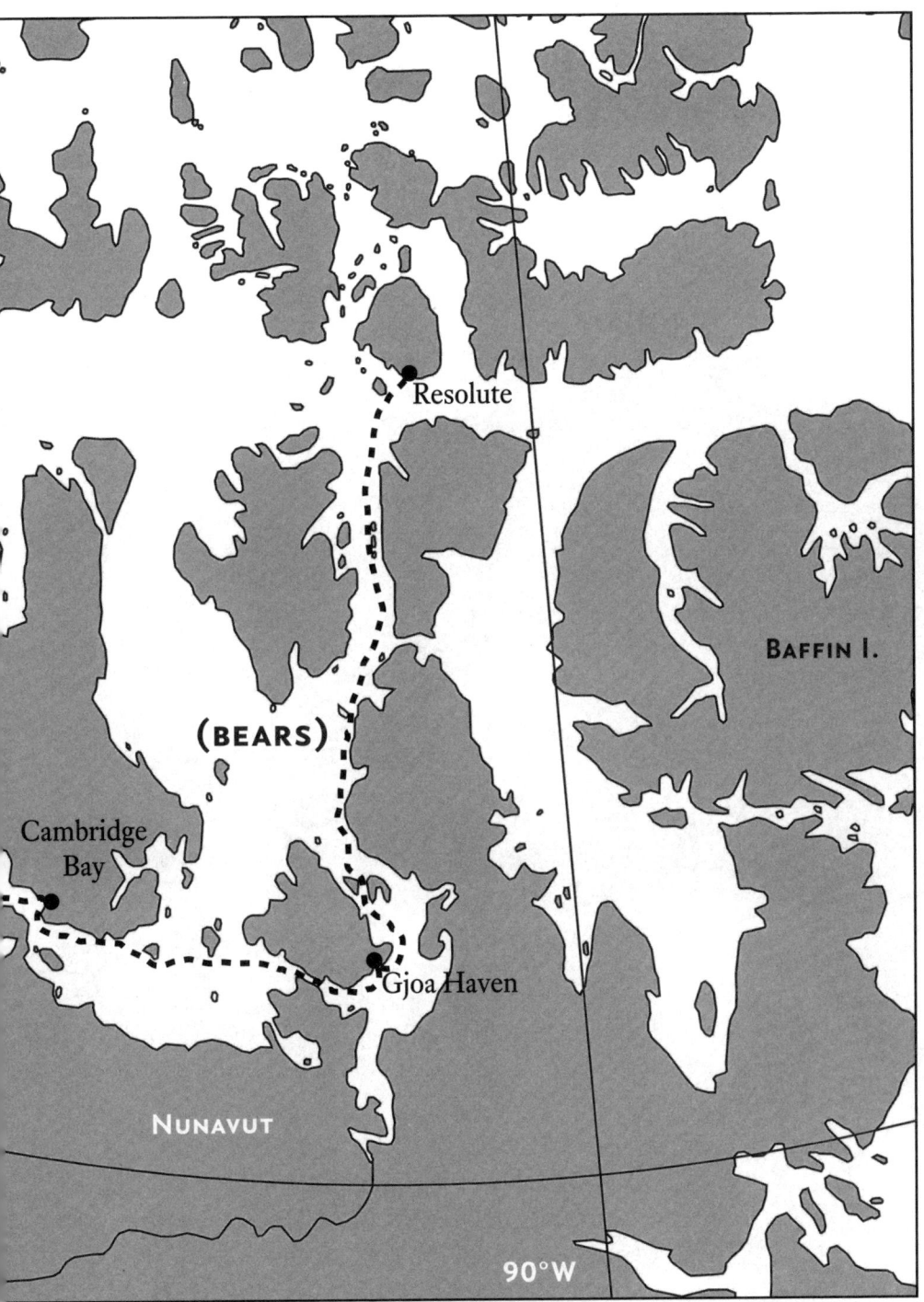

I

DREAMS TO REALITY

Soon after my 40th birthday a mate asked me if I wanted to join him rowing the Atlantic as part of a six man team. For a whole host of reasons it didn't work out for either of us. Shortly before Christmas 2007 we were in a pub and he asked me if I wanted to put together our own campaign for a two man Atlantic attempt. Or something else. I thought for a moment and then, and I can't remember exactly why, I said "Let's row the Northwest Passage." I didn't really fancy the boredom of an Atlantic crossing. Nothing to see but ocean, day after day. Whilst I can understand and would probably relish the challenge, it doesn't strike me as being fun. The Northwest Passage seemed much more up my street.

I've always been a climber, but not a particularly talented one. I climb because of the view and the situations you can get yourself into, and from which you then have to work a way out. Mountaineering was a natural progression from roadside crags, but in my late teens, rather than hard routes in Scotland or the Alps I was fortunate enough to be able to pursue my passion for seeking remoteness in the Andes, and later the Himalayas, the Ruwenzori and Patagonia. I also enjoyed yachting, having been brought up with dinghy sailing and family yachting while living in Greece aged seven to twelve. Having dabbled on the odd flotilla holiday as an adult, I got back into yachting in 2005, vaguely with a view to taking a boat to Greenland. The idea of having everything you need in a boat in which you can journey exactly fits with my attraction to self-contained mountain expeditioning—small groups of climbers carrying your own gear rather than a massive Himalayan trip with yaks, porters and cooks. I also have an innate aversion to employing guides. Some may call it arrogance, but for me travelling and expeditions are about freedom and self-determination. My philosophy is that if something is too dangerous for the team to deal with without a guide, then we shouldn't be doing it. I have almost exclusively organised and led all the trips I have been on myself—partly because I was rarely asked to go on other peoples' expeditions, but also probably because I wanted to pursue my own ideas. I was fortunate that a career in the Marines had provided plenty of opportunity for adventure, both in work and during periods of leave.

My interest in the Northwest Passage lay not so much in the history, but the remoteness. I had read some history, largely an account of the expeditions that the then Second Lord of the Admiralty, John Barrow sent there in the nineteenth century. After initial exploration of the possibilities of a route to connect Europe with Asia, long before either the Suez or Panama canals, it was the determined effort of Victorian Britain through Franklin's expedition of 1845-48 that amazed me. It has been compared to the effort to put men on the moon, which is probably an exaggeration in terms of the technical and financial effort expended but not in the depth of the unknown that the men experienced. Franklin's expedition met with spectacular failure, most probably because lead used in the solder on the revolutionary tin cans poisoned the crew. The ships were eventually lost off the north coast of King William Island right in the heart of the passage. What was more incredible was that they went lavishly equipped for several years at sea with all the trappings of Naval life including candelabras for use with dinner — but no sledging equipment. Between 1847 and 1859 a total of thirty-six expeditions searched, initially for the men themselves, and then to try to establish what had become of them. It quickly became clear that the men had suffered the most appalling hardship, and had almost certainly resorted to cannibalism as they desperately searched for a route south to safety. None survived. I quickly realised that whilst we weren't taking candelabras or any other luxuries, and were sailing a tiny boat just a fraction of the size of their proud ships, no matter what happened to us on our journey our experience could not compare with those of the early pioneers. Despite us having charts, global positioning systems and satellite phones it would certainly offer a host of challenges of its own.

Following several further abortive attempts in the late 19th century, it took until 1906 for the Northwest Passage to be navigated. Roald Amundsen, who was later to beat Scott to the South Pole, took three seasons to force the passage, wintering twice in the Arctic and learning from the local Inuit as he went along. The real attraction of the Northwest Passage to me was in the very fact that it was a journey through interesting remote waters but never that far from land. This meant we could not only observe the (we hoped) stunning scenery but also seek shelter in a storm. I wasn't sure if it had ever been rowed, but on early investigation of the distances involved and the ice coverage, I quickly convinced myself that this was going to be hard enough as it was without deliberately shunning the use of free wind. After all, I wasn't going for the purpose of doing a first or breaking a record, I was simply going to have a look around. And so the concept became that it should be an open boat that could be rowed or sailed.

A strange set of conflicting factors were forming in my mind—size leads to cost, and I didn't know how I would fund it, I needed an 'angle' around which to raise the funds, and so the idea of a first traverse in an open boat was born. It had to be an open boat to distinguish it from a yachting trip, and perhaps more pertinently I knew of no-one who was prepared to lend me a yacht to go through the Northwest Passage.

I had been inspired by H.W. Tilman, who deliberately took his sturdy ex pilot cutter yachts to the far north and the far south through the 1960s and 1970s. Tilman was very much a modern day explorer, having been involved in a series of expeditions with Eric Shipton in the Himalayas before World War II; he then earned a formidable reputation during the war. He spent his retirement conducting a series of exploratory trips with volunteer crews, first far south then north around Greenland, although few of his crew made a subsequent trip with him; most were put off by his ability to endure the harsh conditions. Like many people I was also in awe of Ernest Shackleton's famous open boat journey from Elephant Island to South Georgia, conducted out of necessity to survive when his entire crew were marooned in Antarctica after his ship sank, having been crushed in the ice. In a remarkable piece of seamanship, and no small amount of good fortune, they steered a converted lifeboat over 800 miles across one of the most dangerous pieces of ocean on the planet.

As with previous ambitious projects, I simply refused to believe that it wasn't possible. Initially, the plan was to 'just' attempt the central part of the passage from Kugluktuk, formerly known as Coppermine, to Resolute, a distance of about a thousand miles, in about five weeks. I bought and read a series of books on high latitude sailing and kayaking. I was particularly inspired by a book that had just been written about a circumnavigation of Spitzbergen in 1991 by an old friend of mine from the Marines, Phil Ashby and the author Peter Webb whom I had met briefly at Phil's second wedding a few weeks earlier. It was a remarkable feat; two nineteen-year-olds with minimum safety equipment and an old Norwegian-designed open rowing boat, with a makeshift looking sail. A quick search of the internet for a sturdy boat that could be sailed and rowed led me to Norseboat, a small company in Nova Scotia making 'Sailing-Rowing Camp Cruisers.'

I read Frank Dye's account of taking a 16-foot open Wayfarer dinghy to Iceland and Norway from the UK in the sixties. Reading this remarkable book served two purposes; it made me realise that such voyages could be achieved with the right mental and physical preparation and adequate risk assessment of such a venture. I was particularly worried by his account of when they capsized in a storm. The boat rolled, of course everything got wet and they lost some equipment, but they survived. I seriously admired someone prepared to challenge the sea in such a way but certainly wasn't prepared to take the risk they had. They were without reliable communications, a life raft or other safety equipment. However, it was clear that he was a master helmsman with years of experience, something which I patently didn't possess.

I always wondered how many adventurers had set off to wild unexplored places, and were either lost at sea, or spent months or even years marooned on Arctic islands never to be heard of again. Until recently we only knew the stories of the incredibly talented or lucky who got through an ordeal and lived to tell the tale. We could benefit from modern technology: satellite communications, emergency beacons and a self-inflating life raft and GPS navigation, but even so, capsize was still my biggest fear and remained so throughout the expedition. Returning to Frank Dye, whose inspiring quotation we used to introduce this book, I was also struck by the superb photograph of Dye's companion carving a slice off a whole cooked chicken that seemed to make up the majority of their rations. We would take the finest lightweight dehydrated food.

In terms of training, I regularly had to embellish the truth with people to help my own credibility. I fully intended to do a trial in the summer of 2008, sailing a dinghy to the Scilly Isles from Plymouth, but it never materialised. I knew I could sail a dinghy because I had done so extensively as a child living in Greece, but that was a Minisail—an early version of a Topper. Flat, fast, and simple, with no foresail. I'd never been attracted by the idea of sailing a bigger, slower, more stable Wayfarer type boat very far, as it seemed boring, and yet suddenly I was committing to spending several weeks in something similar. Many people asked me how the rowing training was going, and I had to admit I'd never rowed more than a few miles on water. I can put in a reasonable showing on a Concept II Ergometer (Rowing Machine) but as any proper rower will tell you "Ergos don't float!" I took some solace from recalling a very old friend Jason Lewis, (whom I hadn't seen for fifteen years) who had pedalled his way around the world (including the Atlantic and Pacific in a pedal-powered boat) taking most of the ensuing fifteen years in the process. When asked about his prior training, he replied simply, "Why prolong the agony?"

So as summer 2008 became autumn I started, nervously at first, to advertise my intentions. As with some of my previous exploits I was worried that onlookers would deem my proposal too dangerous for my experience in the field. I read as much as I could and started to communicate by email with people who had travelled in this region. Even at this stage, the best route information I could lay my hands on without serious investment was Google Earth! I had a large scale version, constructed by printing in colour on A4 and sticking all the sheets together with a gluestick.

I had a list of seven possible partners for the trip. My original transatlantic partner had other commitments, leaving just six. Out of those six one name, a fellow Marine, particularly stood out as being ideal. I already knew Tony Lancashire well, he having worked for me for over a year, and then having seen him when he accompanied me on a winter sailing and mountaineering trip to Norway earlier that year. He could sail, although like me he was more yachtsman than dinghy specialist; I knew he was uncomplaining and physically and mentally robust. Most importantly, I enjoyed his company. He is understated yet gregarious and he could get things done through force of personality.

T I'd known for some time that Kev was itching to pull together an expedition in the North but I wasn't sure where his next adventure was going to take him. I'd heard rumblings of sailing to and then traversing Greenland but there also seemed to be a trans-Atlantic idea still running in the background somewhere. Needless to say I was keen to find out if it was something I could get involved in and interested to discover who the competition might be. We'd been away to Norway the year before and seemed to share a similar philosophy on adventuring so I knew I was in with a chance but I was also deeply aware that he was my boss, and that's not always a recipe for success.

The Norway expedition had involved taking a 39ft Hallberg Rassy yacht owned by the Royal Marines up into the inner leads of the western coast of Norway in the middle of winter. Sailing in those latitudes in winter was rare enough. To drop off a shore party that then went on to climb up onto the mountain tops and ski down the other side was even rarer. While not especially remote, the expedition was challenging enough to push everyone outside their comfort zone. A night spent desperately battling to save the yacht from a fierce katabatic gale and three days stormbound on the icecap were proof that we could cope with the unexpected, but were they also portentous predictions of events to come?

Kev and I complemented each other well and with subtly different strengths and weaknesses we had worked well as a team. The question remained did Kev see it the same way and would that fledgling team spirit stand up to the rigours of a much longer expedition with just the two of us packed in a much smaller boat? If selected I would have to hope that it would, otherwise a long and miserable spell at one end of a tiny boat awaited me.

Fortunately it seems he did feel the same way, or at least couldn't find anyone else with the time and motivation to make it happen. In September 2008 Kev tentatively approached me to see if I would join him in attempting to transform an interesting idea into reality and start getting the expedition off the ground. I was delighted; the only problem was the expedition still only existed in our heads and I hadn't even formally secured the time off I'd need from work.

K In the meantime, I had to work out a funding plan. The boat was likely to be approximately half of the overall costs of the trip. My plan was to use Tony's and my cash, augmented by any military funds I could attract, to underwrite the operating costs of the expedition, and seek commercial sponsorship for the boat purchase. As with many of these ventures, I mulled over the charity angle but had to be totally honest with myself and all who asked. I wasn't running a marathon at my own expense to raise money for a worthy cause, I was engaging in what I perceived to be a self-indulgent trip to a part of the world that fascinated me. The compromise eventually revealed itself in the form of a service charity called "Toe in the Water" seeking to use competitive yachting to re-inspire, re-integrate and re-motivate servicemen injured in the course of their duty, primarily in Afghanistan. Their core principle is that everyone on board can play a nearly equal part in crewing the yacht, and I thought I could see a future where sailing expeditions to exciting (high latitude) destinations could be undertaken with a half able-bodied and half disabled crew. The funding plan evolved and we decided that on return the boat would be sold with the proceeds going to charity. We anticipated getting approximately half its retail price, meaning in effect a donation to the expedition was a 50% donation to the charity. There was an element of mutual benefit in our association but we were at pains to stress to all sponsors that we weren't doing this solely for the charity.

In late November I had done a deal with my appointer (personnel manager) that I would be released from my job in the Ministry of Defence in July 2009, would be placed 'in the margin' to go on the expedition, and would then deploy to Afghanistan in October. I was delighted. It was looking more likely, and I was hoping that Tony could also get time off.

The very next day I was moving my office space in the Ministry of Defence. Despite being offered assistance to move the large box into which I had packed all my files, I decide to carry it alone. It was predominantly a protest at the huge effort that had gone into planning the move of a few people one floor down to an almost identical space. Having struggled with the box, through doors, down stairs, refusing help at every possible turn I placed the box down, hardly bending my knees and could feel an ache in my lower back. It had happened before, it was Friday and I travelled home by train and thought little more of it. That weekend, climbing a tree with my two boys, I got home feeling a little uncomfortable; half an hour later I couldn't move. I could lie on the floor but anything else was agony. The following Monday morning, it felt better and I made it back to London, but literally only for a few hours before I had to give up. I knew I was in serious trouble. It took an age to cover a few hundred yards. Into the hospital from the taxi (200 metres), into my flat from the taxi (80 metres) and then to find a bus or taxi to the railway station (300 metres)—each took 20-30 minutes. A few hours later

I was back in bed at home, contemplating the damage. I called in a favour and got myself into the Medical Centre in Lympstone, Devon (the training base and home of the Royal Marines) for a first assessment with a doctor and physiotherapist.

I decided to be honest. "How long will it be? When will I be back at work? Will I need an operation? What are my chances of rowing the Northwest Passage next summer?"

I was very miserable, both for the sake of my back in the future, and for the expedition even if my back proved to be delicate but manageable.

The response was vague but positive. "Don't know, could be a couple of months. Back at work not before Christmas. Operation possible/probable. Need to scan first. Well, rowing is about the best thing you can do. Everything is kept in line, unlike ball sports."

I didn't even want to think about the rough seas and the banging, not in my state. Back to bed, and limited swimming and a few exercises. My father came down the following week to keep me company during the day. In the meantime, I had my laptop, propped up in bed. I could draft the proposals for the expedition. Further investigation into the charity revealed the name of the founder, a young Army physio called Holly King, who worked at Headley Court, the Army's rehabilitation centre. I tried to ring her, with no intention of mentioning my current state.

"Holly's been posted. She now works at the Commando Training Centre, Lympstone."

It dawned on me that she had been in the next room while I'd had my consultation. I knew I had no choice, but if I was going to progress this thing, hoping my back was going to be OK, I had to leave all my credibility at the door and tell her. Not at the next consultation, but the one after. I wasn't that brave, and there was some progress with my back.

I had a scan which fortunately revealed nothing, and stuck with my physiotherapy exercises, swimming and cycling. No rowing yet. Over Christmas I fell off my bike on some ice, having only recently converted to clip-in pedals. Without these I would have been fine, but as with a clip-in pedal novice who forgets his position at traffic lights, I could not release the pedal and my knee hit a rock (I was off road). I cycled home feeling the blood running down my leg and shortly afterwards fainted in my kitchen, I presume from the shock and pain. A quick trip to hospital, a few stitches from a delightful nurse who knew both that I had fainted and that I was a Royal Marine. I bet she mentioned that down the pub that night! Overall, my recovery continued unabashed and I think by that time I began to suspect that my back was going to be OK. All round though, my credibility was in tatters and we hadn't yet raised any money.

As my initial plans were forming in late summer I had spoken to various friends working in industry who thought that their company might donate several hundred pounds in return for a logo on the sail, and maybe a presentation on our return if it went well. Then, in September, Lehman Brothers collapsed and the financial crisis (Credit Crunch) began. Offers of sponsorship dried up within days. I seriously doubted that we would ever find the money but persevered with my planning. As ever, the eventual funding came from unexpected sources. Despite what I considered carefully targeted approaches to commercial companies, even those with links to the military produced very little funding. With the war in Afghanistan reaching new levels of intensity every day, I failed to see how the Global Credit Crunch could have affected their business. Undeterred I approached a variety of Trust Funds, and struck lucky with the Scott Polar Research Institute who not only gave us some funding but also much needed credibility.

My confidence had taken an early knock when I had advertised our expedition aim on an early version of the website as "to be the first to navigate the Northwest Passage in an open boat." Some well-meaning web surfers pointed out that my original plan to cover 1000 miles between Kugluktuk and Resolute wasn't the full Northwest Passage which runs from the Bering Strait to Baffin Bay – a much longer distance and outside the time I had available. A less polite email pointed out that two Canadians had traversed the Passage from Inuvik to Baffin Bay on a Hobie Cat over three seasons in the 1980s. A Hobie Cat is a 17 foot catamaran used normally in beach resorts. It is fast, light and has just a net 'trampoline' to sit on, so no shelter at all. I was gutted—how could I have been so stupid as to not have found out about them? It didn't help that the Canadian emailer went on to say how galling he found it that the Brits were always trying to do something first in Northern Canada which, he went on, implies that the Canadians aren't capable of it. I amended the website to remove the claim, bought the book, which was out of print, and was hugely impressed by their fantastic achievement.

Much later, after the expedition was over, I also found out about a couple of ex-servicemen who had a very similar concept to us in 1988. Mike Marriott and Mike Jacques started out from Nome, Alaska in a 16 foot Falmouth Bass Boat, *Tuluk*, and sailed over 1000 miles as far as Komakuk Beach, just past the Canadian-Alaskan border but before the real Northwest Passage begins. I understand they ran out of sponsorship and never returned in subsequent seasons.

I had a brief dalliance with a TV production company who promised much, on the basis that we took a celebrity in the boat as well. Before I had chance to formally decline, the credit crunch made the whole project less attractive to the company and communications dried up. We had to remember the reason why we were doing this; the attractiveness of 'a first' was primarily to attract sponsorship and not to try and lever our way into the record books. We decided not to attempt any other kind of contrived first—'First in one season,' 'First in an open monohull,' 'First by two blokes wearing ladies underwear'… à la London Marathon. We wanted to remain in control, and the real aim of the project was two blokes in an open boat in the wilderness without support crews.

T   By this time I was at the United States Marine Corps Staff College in Quantico just 30 minutes south of Washington DC. It was a fantastic opportunity to sample everything that life in the capital of the free world has to offer, but not ideal for planning a major expedition with another bloke 3000 miles away in London. Up until this point the project had very much belonged to Kev. I'm not exactly sure when it stopped being his dream and became our reality, but by mid-October I found myself at the Annapolis Boat Show with a tentative appointment to meet with a Nova Scotian boat builder named Kevin Jeffrey.

Up until this point I had been heavily involved in the administration associated with moving my world over to Virginia on the East coast of the USA. Breaking my shoulder in a rugby match on my birthday within a week of arriving in the States did little to add to my preparations for a major expedition to the Arctic. So arriving at the Boat Show, fresh out of a shoulder brace and with 6 inches of titanium in my shoulder, marked the start of my engagement in the expedition planning proper. Thirty-five degrees in blistering sunshine and a rum & Coke in hand, I found myself wandering past millions of dollars' worth of motor cruisers in search of the diminutive Norseboat stand. I was with a friend Jeff from the United States Marine Corps, who had come along to show me around, and I suspect check out the Brit's latest crazy idea. When we did eventually find the Norseboat, one look at Jeff's face said it all. A lovely looking, and no doubt very capable day sailer, the Norseboat 17 was above all very small and very open. It was hard to imagine it crashing through the English Channel never mind big Arctic seas. If truth be told I was struggling to see exactly where Kev and I and all our kit would possibly fit.

Kevin Jeffrey himself was something of an enigma too. Behind the beard and well-oiled sales pitch is a man fiercely proud of every one of the boats he designs and manufactures. On the strength of a couple of vague emails from the UK and a single phone call from a pair of odd British Royal Marines, here he was animatedly discussing ways to support our trip to the Arctic. One thing was certain—the 'camp cruiser' would need some modification if it was to stand up to the rigours of a 2000 mile journey through ice choked waters of the Northwest passage.

We were looking to find a balance between weight and stability, or more importantly, sea worthiness. In the open water at the western edge of the passage we could expect big seas rolling in across the Arctic Ocean from Siberia, yet it was also a distinct possibility that we would have to drag the boat over ice later on in the trip. The Norseboat was built to a traditional design, the hull based on an 1800s Nova Scotian fishing boat with a modern, and what appeared to be robust and simple, gaff rig. Unlike an ocean-going rowing boat, ours would not be self-righting and had no watertight cabin. It was a true open boat.

Two more rum & Cokes and a few rough 'back of a fag packet' sketches later and I was beginning to see the potential in the boat. She was small enough to pull up the beach or drag over the ice if required, robust enough to cope with big swells and the occasional ice floe and, critically, cheap enough to fit our budget. All we had to do was:

- Introduce extra buoyancy
- Reinforce the bows

- Raise the cockpit floor to create water tight compartments and limit the amount of water she could ship in heavy seas
- Design a self-righting mechanism—maybe
- Design and build two rowing stations
- Install a solar power electronics pack
- Strengthen the dagger board.

It was a long list of modifications that quickly ruled out any option to buy a secondhand boat or a standard one off the shelf. We'd reached a decision point that might threaten the viability of the whole concept. Fortunately right from the start Kevin Jeffrey was almost as inspired as we were by the prospect of sending one of his boats up into the frozen north, and immediately set about drawing up some significant modifications to his standard product. That night as I drove back to Quantico with Jeff I felt for the first time that we had a project that was really going somewhere. As it turned out 'getting it somewhere' was to be more of a challenge than we first thought.

K   With Tony responsible for boat design, I started tentative enquiries with a freight company to deliver the boat to our scheduled starting point at Kugluktuk. It proved problematic almost immediately. I had no proper maps of Northern Canada and couldn't seem to get through to anyone who understood my problem. I made a couple of abortive phone calls to locals in the northern settlements on really bad telephone lines—unsurprising given that it was mid-winter and the weather was probably awful. Eventually I found a company who said they would road-freight the boat to a place called Hay River and then take it on the barge from there. Stupidly, I didn't enquire as to the actual route; having worked out that there were no roads, I assumed it would be taken down a river to end up at the mouth of the Coppermine River, our start point in Kugluktuk. With this problem solved, I moved on to other issues.

It wasn't until the end of February that we were advised of a change to the barge schedules which meant that the boat could not be guaranteed to be in Kugluktuk before the end of the second week in August! This was potentially disastrous. There were so many variables, and we had to assume a distance per day to calculate how far we could get before the ice and the weather closed in. I tried endless Excel spreadsheets that were all apparently hopelessly optimistic compared to other small boat travellers. But I argued that we could be faster than the kayakers because we could keep moving 24 hours a day. Was 4 knots average in the right direction possible on a good day? How many good days could we expect? What about rowing? I pored over the Arctic Pilot for ideas on prevailing winds. Common wisdom said that there was a very slow current generally setting west to east but I knew it was winds which really mattered and they were 50:50 predominantly west or east. My planning figures were to move on five days of the week, the others allowing for bad weather and stops in the few towns en route. Of those five days we need to do 50 miles per day in ice free waters and 35 miles where there is 1/10 ice. Were these figures ambitious? Maybe, but then on a good day with the wind behind us I was convinced we could do 100 miles. When friends asked me about the trip, I felt the need to explain these calculations. Mostly their eyes glazed over but Tony was unperturbed by my worries, outwardly at least.

T Getting hold of accurate information for Northern Canada was proving to be far harder than we first suspected. In essence we were planning a trip to somewhere we'd never been, without any decent mapping and with no realistic idea of what progress we could expect to make. (It is surprisingly difficult to plan a 2000 mile trip using Google Earth). As each frustration to our plans emerged Kev produced another spreadsheet in a range of colours that proved we could just about achieve the required distance in the given time. Then the conditions would change again and out would come another spreadsheet showing that we could still achieve it but in less time. As each new challenge presented itself we found ourselves becoming increasingly guilty of resolving them by subtly altering our planning assumptions to allow for a slightly quicker average boat speed or fewer rest days or less ice coverage. In our desire to meet our target we were straying into that classic mistake of chasing the error, willing our calculations to support our aspirations. It was not a good place to be, and the constant moving of the goal posts was starting to frustrate us both. If we were to stop the expedition slipping away from us, we had to come up with a radical re-think.

K In a particularly long Skype call, Tony and I discussed the options. I suggested, "We could start from the other end—can we get the boat to Resolute, or even Pond Inlet?" We had already looked at extending the route in that direction. "I definitely don't want to delay the whole trip for a year, we'll never get the time off."

T With the proposed route reversed and a start point in the east, I started looking at options to move by air. The RAF could perhaps get us into Edmonton, but there was no guarantee on the date and no way forward from there. Reluctantly I turned to the commercial world and found a small airfreight company operating a Douglas DC-3 of Second World War fame that could just about squeeze the boat in through a side door. They agreed they would fly it and us into a small airstrip at Pond Inlet on the eastern end of the passage. Things seemed to be picking up again until a few days later when their quote came through at more than the cost of the boat itself and well outside our resources. Even if we could negotiate a split load and share the costs with one of the mining companies operating in the far north, the costs would be crippling. Piggybacking on one of the few research vessels routinely visiting the eastern edge of the Passage was within budget and again for a time we thought we had a solution. Their timetables however were agonisingly too late in the season to allow a start from Pond Inlet or Resolute without being caught in the ice mid-passage. As the impediments mounted I began to sense Kev had real concerns about us even making the starting line. Even my overarching sense of optimism was starting to look faintly ridiculous in light of all the logistical difficulties.

K As if to appease those who said our planned route wasn't the full passage we had one final conversation: "We could switch back to a western start, leave even earlier and go from the road-head at Inuvik."

Tony warmed to it, "OK. We'll just have to go for it! Start as early as possible, ice permitting. And while we're about it we're not stopping in Resolute. The aim is to go all the way from Inuvik to Pond."

In purist terms even that wasn't the full passage, but it was the route taken by the Hobie Cat in three seasons and it did include all the historic central section, linking the open water of the Arctic Ocean with the Atlantic Ocean in the east.

T   In a stroke we had just added 600 miles onto the distance we needed to traverse and brought our departure date forward by over two weeks. It was going to be no simple undertaking and we were guilty of resounding 'mission creep'—but it was a plan!

K   I was delighted that we had a plan that only involved road moves rather than putting the boat on a barge. I discovered that the barges that I had originally thought maybe ran once a week, actually ran once a season! I was getting a sense of how remote this place was. The danger was that we wouldn't complete the full distance and so would potentially miss out on the most interesting scenery that lay as we turned north up Franklin Strait, past where Franklin's ships had been lost coming from the other direction. We could spend a summer on the periphery of the Northwest Passage without getting into its heart. We had set ourselves a challenging target requiring a combination of reasonable weather and favourable ice conditions and it demanded all-out effort from the start.

One of the key milestones in planning the trip was having our plans examined by the Major Expedition Committee. The committee was run by the Royal Navy to try and ensure they were not putting their name, people and funding at unnecessary and poorly thought through risk. I spent a lot of time preparing, as it is not uncommon for expedition leaders to have to return to the committee several times having re-worked some of their safety procedures. This expedition was definitely going to be classified at the top level of 'Remote High Risk' so I knew they would be extra inquisitive. My presentation was weighted towards two aspects—demonstrating that we had studied the ice charts thoroughly, and that the safety procedures to be employed were simple, robust, and sufficient to reduce risk to acceptable levels. I boiled my safety philosophy down to three themes—embrace Technology, Patience and Discipline. Put simply, we would use satellite communications to get the best weather and ice predictions, courtesy of the Royal Navy meteorologists in Northwood; we would be prepared to compromise our aims and sit things out rather than risking a dodgy crossing; and we would have the discipline to drop sail, put on dry-suits and employ strict Go/No Go criteria.

Tony and I had decided that the boat would be without a formal skipper and we would very much be two equal partners in this venture. Although it is easier to say than to do, we resolved that we would always adopt the course of action of the most cautious. So if I wanted to try a crossing in a storm and Tony suggested we sit it out, we would sit it out.

T   Reaching this decision well in advance of even setting foot in Canada was pivotal and I am convinced avoided much resentment and potential disaster later on in the expedition. Inevitably our subtly different approaches to managing risk could result in wildly divergent responses to testing situations. Having previously agreed on always taking the safer option took most if not all of the sting out of the decision. On top of that, Kev is significantly more senior in the Royal Marines rank hierarchy than I am and for over a year he had been my direct boss. Whilst that in itself did not present any inherent difficulties, and in the comfort of the UK we were well able to draw the line between the workplace and our social life, it was not inconceivable that tired, cold and under stress, we might revert to the old structure. It is to Kev's enduring credit and my great relief that never once in the course of the entire planning and execution of the expedition did he ever try and 'pull rank on me.'

K   My performance in front of the committee must have worked because after a few easy questions I was endorsed by the committee and plans were moving forward again.

In April, Tony came back to the UK and we had a rare chance to meet face to face. As planned, he brought all the charts that he had secured free of charge from the Canadian Hydrographic Service. We covered virtually every inch of carpet in my London flat with the 56 full-size charts, and began putting them in order and examining the route. Although they generally lacked detail, this only added to the excitement as to the remoteness of where we were going. The Admiralty Pilot, on many of the inlets off the beaten track of the 'Normal Route' through the passage, simply said "based on a survey in 1860, little known of dangers or depths." As we were shallow-draft, and planned to stay in touch with the shore where possible to give us the option of riding out a storm, we would be going right into these virtually uncharted areas, in some cases, possibly for the first time since 1860.

T   Meanwhile in Nova Scotia Kevin Jeffrey and his team at Norseboat were working hard on incorporating the long list of modifications we had discussed. The time difference between Kev O in the UK and Kevin J in Canada meant that I took on much of the responsibility for dealing with the design and delivery of the boat. The global downturn was evidently having an impact on Norseboat and as the build ran into difficulties and began to fall behind schedule I found myself walking a difficult line. Back in the UK Kev was getting increasingly and vociferously frustrated at the slow progress, and I was bearing the brunt of his frustration. He had a point but I was conscious that Kevin J was offering us a substantial discount on our boat, leaving only a minimal profit margin. Understandably in very difficult times he had to focus on the more profitable parts of his business, but on occasion I did fear that we were not going to get the boat in time, or even worse, that the firm would fall victim to the recession and we wouldn't get the boat at all. Having dealt with Kevin J on almost a daily basis I was impressed by his commitment and personal stake in this venture. I remained convinced he was doing all he could to deliver the best possible boat to us and despite the delays I was quietly confident that between us we would be able to tick off everything on the list. The only problem was would we do it in time.

K   When we received some photographs by email of the boat in an early phase of construction, it was both exciting and daunting. I negotiated a long weekend to go and visit Tony in Virginia, to where he had arranged for the boat to be delivered. Whilst it would be unfair to say I had my doubts over Tony's commitment, it was true that I occasionally doubted how organized he was in getting things ready for my aggressive timeline. He was in charge of managing the boat build, and I had hoped that the boat would be completely ready before I arrived, so we could spend as much time as possible in the boat testing it, working out procedures, and most importantly getting experience in a relatively benign environment sailing her. This was supposed to take the place of the trial trip to the Scillies which hadn't materialised the previous summer. As with all these things, delays had occurred and whilst the hull itself was ready, Kevin Jeffrey was going to come down to commission her the very weekend I arrived to run our trials. My plans for spending three days sailing night and day up and down the Potomac River received their final blow when I heard that Lara, Tony's girlfriend, was going to see Tony on the very same flight that I was on.

It is worth, at this point, recalling a conversation I had had with Tony months earlier when I was looking for a partner for the trip. Lara had just returned from Makalu—the fifth highest mountain in the world—having become the first British woman to summit. A Navy doctor, she was also the first woman to pass the Commando course in a single attempt (one other had passed a few years earlier but only by returning on a subsequent course to finish, having become injured). She was also about to leave for Afghanistan as a doctor deployed right into the front line. When I had first mooted the idea of the Northwest Passage, he said, "I've got to do something pretty adventurous, not only does Lara have better climbing 'dits' (anecdotes) than me, by the time she gets back from Afghanistan, she'll have better operational dits than me."

I have to admit that initially I was somewhat miffed at the last minute nature of the planning for the weekend, but I knew I had to go along with Tony's easy going attitude to life which hadn't prevented Lara from coming that weekend. Whilst with other boyfriend-girlfriend relationships, this would have been catastrophic to a serious expedition boat trial weekend, Lara could see the position clearly.

T   Kev's arrival in the States was sandwiched into a busy schedule for both of us. Later in the timeline than we would have liked, it was the only weekend we could both manage. Unfortunately it was also the only weekend I would get to see Lara for some time. I knew this wouldn't sit well with Kev's enthusiasm to get out on the water testing the boat but sometimes there's a compromise to be struck and whilst I didn't relish annoying Kev I was far more prepared to do that than annoy Lara. In addition it was becoming painfully obvious that the reality would not match our aspirations for the weekend. We hadn't yet laid eyes on the boat and there were bound to be a host of issues to resolve. As long as we could identify the scale of the problem and get her into the water for a limited trial, I would be content. I determined to let Kev reach that conclusion himself.

K   Soon after we arrived, Kevin Jeffrey turned up, having driven almost solidly for two days, towing a beautiful looking boat. He is the sort of bloke that you just naturally warm to. Passionate, softly spoken and casual, it just never entered my head to be annoyed at the lack of completion of the boat. I suppose it was partly because we felt we needed to impress him. We were still suffering, me maybe more than Tony, from that fear of being ridiculed for our lack of experience. There was more than a nagging doubt in my mind that we would maybe get fifty miles into the trip and find that the seas, the temperature, the ice or whatever would end our expedition, and whilst I was of the view it was better to have tried and failed, I wasn't keen on that sort of ignominy given the investment of money and energy into the project. I felt a sense of satisfaction that at last we had a boat, as if all before this had merely been a paper exercise and that now we were really going to go to the Northwest Passage.

As for the boat, she had a look of class, albeit unfinished class, robustness and such beautiful lines. We had bought the Mercedes of dinghies and we were both delighted. As to the amount of work still to do, I was classically caught between wanting to find someone to blame, whilst being so attached to the project that to admit things weren't alright weakened our tenuous claim as a credible expedition even further.

Our apparently unprepared position, although unintentional, was absolutely our responsibility and we had to get on with it. The following day was spent assembling final bits of the boat, re-sealing watertight containers, fitting solar panels. I was relieved that although we hadn't had a significant part to play in actually building the boat as I had originally intended, we had now seen underneath all her clothes. The one real problem was the sliding seat system. I had misunderstood Kevin J; I thought it was a standard option on his boats, but actually he had improvised. What he had was a length of track from the mainsheet traveller of a yacht and the caster traveller system attached to a hand crafted wooden seat. It was neither robust, smooth nor comfortable and it wobbled a lot. I was tempted to say "OK we'll make it work" but it just didn't feel right, as we had to plan on spending many an hour sliding up and down the track in days of a dead calm.

In the space of the late morning, incredibly, we had sourced a proper sliding seat system from a retailer we found online who lived about 30 minutes away. Leaving Kevin J with his sealant gun, we set off straight away, meeting Mark who ran a sort of rowing business from the sizeable workshop in the basement of his house. Mark was incredibly helpful, and we quickly had two systems and the means to bolt them together. We were back in time for lunch—it was one of those days when we just had to get on. However, some of the other residents in Tony's apartment block had complained that it was "against the regulations to work on a boat in the car park." I had two days left, the Northwest Passage was now less than two months away and we were nowhere near getting the boat in the water. I was incensed. Tony, with considerably more patience and understanding of the American psyche than me, concluded that there was nothing to do but move. All was resolved when Kevin J came up with the idea of working on the boat in the sizeable car park of a yacht chandler that was fortunately only a few hundred metres away.

Lara was tasked with finding the right sized nuts and bolts in the chandlery as we fitted the sliding seat system until late in the evening. It looked fantastic—like it was meant to be there. And we'd fitted it, with Kevin's considerable assistance of course. It had been a good day but my dream of testing all the features on this simple boat and working out stowage plans and cooking ideas were now but a distant memory.

T   Whilst it was relatively minor in nature, I don't think either of us had anticipated the volume of the work that needed doing that Friday. It was however enormously satisfying to have worked on the boat ourselves and invested something of ourselves in her finishing touches. Quite apart from the practical benefit of spending the day getting to know how everything was put together, I now somehow felt I had a vested interest in her that went beyond being a passenger. We had debated all sorts of clever, witty names for her but in the end opted for the simplicity of *Arctic Mariner*. A simplicity that was matched by her initial naming ceremony in the chandlery car park, with her name handwritten on a piece of green tape attached to the transom.

K   Saturday was the day we were finally going to put the boat in the water. After more delays, on a muddy beach on the Potomac River, having learnt the simplicity of her rigging, we launched *Arctic Mariner* with little ceremony. As I stood on the tall jetty beside her, looking down into her tiny cockpit with the sliding seats poised ready, I experienced one of those rare moments of pure anticipated excitement. Was it really possible that we could navigate the Northwest Passage in that? I was neither convinced nor sceptical. The boat was a vehicle for self-contained adventure. We would go on a journey, and she would be our home.

The first sail was with Kevin J, and Lara, whom I had to persuade to come along, so did she not want to intrude. Tony and I found our new boat steady, good to row, easy to sail, and great fun. Kevin J had tracked down another Norseboat owner Phil McLean who had driven down and was out in his boat with two of Tony's friends from Staff College who had helped with the launch. The wind picked up, and we had a great sail down wind, with the considerable current, clocking nine knots over the ground. I think we convinced Kevin that we could sail, and all was well in the world. Back on the beach we conducted a righting trial, proving that we could right her in the warm calm waters of the Potomac, with almost no gear in her. I could see it would be very different in an Arctic storm. And the watertight compartments leaked. It was something else to add to the jobs list that Tony would be left with as I flew back to the UK in less than twenty-four hours.

With the wind freshening Tony and I went out to do what we had planned for this weekend, which was to sail and row together. Having reached across the river, (meaning that the wind is coming across the side of the boat) we found ourselves considerably downstream. We reefed the sails, which while easy in these calm seas, as in any boat, does nothing for their shape. Then we found her incredibly difficult to tack (turning the boat through the direction of the wind). In the combination of wind, current and waves she just wouldn't go round. Neither of us wanted to admit it but this was not good. We were now even further downstream and after a couple of eventual tacks and beating (making the boat sail at an angle into the wind) back upstream we decided we had to row. And so, in over 20 knots of wind, being swept downstream, Kev and Tony, soon to attempt the Northwest Passage, did their first tandem rowing. It was hard work, inching back against the current and trying to stay vaguely in time and steer the boat while 'catching crabs' or crashing oars. By the time we got close enough to the beach to be out of the mainstream I noticed that our fixings for the rowing track were now loose having done less than an hour's rowing!

It was at this point that the group of Tony's friends and our new-found friend Phil really came into their own. Drinking beer and eating pizza on the beach in celebration of the launch masked the issues which otherwise could have left us dejected and miserable. The day had been a Curate's Egg. Tony seemed to have tasted the good bits, and whilst I was delighted with the earlier sail, I was left with some big questions—oh, and some nasty blisters on my hands that I didn't over-advertise. Finally, that evening we had to drop the boat off its trailer because Kevin was returning with the trailer and of course we hadn't purchased a trailer for our one-way trip through the Northwest Passage. We soon realised that this was a big heavy boat which two of us could not man-handle on land. Our beautiful new boat looked forlorn propped up on the hard standing next to all the decaying boats. Oh, and it had landed heavily as it slid off the trailer. Still, it wasn't to be the last time it got some rough treatment.

Kev's weekend in Washington had been a whirlwind of activity, punctuated by finally getting our hands on the boat and successfully sailing and rowing her as a team for the first time. We had proved the basic concept but we were still a long way from being ready for the Arctic, and I was painfully aware that the vast majority of the final fitting-out of the boat would fall to me—and at an incredibly busy time for me, approaching the end of my year in the States.

I was particularly concerned at the weight of the boat. I was left unable to sail *Arctic Mariner* as a new bespoke strengthened mast did not fit the boat and had to be re-engineered. Consequently I had her out several times on the oars and it quickly became apparent that even lightly loaded she was no shark through the water. A combination of friends graciously gave up their time to help me get to know her better and hopefully improve her speed under oars. Most notably Jeff, Tye Gilbert and Mark Cox were tireless in their logistical support, mental encouragement and physical muscle, but despite our best efforts we were never able to coax more than about three knots out of her for any sustained period of time. In fact all I seemed to be achieving from the regular trips out was an increasing bill at the isolated but fabulous waterfront bar, and a growing appreciation of just how difficult it would be to manoeuvre *Arctic Mariner* in and out of the water. Again my Quantico friends were central in both building up my bar bill and adding to my concerns about her manoeuvrability.

K Our plans for Tony to sail the boat every possible minute to gain experience were thwarted by the missing mast and even when the new mast did arrive, he was in the middle of his course final exercise which took out all the evenings and weekends for a fortnight. Suddenly Tony was getting ready to return to UK, and had to pack the boat, and prepare it for it to be shipped up north. He had already sourced a myriad of stores for the boat. In what was becoming typical for the expedition, everything seemed last minute and he had the transport company arriving the day before he left for UK, and no cradle on which to transport the boat.

T Unable to get the required sailing time in I swallowed my concerns and contented myself with working through the huge list of things still to be done. In the short term I needed to find someone willing to lend us a trailer to move the boat on, and a huge amount of stores still needed to be sourced, paid for, manifested and packed. With a week to go the life raft and its associated freight permissions had still not arrived. I needed to manage the pickup of the boat on a limited-access military base, by a freight company coming from 1500 miles away, before I departed the country, but after the last of the stores arrived. Finally, somehow I needed to build a cradle for the boat to travel several thousand miles on. The maintenance team at Quantico were fabulous in meeting the last of the requirements, designing and knocking up a wooden crib in the space of 4 hours for nothing more than the satisfaction of being involved. Even so we were almost defeated at the final hurdle when the freight truck was delayed and I was forced to use every trick in the book to prevent my volunteer forklift truck driver departing before the rig arrived.

K With the boat finally on the move and Tony back in the UK, but incommunicado on another exercise on Salisbury Plain, I soon discovered our problems were far from over. Everyone always said that getting the boat, ourselves and all the equipment to the start line was the hardest part of the trip (partly because it also involves raising the funding) and we weren't there yet. Late one night in my flat in London I received a phone call from 'Dragos' who had been organising the freight. Having not exactly covered himself in glory over the whole business of the barges and getting the boat to Kugluktuk, I was a little uncomfortable using him but couldn't see the difficulty in driving the boat to Inuvik. I had even thought about trying to save some money and tow it there ourselves, until I realised it was four thousand miles!

Dragos explained the problem. "The boat is now in Edmonton and the Canadian Customs wants to inspect the shipment."

Thinking that we had some life jackets with compressed air canisters, I was instantly anxious, "OK, shouldn't be a problem"

Dragos then got to the point, "Do you have the purchase receipt for the boat, showing that the tax has been paid."

I thought to myself, "Shit, how much tax haven't we paid. Why didn't Kevin mention the tax issue?"

After a plea of "we're doing this to raise money, we're going to sell the boat at the end" that I soon realised was pointless, and with the tax on the boat amounting to Cn$1120, or nearly £700 that we didn't have I knew we had no choice but it really pissed me off. We would just have to pay, potentially more out of our own pockets.

When you looked at it in the cold light of day, it did look suspicious. We had bought a boat in Canada, not paid the tax because it was exported to the US, and then six weeks later we were re-importing it into Canada!

Over the course of a frustrating three days, we then heard that the freight company could claim the tax back, and we didn't have to pay it! I didn't ask how the bureaucracy worked, but then came the bad news, the Customs were charging us Cn$1895 storage charges, and this was partly because all was resolved on a Friday afternoon and the boat couldn't be removed until Monday morning. The shipping company worked really hard to minimise our costs, and in the final twist a very kind Dean Smith of Allen Services offered to take the boat to Inuvik free of charge on a part load he was taking there, and Dragos deducted this leg from our final bill. We were still down in cash terms, but nowhere near as bad as we might have been, and we had a boat in Inuvik.

Food, however, was proving my least expected worry. To save the hassle of buying all the food locally to supplement a few freeze-dried meals taken out in our luggage (the usual palaver I go through to save money on expeditions), I thought that this time I would do it properly. I held a meeting with a specialist company, talked nutritional requirements, and selected our varied menu based upon three days dried and one day wet (like tinned food but in foil pouches). Space and weight were a significant issue, albeit maybe less than if it was going in rucsacs on our backs. With literally two weeks to go, I received a phone call from the company explaining that they were not allowed to import foodstuffs into Canada. Again, I was seriously pissed off. It was surmountable, but involved carrying loads more baggage and purchasing the rest in Canada. And it was so avoidable; even I could have told them that it would be an issue importing foodstuffs into North America but I assumed that as experts in freighting expedition food worldwide, they had a procedure to comply with the bureaucracy.

One of the last things to be sorted was our shotgun. Highly advisable for protection against bears, I had asked lots of people how to rent a firearm. I assumed this would be easy, given the amount of hunting that goes on in Northern Canada. Some said they just used bear pepper spray, and that a gun wasn't required. Others said it was essential. Whilst I admit to being slightly laissez-faire, Tony was adamant we needed a gun, and that we should also have trip flares for round the tent. I found a gun shop in Edmonton, and after the British Defence Attaché, Brigadier Simon Knapper agreed to be our sponsor we could 'buy' a weapon, which we would then sell back at the end of the trip. I would call that renting but there is no such thing as a rental firearms licence if you are operating alone.

Tony and Lara came down for a weekend to sort all the final arrangements in late June. Although we planned to finalise everything, I was beginning to understand that Tony just doesn't operate like that. In fact, within an hour of arriving—with Lara due to arrive later—Tony and I were in a pub in Honiton watching the rugby international with three very pissed South Africans. We still had lots of boxes of new gear, from anemometer to handheld radio, to iPod speakers and cameras, virtually all untested. This wasn't how it was supposed to be, we should have had the boat for six months, tested all the electrical systems and cooking options. I had a car battery in my study that was replicating the solar panels and battery that we had in the boat that was thousands of miles away. It all seemed to work. I could charge the netbook, satellite phone, GPS, camera and radio. And I'd soldered a lead together that meant we could power the iPod speakers from the car battery. We didn't need to take loads of AA batteries, saving weight. Or so we thought.

The other perturbation of the weekend was that the new bedroom that my wife, Amber and I had ordered five months previously was being fitted on the Sunday. I explained to Tony the obvious relevance of new bedroom furniture to my participation in the expedition and, in the midst of a British heatwave we removed the old fitted wardrobes early Sunday morning. The old bedroom carpet was unceremoniously dumped out of the bedroom window where it remained until the following weekend along with a pile of old cupboard doors and broken chipboard.

Lara spent hours sorting our medical kit, trying to reduce the bulk and weight to the absolute minimum. The components originally filled a large rucsac. When Tony and I looked on incredulously at all the stuff, Lara took us both out on to the patio for First Aid training, with her now daysac-sized case bulging with dressings, splints, tourniquets and even morphine. In a sobering hour, we covered trauma injuries and resuscitation. A quick demonstration of the new military issue tourniquet so widely used in Afghanistan added to the dawning realisation of just how isolated we were going to be.

"You only put this on to save life—you're going to lose the limb," she explained. "How long will you have to wait for rescue?" she asked me.

"Up to 48 hours" I replied, going over in my mind just what that 48 hours would be like if one of us had a serious crush injury, or lacerations from a bear. Although I worry about some things, getting injured isn't normally one of them. But I could sense the feeling of responsibility that Tony and I had for each other. There was going to be no-one else. We asked about other medical procedures, to which Lara replied, "You're not qualified to do it, you'll do more harm than good, stick to the basics and you'll be alright. Probably." I trusted her judgement that we had what we needed, including a vast array of fairly powerful drugs, and a neatly printed, waterproofed idiots guide to using everything that ran to eight sheets.

T   Kev's spreadsheet campaign was invaluable during those final few weeks and he worked wonders in fighting through the customs difficulties associated with crossing the Canadian border and finalising our shotgun in particular. There is little doubt that without his drive and tenaciousness we would have struggled to resolve all the myriad issues on the run up to departure. It was a theme that was to characterise our time in the boat together over both of the next two summers, and one for which I was repeatedly thankful. It was also at this stage that I remarked in my journal on one of Kev's other persistent tendencies that was to run throughout the expedition.

"I found it slightly frustrating today the way Kev jumped around from one subject to another when we were trying to pack. Half way through checking off a long list of kit he'd get distracted and dash of to fiddle with something in the garage or some other distraction, dismissing all the reasoned argument for taking some item of kit in a flash and switching tack completely. I can't really get annoyed though because I recognise the same excitement in myself."

K   The very last weekend before we left was even more chaotic. Tony finally arrived on the Sunday late afternoon while I was in the middle of a surprise champagne and cake party that Amber had organised. Initially I just wanted to go and pack, but people drifted in and out most of the late afternoon and early evening. Actually it was just what I needed, a chance to see people, knowing full well that I wasn't going to have much varied human company for the next two months.

The last item (canisters for our charts) arrived the following morning, just in time although I had originally ordered them four weeks previously. The satellite phones worked in that we could send and receive email but it all seemed a bit fragile, both physically and electronically. The speed of transmission is so slow that we devised a system where all email traffic was routed through our rear link man, an old friend in the Marines called Dan Bailey. This was essential so that firstly he could collate all messages into one to save transmission time, and also crucially he could filter out the well-meaning, morale-raising multi-mega-byte video file that would clog up our system and prevent us receiving vital weather information. This meant that he alone knew the email address for us on the boat, and I rigorously enforced this. Even Amber and Lara didn't know it and had to send messages through Dan.

T   The surprise party at Kev's place on the day before we departed was a well-deserved tension release valve that I think we all needed and it gave me an opportunity to meet some of Kev's closest friends, but it put even more pressure on our last minute packing. Dinner was scheduled for 1800 the next evening at my cousin's house in London, who would then run us all to the airport in the morning. By the time we finally pulled out of the drive at 2130 with a three hour drive ahead of us the plan had changed to a night in an airport hotel. Ironically after all the bustle of the preceding days, weeks and months the drive through the night to Heathrow was surprisingly relaxing, stress free and actually quite enjoyable. We were finally on our way.

II

MACKENZIE AND TUK

My journal from 20th July 2009 sums up my mood on departure:

> *I awoke the following morning to the first real tinge of excitement. So far there has been so much admin to do it's been difficult to think about the trip itself. Last night Lara asked me how I felt about our adventure; if I'm honest I didn't really know how I felt, it's simply been something looming on the horizon, now it appears the horizon has come to meet us.*
>
> *Looking back the last six weeks have been a little manic squeezing in a job move, a house move back from the US to northern Scotland, a birthday and co-ordinating all the moving parts for the expedition. Simply collecting my kit together in one place has been a challenge involving endless trips up and down the motorway gathering my scattered belongings from various military bases, storage spots and houses of friends and family. I began to feel a little guilty too for dragging Lara up and down the country sleeping on friends' floors or spare rooms. At one point she turned to me and claimed 'Our relationship seems to be founded on the quality time we spend in the car.' Hmmm, perhaps not the best way to begin a trip away to the other side of the world in a tiny boat.*

On the day of departure we dragged our nearly 100 kilograms of luggage with us to the Thomas Cook desk still not sure if my attempted charm offensive had worked, whether our extra baggage allowance had come through, and if it hadn't whose credit card was going to take the hit. Kev's decision to put all his hand luggage into a bright blue canoe bag (to save checked baggage weight) was already beginning to look questionable as he wandered through the airport in his Crocs with the canoe bag dragging along the floor behind him resembling a tramp at Waterloo station. Twenty minutes of repacking in front of the check in desk, and a little more liberal use of the charm, and we had the right collection of bags at the right weight and had avoided the staff discovering the forty kilograms of food that we still weren't certain would clear customs into Canada.

Lara and I have got used to saying goodbye to each other after a number of times. While I'm sure I'm not supposed to say so, it does get easier and our goodbye was heartfelt but not tearful. Just before Kev and I slipped off through the departure gates Lara handed us both leather bound journals complete with pictures of loved ones back home. Perhaps more than anything this underlined the sense of departing on an adventure and we both greatly cherished her gift.

I raced Kev through the security in a rather childish way, each of us choosing a different lane to see who made the better call. I wondered if this was an indication of the competition to come.

Flying over Greenland we spent half an hour welded to the windows entranced by the immense glacial landscape unfolding below us. Eventually we dropped back into our seats on the first row and Kev looked on rather smugly over the top of his 'holiday read' as I was engaged in conversation by the 70+ lady on my left, a surprisingly interesting Welsh lady with a plethora of sons, daughters, grandchildren and even great grandchildren. She had a wealth of stories from around the world and not for the last time our adventurous aspirations were put back in their proper place. I'm always amazed by the extent of adventurous spirit all around us but even my enthusiasm lagged as we entered the third hour of non-stop talking and I retreated into the 'book.' Before we'd left I'd put together a green plastic file with all the paperwork we could possibly need, including a cut down version of the *Admiralty Arctic Pilot*. As I flicked through the first pages of the *Pilot* in slow time I felt the first inklings of disquiet returning. Distances that seem so small and inviting on the chart take on a new dimension when you impose our tiny boat on top of those huge expanses of sea ice and tundra and try to imagine their extreme remoteness.

After arriving in Edmonton we had gradually ticked off most of the worries that had accumulated as a result of our last minute planning. We collected our shotgun from a very helpful Gord McGowan of *Milarm,* a medium sized gun shop just out of downtown Edmonton. It contained more weapons than I had seen used in small wars. Gord was clearly a heavy metal fan, judging by his tattoos and denim jacket. I looked for his Hell's Angel motorcycle but he seemed to be using a pick-up to get to work that day. We then almost cleared the *Mountain Equipment Co-op* of their supplies of 'Mountain House' dried food, to make up for the debacle of our supplier not knowing about import restrictions.

Two further flights northwards were required just to get us to our starting point, and First Air, the Canadian airline that had agreed to sponsor us, were fantastic in easing the whole process. I was surprised how easy it was to transport a shotgun, and after another airport repacking session it was Kev's turn to employ the charm in getting all our additional stores freighted up to our mid-point stop in Cambridge Bay. It was more evidence of what I'd seen all along during the planning of this trip. After just a little time people everywhere would start to feel a personal involvement in what we were trying to do and go out of their way to help in whatever way they could. Without this help it is questionable just how far we would have got.

K I had arranged to meet an old school friend and ex-Marine called Rick Storrie who was living with his family in Yellowknife. I happened to see his location on his Facebook page and although I had never met his wife Bridget, and Rick was working out of town, she picked us up after we had retrieved our shotgun which had not appeared on the baggage carousel and was languishing in the hold. We had first-hand experience of the frontier town atmosphere, and the huge mosquitos. As we flew northwest out of Yellowknife, en route to Inuvik, I too was struck by the vast emptiness of northern Canada. Thousands, if not millions of tiny lakes stretched as far as the eye could see from 30,000 feet. In another location, each would be an attraction in its own right, with paths, canoes and maybe a café here and there. But then that would be to ignore their inaccessibility, let alone the mosquito infested swamps that lay amongst them. I had been warned about mosquitoes, especially in the early part of our route. Stories of downed pilots opening their canopies to then die from blood loss had me believe it would be unpleasant whenever we were not moving at speed some distance offshore.

Despite the success so far, my worries weren't over, at least not in my mind. As we cleared one hurdle, I invented another. How are we going to find the boat in Inuvik? What if it had been damaged in transit? How will we get it in the water? How will we load it and keep all the gear secure. I imagined camping next to it on some mosquito-infested shoreline by the town centre. Most of all, I was still worrying about how far we would realistically get, once we got out of the Mackenzie

River delta and out into the Beaufort Sea, exposed to the full force of the Arctic Ocean coming from the polar ice cap. My journal entry for 22nd July:

> *I feel nervous and I'm not sure entirely why. Success is having an exciting and interesting time, not an outcome of getting a certain distance. I'm looking forward to it but have trepidation. Very pleased that I chose Tony (and that he chose to come along)—he is very committed to the whole project.*

Arrival in Inuvik was met with the normal comedy of finding a way into town. Despite the remoteness at the end of the furthest north road on the planet a taxi duly appeared; ours was driven by a West Indian which seemed somehow bizarre. Soon we were ensconced in the *Arctic Chalet*, a winter dog-sledding hostel which we had pre-booked, and then we set about finding the boat. We managed to establish that it was probably back at the airport, and having secured the loan of an old station wagon and trailer we drove back to look round the collection of hangars and prefabs that made up Inuvik airport. We were shown to a tented hangar and inside we discovered our beautiful boat, intact and with all the gear that we had loosely secured under its cover. A helpful forklift driver loaded it on its cradle on to our flatbed trailer and we set off back to town, to a shallow beach that served as a launching area onto the murky but mighty Mackenzie River. We soon realised that the boat was too high to float off without the 4x4 we had borrowed floating off downriver as well. Not for the last time my Crocs came in handy in the mud, and after a combination of pulling the cradle apart, and pushing the boat, she was afloat. I was caked in mud and we were about a mile and a half downstream from our hotel and a small jetty that we were to borrow while we stowed her. I set off rowing upstream while Tony drove the truck. I hadn't found my rowing gloves and was determined not to start the trip with blisters à la Potomac River, so I couldn't pull too hard. However I found it surprisingly easy to row upstream, remembering of course that the boat was virtually empty.

T As Kev set off rowing up the Mackenzie River in a stripped-down boat I couldn't help but remark on how almost comically small she looked. It suddenly seemed inconceivable that we could take her two thousand miles up into the heart of the

Passage. Still, Kev's excitement had been bubbling away all morning and it was impossible not to be affected by his enthusiasm. Throughout the trip he seemed to alternate between deep pessimism and extreme optimism on a regular basis and I know he was particularly concerned about how our adventure might be perceived by the wider community. Today with the boat in the water and able to bend his back to the oars it seemed that nothing could stop him. Driving along the side of the river it suddenly occurred to me that this was the first time we'd been apart in almost a week. I wondered idly how this enforced close proximity would work out over the course of the next two months. So far Kev had been a perfect companion and our personalities seemed to balance each other well. Adventurers, by definition almost, often have big egos and can struggle to bond. With Kev I had no such worries, but I was under no illusion that the pressures in a small boat for such a prolonged period would be insignificant.

K Packing the boat was easier than we expected, but for the fact that we both knew we wouldn't be able to repack the lockers whilst underway as efficiently as we had to start with. We needed more wriggle room, and I feared we would spend a lot of time unpacking and repacking to get to the things that we needed. Before I left England, some work colleagues in the MoD had given me a 'Commando Joe,' an eight-inch tall Royal Marine Action Man figure, on the proviso that he came with us through the Northwest Passage. We fixed him to the mast, permanently acting as look out. All the food was squeezed into the three under-floor lockers, packed in 'one man, one day' clear plastic bags. We had forty-four full man-days of food and five days spare with a resupply planned for Cambridge Bay, which we estimated was at least three weeks away. Under the bow we kept our empty holdalls, all the spare charts, liferaft and sleeping bags when not in use. This was the driest part of the boat. Beneath this there was a large locker which seemed to have everything else in it. Tent, sea-anchor, first aid kit, tools, spares kit, pulleys and line, reverse osmosis watermaker, secondary water pump and not forgetting the bucket which was for bailing, general purposes, and to use as a toilet if required.

The two side lockers were personal space, for the very few spare clothes—we each carried a quilted suit to change into if we got completely wet. We also each had a waterproof bag on deck with everything we would use regularly: cameras, journals, binoculars, VHF radio, ready-use hat and gloves, netbook computer and one of the two satellite phones. The stove also lived in one side along with various presents from Amber to be opened as we progressed. One set of oars were neatly stowed under the gunnels, along with the anchor, and under the stern were flares, inflatable rollers and pump. The stern locker was also the bilge and contained fuel and spare water. The rest of the water and the drysuits lived under the platform that was formed to make our sleeping area over the second rowing station. My journal continues, from 23rd July:

It all seems so close but also so unreal. We have a boat, almost full of gear, but I just can't imagine living on her. Charting, using the netbook computer and satphone. In a storm. So, is it a yacht or is it a dinghy? It's a dinghy that we are treating as a yacht.

We had a last 'night out' in Inuvik, which proved an interesting experience. I had read that the northern communities were mostly dry, or at least alcohol was heavily controlled. These communities have still to recover from the rapid transition from a simple, subsistence-based existence to becoming part of modern day Canada. The indigenous Inuit currently experience high levels of alcohol dependency, teenage pregnancy and unemployment, and a large proportion live almost exclusively on government subsidies. Seal and animal hunting, even fishing are more pursued for leisure than for commercial reasons, and many of the other jobs go to the so called 'Qabloonas' or white men. Although there is supposed to be a transfer of skills and responsibility, this process is taking time. The bar was populated either by hard-living frontier workers or drunk Inuit trying to bum drinks off us, the obvious gullible newcomers in town. I did buy one hapless but chatty individual a drink, only to be chastised by one of the more sensible locals, and then Tony. I claimed I was just trying to get rid of him. Almost everyone we spoke to claimed to have featured on *Ice Road Truckers*, which, given the fact that one of the famous ice roads starts at the roadhead in Inuvik and heads down the frozen Mackenzie to Tuktoyaktuk was at least plausible. Overall, I can't say I liked the town. It was neither welcoming nor unfriendly, but I couldn't really understand what it was doing there. This would be a recurring theme in other communities we visited, although one has to remember the huge reserves of hydrocarbons and minerals waiting to be extracted from this region.

Nobody seemed interested in our plans for the Northwest Passage, but then we were still sixty miles upriver from the delta to the Beaufort Sea, so no yachts and very few commercial vessels other than the resupply barges will venture this far upriver. Even if we had waited for our boat to be delivered to Kugluktuk, some 500 miles east, it would still have passed through here and I felt we had made the right decision to start our adventure from here, even if the town itself left a little to be desired.

I didn't sleep well the last night before departure. It reminded me of those times I had woken up whilst on exercise in Norway, knowing you had half an hour left in your sleeping bag before it was time to emerge from the tent into the cold, pack up the camp and ski through the night. I was half awake, half dreaming of being either plagued by mosquitoes or terribly cold and wet. I take a sort of perverted satisfaction in keeping myself going in the cold and wet, day after day, but it doesn't mean there are no butterflies before a trip starts.

Tony's final journal entry before departure:

T   *Packing the food in individual bags for each day took an age but finally it's all stowed. A day of worrying about what will fit, what won't fit and what will never fit was wasted concern—It all fits—Just! With everything we need for two months alone in the Arctic packed into every available space in a tiny 17ft boat it's faintly astounding how small your world can become at times. We file a copy of our intended route with the coastguard and then in a rather surreal moment, slip off for a final meal at the ubiquitous Pizza Hut, which in this part of the world really is a hut. An odd final meal for the condemned men but afterwards we are keen to be away. With effectively twenty-four-hour sunshine this far north there's nothing to stop an evening departure and it's not long before we're walking down to the boat and the start of our adventure.*

K   As if to magnify the significance of the moment, I said to Tony, "I don't know what is going to happen and how we're going to deal with it, but I can't think of anyone else I'd rather be doing the trip with." I think he appreciated it, but it sort of sounded cheesy. The actual departure was much more matter of fact. There was a party of middle aged ladies who came down to see us off, but with more faffing around they left us to it. With me on the oars, and video camera, Tony cast off and simply said "And so it begins…" It was 1800 hours on 24th July 2009.

With a distinct absence of wind, we rowed for four hours, mostly one on one off. The neoprene pad rowing gloves we had were excellent. It had been another of my fears—how to take care of our hands in the cold with blisters and cuts. The boat felt heavy, because it was! But we were going with a current, downstream, which lulled us into a false sense of security. We were in shirt sleeves, actually quite warm, with a few evening midges. Tony seemed convinced that the rowlocks were in the wrong place; something he had discussed with Mark (who was a competent rower), back on the Potomac. He may well be right, but it seemed to work for me and I could see it was going to become an issue for him because on the river he couldn't keep the boat going in a straight line. That the rowing position wasn't quite long enough was caused by us squeezing two sliding rowing positions into the space available, and I had to sit slightly too far back on the seat. I rowed in Crocs, leaving my Gore-Tex and leather boots for a colder day.

There was a fair bit of local traffic on the river. One or two local fishing dories roared past us, waving and somewhat bemused by the tiny boat without an engine venturing out downriver. One stopped and gave us a five pound Whitefish that we chopped into eight steaks on the transom and fried for an idyllic supper in the reasonably bright daylight of the midnight sun. Easy enough to read by, it still cast an eerie glow across the forested banks of the river.

T   It felt fantastic to be finally away down river, ironically the Mackenzie reminding me of the Potomac so far to the south where we had first put the boat in the water. A long period on the oars is somewhat marred by my frustrating inability to keep the boat in a straight line. I keep reflecting on the decision not to take the time to change the set-up of the oar locks for maximum power and control. Each stroke feels just that little truncated and uneven and I hope that conditions will allow us to sail far more than we row. Almost on cue a steady wind comes up from the south and allows us to hoist the sails for the first time and break down into

An all-too-easy start on the Mackenzie River →

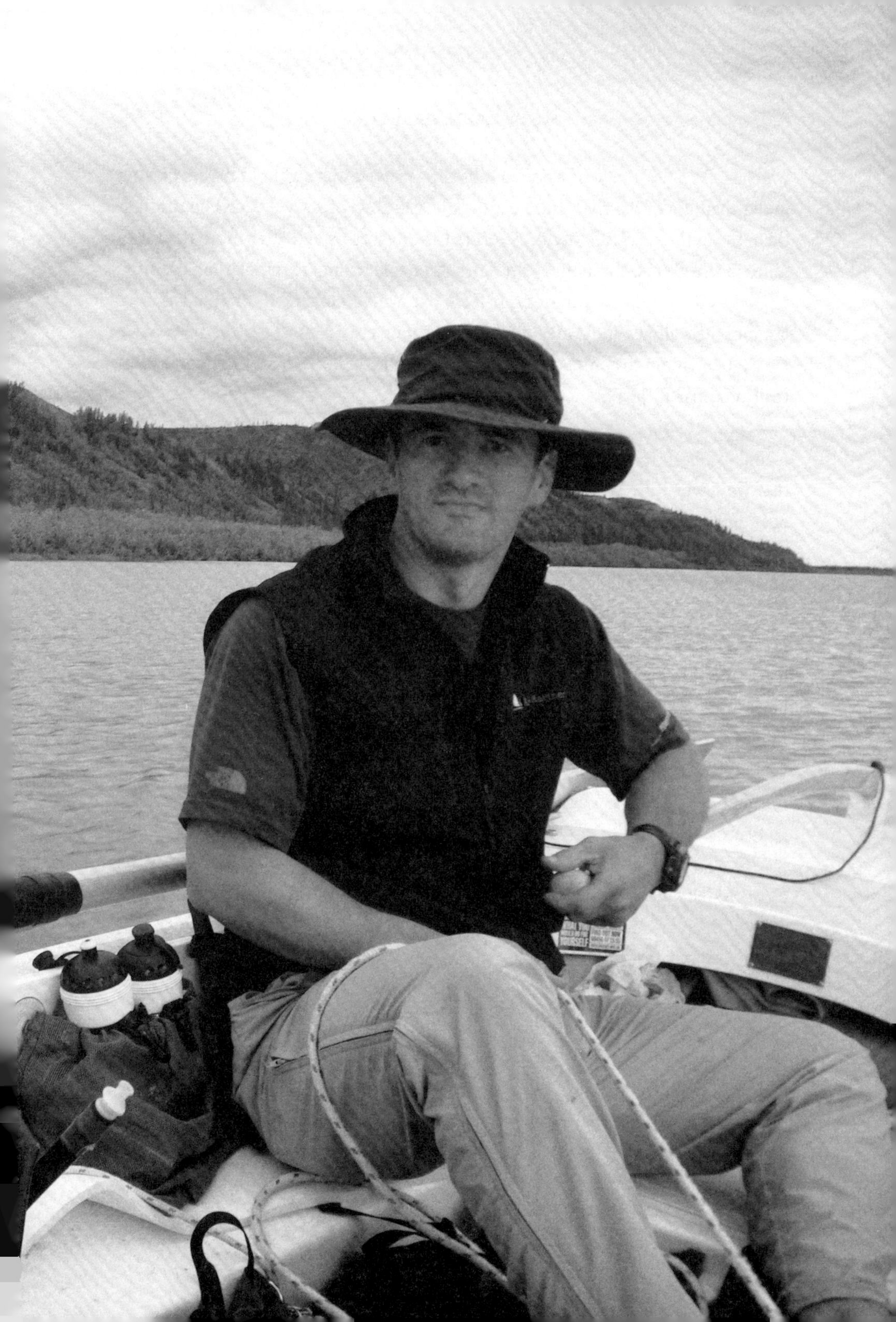

watches. As a low range of wooded hills slips by we catch sight of beavers playing in the shadows of the river and hear the ghostly howl of wolves prowling through the trees in the near full moon. A relaxed start eases us and after more than fifty miles in the first twelve hours I find myself unable to stop extrapolating, optimistically predicting likely progress. It feels like we've embarked on an adventure but more 'Swallows and Amazons' than anything else. Almost guiltily I worry we have fallen victim to complacency and alone on the helm I wonder again if we can really do this? If the pack ice that lies ahead will let us.

K   I think we both felt it was like a weekend away, maybe like the training weekend that we never had. We did put the extended canvas cover over the front of the boat and found that the character of the boat completely changed. Although it was only light plastic covered canvas it created a helming position and a sleeping area, albeit a narrow short one where the plan was to poke our feet up further into the bow. Despite our original plans, and my concerns that it wouldn't stand up to strong winds, this flimsy cover soon stayed up for the whole seven weeks. I had wanted to ensure that the cover didn't stop the boat being classed as 'open' but in the end there was no danger of this. We had to drop the cover, but not fully unzip it, in order to reduce the sail area, known as reefing. I never really wished that we had a waterproof compartment like the ocean rowers have, but the shelter our canvas cover provided was probably essential for us to be on the go twenty-four hours a day.

As we approached the massive delta of the awesome Mackenzie River, its character changed completely. Gone were the neat river banks and hundred yards or so of deep navigable water. The 'river' now appeared to be several miles wide, but in reality most of this was no more than a few inches deep. The wind had swung round to a northerly and we were loosely following some navigational markers but it became clear that local knowledge was essential. As we tacked up the channel, apparently making good progress, the boat would then come to an abrupt halt as we went aground on the mud. We started to become acquainted with the system for lifting the centreboard, which crucially had been fitted prior to the sliding seats. The rope that raised the centreboard ran in a space under the sliding seat monorail that was only just accessible to long fingers before being gripped by a plastic jammer that was equally inaccessible. Soon we had a knot, which had tightened itself under the considerable weight of our steel centreboard, which was preventing us raising or lowering it; and then we were aground, in about four inches of water, stuck fast.

Being completely alone was now a reality. How could we get the boat off and underway? We couldn't cut the line without unpacking the boat such that we could lift it on to its side to reattach new rope. And we were about three hundred metres from dry land.

T   Naked to avoid getting my clothes wet, I climbed out of the boat onto the sandbar and with some difficulty managed to dig out the centreboard and gingerly ease the boat out backwards. My aching blue feet were a stark reminder that despite the relatively mild weather the ice front was a mere fifty miles further north and the water temperature was painfully cold.

K   Further out into the delta the wind picked up and became a north-easterly, so right on the nose. We seemed to be going nowhere, tacking backwards and forwards across the two to three hundred metre channel, and were being pushed back by the choppy seas, especially when we actually put the boat through the wind, known as 'going about.' Rowing together (which necessitated taking the canvas cover completely off) we found we could make progress but it was hard work. As the delta opened out into Kugmallik Bay we found we could sail again but the waves were now up at two to three feet.

T   As the day progressed, the dawning reality of our situation made us both a little nervous about heading out into the Arctic Ocean. The abstract very rapidly became the all-too-real in the shape of long rolling seas crashing into the bows and limiting our progress to a crawl. With the increased seas came a cold fresh wind from the northeast and as the evening advanced we were both tired, hungry and cold. I think the enormity of the challenge threatened to overwhelm us both for a while and in the cold spells on the helm I wondered not for the last time if we could really do this. We both sank into ourselves a little but I think Kev seemed to be a little more subdued, perhaps feeling the responsibility more than I. We got used to the incessant bouncing around but quickly realised that we must do something positive to address the cold and hunger and increasingly despondent state we were falling into. It was time to establish a proper routine and make some hot food.

K   I was very aware that my proposed cooking system had never been properly tested in a choppy sea, and was actually worse than the system Frank Dye had used in his Wayfarer forty years ago. He had built a hanging, enclosed box into which he placed his Primus stove. I had intended to build something but never got round to it. I had a stove mat, made out of an old MDF floor tile (supposedly heat resistant) and some chain that I'd bought in Inuvik. In the end, the strength of my system was in the inherent safety of modern petrol stoves, provided they are filled with the finest quality stove fuel—purchased at vast expense in Inuvik. We also had a spare stove, and a spares kit with which in previous years I had regularly maintained similar stoves. I had ascertained that this was an absolutely essential item. Despite the constant bouncing, it was possible to heat water safely provided I kept a hand and weather eye on the stove and the small yacht kettle over it on the floor of the boat, whilst sitting on the sliding rowing seat. The chain remained unused.

T   Good food is something hugely important to me and I've learnt from experience that my mood worryingly closely reflects the quality of food I'm consuming. Although Kev seemed less bothered, meal times were something we simply had to get right if we were to succeed. We'd had to change our feeding plan at almost the last moment and I in particular had some concerns that the hastily purchased replacements wouldn't live up to the challenge. As it turned out we needn't have worried. Each day consisted of a single bag of food each, containing 13 items. Breakfast, lunch, dinner & dessert formed the core meals, along with soup, chocolate bars, beef jerky, nuts & raisins. One in every four meals was the military 'wet' rations that we were both much more familiar with. The freeze-dried meals were fantastic; add boiling water, seal and leave for ten minutes and then eat straight out of the bag. The only change to this routine, used in almost all weathers on both years of the trip, was that in 2010 Kev used the warm bag as a heater inside his jacket. It being American-made, we didn't always understand from the labelling on the packet exactly what was going to be revealed inside. One evening as Kev was cooking, I asked him, "What have you got for us?"

"Vegetable Stew with Beef. Shouldn't that be Beef Stew with Vegetables?" he replied sardonically.

K The stove stayed on to make a hot drink, and although quite a bit of hot water and tea spilled, it simply ran into the bilge in the stern and was pumped out along with the seawater that washed into the boat. As ever, we felt significantly rejuvenated after hot food and drink, and I was delighted that it had worked even in this weather. It was a significant milestone; gradually we were proving our concept of twenty-four-hour travel and developing a routine.

In marked contrast to the Mackenzie River delta, once out on the Arctic coast proper the scenery was incredibly dull. We could occasionally see land, but it was so low lying and featureless it appeared literally as a line on the horizon. More than a few miles offshore and that disappeared, and we would be deceived into seeing islands that were in fact just very slightly higher ground. The only things of interest were the 'pingos,' areas of tundra forced up in a symmetrical hummock by the expansion of ice forming beneath them. Interesting but not exactly spectacular. Viewed from the air, or indeed Google Earth, the entire peninsular resembles an extreme Swiss cheese. It is hard to differentiate between water and low lying swampy sand, and sea. It is a classic littoral but without any man made features to add interest. Overall, it was to be expected having studied the charts, but it was disappointing. One of the reasons I came to the Arctic was to see mountains and glaciers crashing into a sea littered with ice. I knew this was more likely at the other end of the passage, but as I looked out over the brown sea, still stained by the river delta outflow I wondered how monotonous this journey would be. That said, as if to remind us where we were, earlier we had had a magical glimpse of a caribou shuffling along the shoreline.

It was now 2230 and we settled into our second night afloat and the reality of long cold watches in big seas and strong winds. We were faced with the first real decision point of the trip proper—whether to push on, making about two knots in the direction we wanted to go but having to tack laboriously back and forth, or turn south to stop in the shelter of the tiny Inuit settlement of Tuktoyaktuk.

Neither of us was keen to head in so early in the trip and we resolved to carry on. As the wind picked up and we struggled to fend off the cold we were reluctantly forced to reverse our decision, a sense of despondency and fatigue driving us in.

T It was the right decision but the painfully slow approach through the early hours of the morning somehow felt almost like an admission of defeat. Kev seemed especially despondent. At 0001 on the 26th July I woke him from a fitful sleep curled up in the bow to wish him a happy birthday. He grunted his thanks rolled over and fell back asleep almost immediately. The approach to shore was hard but for me at least, with a clear target in mind, some of the earlier optimism returned as I wrote in my journal:

> *We are learning patience and while we're at it, learning that we can administer ourselves at sea. We can eat, sleep and continue to function.*

K We beached the boat in the bay at Tuktoyaktuk around 0530, and settled down to sleep only to be woken a few minutes later by children who had come to investigate the new arrival. During the eternal daylight of summer, many Inuit children adopt an unusual body clock that sees them awake most of the 'night.' We were as friendly as possible, and eventually they left us to catch a few hours sleep.

I took a short walk into town and took time to reflect. It was my forty-second birthday, we'd covered 115 miles in thirty-six hours but we had a long way to go and I began to feel that maybe we couldn't do this and that if that was true, I'd be letting everyone down. Many people had believed in Tony and me and our plan but the goal seemed very distant. I asked myself why I always have to attempt the unattainable. I had attempted a mountain biking trip to the Himalayas in 1988 to cycle to the basecamps of all fourteen of the eight thousand metre peaks. Everyone said it couldn't be done, but I had read *Bicycles up Kilimanjaro* by the Crane brothers and was convinced you could cycle almost anywhere. I got to five basecamps including K2 high on the Baltoro Glacier before suffering compressed nerves in my shoulders from carrying the bike. The expedition continued, or rather, my main partner in this five person trip continued mostly carrying his bike, much as we had done earlier, to ten basecamps. He went on to be my best man, and then lead a group which became the first to cycle from the Dead Sea across Asia and then summit Everest, the Longest Climb on Earth.

Was this going to end a few more miles up the coast, and even if it didn't would it just be relentless and not enjoyable at all? I spoke to Amber on the satellite phone and realised I was quite emotional and missing her and my two young sons. I wondered whether I needed to come and do this trip to reaffirm my contentment with family life. Not that I was unhappy before I had come away, and so I put my reasons for coming all this way and putting myself through this down to having always wanted to live a life of extremes, within certain boundaries and constraints, one of which was, of course, my family.

My journal for 26th July, my birthday, reads

It's early days – we've been gone less than 48 hours. We need to break the journey down into small goals. We've got time. There will be successes, if we get the right winds.

Later I talked through my concerns over the trip with Tony, who was more upbeat than me. We set ourselves a new target in the back of our minds of our mid-way stop, Cambridge Bay. Surely we could work along the coast to there in the time we had. We would sail when we could, row when we had to and camp on shore to catch up on sleep when we needed to. Not for the last time, we were re-assessing our definition of success. We told ourselves that to be too focussed on the whole passage was dangerous, which in reality it probably was.

Having purchased another ten-litre container of water, we re-stowed some of the gear incorporating the lessons of the past two days. The town mayor came to see us, presenting us with Tuktoyaktuk T-shirts. Finally the locum vicar arrived. A bearded, genial and softly spoken gentleman probably in his late fifties introduced himself in an English accent as Andy Yorke from the Isle of Wight. Rather bizarrely for such a tiny remote settlement, he had spent ten years here in the eighties and had returned to cover for the current vicar's vacation, bringing his family for a holiday. We accompanied them visiting some friends from when they had previously lived here, and sampled caribou meat dipped in Whale Oil and later smoked Arctic Char. It was wonderful to be welcomed so warmly, albeit tagging along with Andy and his family. For us it was a very rare and privileged insight into modern Inuit life. Despite the traditional food, a large Plasma screen dominated the living room displaying typically bland daytime TV. Of course, we had nothing to give in return, partly because we were travelling on a small boat and partly because it would be difficult not to appear patronising. Later, Andy and his family took us round 'Tuk' in the evening to view the pingos up close, along with eagles and other large birdlife. They introduced us to the 'Tuk Wave,' the almost incessant motion of ones hands to keep the midges away which were unpleasant but not unbearable. I had enormous respect for what Andy had achieved living here, but despite the inherent excitement that I always felt about remote frontier towns, I had to admit that I couldn't live here for very long.

As we pulled up back at our boat, and before we had opened the doors to the mosquitoes, Andy explained that he had been here in 1986 when the two Canadians aboard *Perception,* the yellow Hobie Cat on the Polar Passage expedition, had passed through. They were the first to sail the Northwest Passage, and I remember reading that they had completely re-stowed and left a large amount of unwanted kit in Tuk. Being reminded of that made me feel a bit better about our situation. Andy had said a prayer for their safe passage and asked if we would like the same. Neither Tony or I are particularly religious but having spent the afternoon in such fantastic company it seemed appropriate. He asked the Lord to give us the wisdom to know when it was safe to travel and make progress in our boat. It had been an emotional day, and despite its inauspicious start, a really memorable birthday.

An hour later we were sailing fast up the coast with the wind coming directly from the side, called beam reaching. The wind was steady and coming directly off the land, so there was no swell or chop on the sea. With nothing to slow her down, the boat was doing over six knots and we were eating up the miles into the evening.

T   A long sail through the night gradually morphed from an exhilarating and fast beam reach into a beat into the face of a cold polar wind. We had debated how far to venture from land, with my voice on this occasion being the more adventurous in chasing boat speed. More importantly, sailing out of sight of land was another step in building our confidence in the boat and ourselves. Still the feeling of isolation you experience on watch was a new experience. Just the two of us in our tiny boat, and Kev was wrapped up in his cocoon sleeping bag with his Gore-Tex bivvi bag pulled up high over his head. I felt small and insignificant in comparison to the latent power of nature surrounding us but surprisingly not intimidated. We can't fight the forces of nature but we are perhaps learning to read her moods and use them to our advantage. Perhaps the only real problem is that Bootnecks (a slang term for Royal Marines) do tend to see themselves as somewhat indestructible and it takes a lot to change that mind set and turn down a challenge.

Sailing through the night was both mentally and physically tiring and the lack of sleep began to show on both of us. Through unspoken mutual consent we agreed to leave the iPod playing throughout the night to help keep us awake. On my second period on watch after two hours frozen on the tiller and several shadow-boxing combinations simply to try and keep the blood flowing, my eyes kept shutting. Moments later my tiredness evaporated as I sighted our first iceberg. This 'first ice' inexorably drew me towards it in a way I hadn't anticipated. A couple of long needless tacks ensured we were on course for a close pass before I woke Kev and pointed it out.

K Having done a long, cold watch in the early hours, Tony woke me at 4 a.m. to point out a huge lump of ice which had emerged from the early morning mist. The small iceberg was beautiful with deep blue colours on its underside and contorted formations where it had partially melted. We could hear the sea lapping at its underbelly. Suddenly I could remember why we had come all this way. Part of the fascination was thinking how far this piece of ice had travelled; up here it probably hadn't calved off a glacier. It was more likely that it had recently been part of a pressure ridge on a huge unbroken ice floe that formed last autumn, and gradually by the heat of the sun and motion of the waves it had broken free, changing every day as it melted and pieces dropped off. It had its own sad tale that nobody could know, and in a few days it would end as a small chunk of ice that would disappear into the vastness of the Arctic Ocean.

T Over the course of the trip we were to see thousands of similar large chunks of ice but this was our first encounter and it called to us like virgins at the school dance. The action of the waves had carved intricate shapes into its flanks or else smoothed them to polished perfection. At its heart it lifted its skirt to the swell to reveal a deep blue underside curving out towards the boat. Conscious of the risk of approaching too close I circled the ice at a distance of about twenty yards marvelling at this, the vanguard of the ice sheets to the north and imagining vividly what lay just over the horizon awaiting us.

K   To stay on the same tack we were now some way offshore, and once on watch I contemplated our surreal situation; our tiny boat, the vast sea with a few icebergs dotted across it. I was enjoying the calm remoteness of sailing on our own on a sea that just a couple of weeks ago was frozen. Later in the morning, after the wind had died, the stillness was incredible. As huge flocks of sea birds swooped in perfect formation, Tony observed, "It's almost as if you can hear their wings flapping."

T   Again on watch, ghosting through the pale watery light of the early hours on a steady but light southerly wind, I gradually became aware of a gentle exhalation several feet behind me and just off to port. Almost immediately another louder whoosh of exhaled air came from little more than five feet off the starboard beam. As we sliced through the dark Arctic seas a collection of infinitely more graceful travelling partners briefly permitted us to join them. For the next ten to fifteen minutes *Arctic Mariner* journeyed in the centre of a pod of at least 20 pristine white beluga whales. In the pre-dawn twilight their ghostly presence was more often sensed than seen, a rush of exhaled air or the occasional glimpse of a pure white back curving gracefully below the surface. Perhaps they interrupted their stately progress northwards to come and investigate our dark-hulled sailing boat, or perhaps we were merely fortunate to be heading on parallel courses for a while. Either way the experience enchanted us both, leaving us silent for long minutes afterwards. These were the memorable experiences we had come here looking for, not a desperate rush to some distant finish line, and that night my lingering doubts were firmly locked away.

    As the wind dropped away we opted to sail and eventually row, back towards land. Grounding ten yards short of a long white sandy beach with a grassy bluff just behind, we debated how best to secure the boat in these benign sunny conditions. A nagging voice in my head seemed to say "This weather is a passing gift, there'll be a reckoning to come," but for now we were content to take what we had and bask in the strong sunlight.

K With the direct heat of the sun it was warm enough to sit in shirt sleeves, although before long the sand flies arrived in droves. We walked ashore with the intention of test firing our pump action shotgun, carried as protection against bears. For a target, we found what we assumed to be a part of a whale vertebra. It was about thirty centimetres across, so from a distance of about thirty yards made for a reasonably challenging shot. We had been advised to load the magazine with shot first, to scare the bear, then slug, then shot then slug etc. The slug rounds looked menacing enough being over an inch long, but people we had spoken to said it would take more than one round to stop a charging bear.

Despite my profession, I still have a healthy respect for weapons of any sort, and we were careful to ensure we knew how the safety catch and load worked. We fired a shot and a slug each, both hitting the vertebrae with the slug round. Although Tony just clipped the side of it, mine split it into several pieces. Despite this, I was still happier that Tony was the main 'operator' of the weapon, and he naturally carried it, while I carried the cameras. Soon after the firing, we spotted a small caribou loitering around the sand dunes behind the beach. We had already decided amongst ourselves that we weren't going to supplement our food with any fresh meat, it simply seemed unnecessary to destroy one of these magnificent creatures. His downy hair-covered antlers were not fully formed but still superb. Back in the boat, we were half dozing, writing journals in the late afternoon sun when we heard a gradually increasing low clattering sound. As we looked up, four full grown caribou galloped along the beach five feet from the bow of the boat and away out of sight. I looked at Tony. We didn't need to say anything. We were both already overwhelmed by the experiences of the afternoon. There was something very special about our tiny boat alone on this vast expanse of beach, and I contemplated the possibilities of what lay in the journey ahead. I wrote in my journal entry for 27th July:

I need to remember this, because just as I haven't enjoyed every moment (far from it) of any trip I've been on, you have to go through the hard times to get to the special ones. It's a life of extremes.

I even managed to get the netbook to take a charge after the bright sun had topped up the batteries. I was already starting to be slightly worried that the battery needed to be almost fully charged to get any charge into the laptop battery. And we had no alternative. We downloaded a whole load of messages, culled from the website by Dan back in the UK and then sent as one long email. It really acted as a lift, a reminder of home, but tonight we didn't really need the lift.

The wind continued to be fickle and unhelpful. After rowing for an hour or so I was feeling an ache in my lower back. My mind returned for the first time in a long while to those awful days seven months ago when I was virtually bed-ridden. To have got the boat in the water up here, it would be awful to have to stop for that. I tried to put it out of my mind, but realised I had to tell Tony, who typically and predictably was uninterested. After all there wasn't much we could do about it. I just had to be careful, but I dreaded the thought of weeks with an ache, having to be bent double to get in and out of sleeping bags under our canvas cover, and the boat bouncing around. We changed direction by 45 degrees as we rounded a headland, and what wind there was seemed to still come from the bow. It is easy to get despondent but in light winds you have to remember that the wind vane is also affected by the motion of the boat so it will always appear to be more into wind than it actually is.

We tried to minimise the use of the GPS because it was another unnecessary drain on our power. Besides, the long lead that we had from the 12-volt socket in the bow was difficult to keep out of the way, and I could easily see it getting wet. We had some batteries but not that many and I regretted not having thought this through and brought rechargeable batteries that we could charge when the sun shone. As a result, with very few reference points from land, and often being out of sight, we navigated quite a lot using the compass. In reality we set course using the GPS to give a direction on the compass and then switched the GPS off. It helped to not think too much about the actual direction shown on the compass because the magnetic variation caused by the difference between True North and the North Magnetic Pole was over 40 degrees, being so close to the magnetic pole. In most latitudes this difference is less than five degrees. This also caused the compass to react very slowly but in its oil-filled case it coped well with the continual bouncing around.

I remember thinking we were like a tortoise, slow steady progress into wind carrying our house and all we need with us. Whereas the Polar Passage team on the Hobie Cat in the eighties were definitely the hare. They could sail closer to the wind and much faster but they had to stop every eight to ten hours, get to shore, drag the boat on to the beach and put the tent up just to get to the stage at which we were starting to cook, still making slow progress. To alleviate the boredom, we listened to the iPod for several hours each day, unaware of how much power this was draining from the battery. My iPod had been well stocked by Amber with three playlists—General Favourites, Motivational Rowing Music and Mellow Listening. As we sailed along, listening to the mellow one, in the sunshine, with more icebergs in the vicinity and another sighting of belugas, *I'm on the Top of the World* sung by Karen Carpenter struck up. We didn't sing along, but this was probably only because it was early in the trip and we didn't know each other that well.

As we progressed further along the coast, day routine became night routine but in reality there was no difference. The sky remained the same, the time on our watches only relevant in that it determined who helmed. The sea became rougher and the wind increased, still coming from the general direction we wanted to go. Making long wide tacks we found ourselves quite a long way offshore; we had long since lost sight of the thin strip of land. I measured the wind speed at only sixteen knots and although impressed by the way *Arctic Mariner* rode the waves I couldn't help but ponder our true viability in big seas. We reduced sail to its minimum but we realised that in much stronger winds we would only be able to go generally downwind. In order to get any drive into the waves the boat heeled over too far. It didn't feel dangerous but I knew how alone and exposed we were and I still dreaded a capsize if a sudden squall hit us. We decided against crashing into the waves all night and ran for shelter. Tony was his consistent, measured, calm self. I was glad he was here.

Before we were near the vague line that constituted shore we were negotiating a myriad of sand bars. We grounded and realised that as we were still several hundred yards offshore there would be no getting to shore. We assembled our tiny anchor and were impressed at its holding in the sand. Tony donned a drysuit to walk it out away from the boat to set it and we finally ate at 1 a.m. This area has been reasonably exploited for its hydrocarbons already, and no doubt this will expand over the next few decades. It seemed so isolated and desolate that it didn't detract from the perception of a true wilderness any more than Tuktoyaktuk or the Radar reflector beacons that we occasionally saw marked on the chart adorning some windswept low lying sand dune.

T After the intelligence test of assembling the anchor and a well-deserved meal we took a little time to reflect on our surroundings. McKinty Bay is a broad, shallow bay made up of what geologists firmly believe to be heavily oil bearing strata. Our anchorage was therefore overlooked by a several inquisitive seals and a huge isolated drilling rig 3-4 miles out in the bay. Mulling over man's growing impact on this otherwise untouched pristine environment lasted just three minutes before my eyes closed and I slipped into eight hours of oblivion.

Sleep makes all the difference, we both woke refreshed to flat calm conditions and sunshine. We lifted anchor at 1000 after a slow breakfast and set out by oar power. Kev rowed first making good progress at about two knots. After about half an hour he called me to look at another white beluga pacing us at about thirty yards off the starboard beam. I took the oars for the second hour pulling strongly now with the desire to get out of sight of the oil platform, as an indication of progress if nothing else. Towards the end of my stint the wind came up again and we hoisted the sails. Beating again we were rapidly making progress towards another mini ice berg. Kev suggested we get a photo stood on it. I was more cautious but easily persuaded so we continued on towards it. Looking at it more closely, Kev had to admit that there was no easy way on to it, but his eagerness to try perhaps demonstrates our different approach to risk.

K Our latest problem was water. We had been on board for four days, two without getting out of the boat, and the low lying shore, even when it could be reached, yielded no fresh water. Cape Bathurst was our first real goal for a number of reasons. It was the most northerly point on this part of the trip, it seemed to have some hills and maybe some rivers, but most of all it was at the end of our first true open water passage across Liverpool Bay. A forty mile crossing and we would be twenty miles from land in the middle. Already we were longing to travel down the narrow passage that separated it from a small island, the Snowgoose Passage. We weren't out of water but we decided to try the Reverse Osmosis Watermaker that turns seawater into fresh. It was one of our essential safety items. With it we could survive almost anywhere. Without it, we had maybe a week at most without finding fresh water. I had borrowed the unit from the Marines, and it was quite old, but I had tested it in my kitchen before we left. These devices are far from simple and they need to be looked after. They basically work by forcing seawater at very high pressure through a very fine membrane and as such they are quite hard work to use. They would be ideal as a physical exercise machine because you cannot rest. You have to maintain the pressure and pump steadily. If you stop, you waste another minute to get it back up to pressure, during which the machine produces salty water. With the inlet hose dangling over the side and continually pumping for five minutes we had made just over a cup full. We filled one of our 750ml ready-use bottles and packed it away.

T   As the day progressed the wind picked up and the air got a lot colder. We roar up to Philips Island at over 6 knots only to turn the corner at the top of the Tuk peninsula to find a long sandy island where our charts clearly showed a mile-wide gap in the sandbar. When we realise that the chart was last surveyed well before we were both born the reason becomes clear. As we set about discovering a new way through the maze of shifting sands my mind wanders to those that worked so hard to chart these waters in the 18th century, often with disastrous results.

K   Tacking backwards and forwards, I noticed the two different styles of helming between Tony and me. Tony has done lots of racing, and prefers to maintain good boat speed even if that means he can't point quite as close to where we want to go. I like to 'pinch,' sailing close to the wind, slowing down a bit but at least you feel as if you are going in the right direction. Each has its merits, but in the absence of any data about the currents it was difficult to assess which was best. I tried to adopt more of his style but when the mind wanders… I suppose we agreed to differ. There was no argument but as we got more tired it was a source of tension.

As the wind picked up and the waves knocked the bow back, the hours dragged on and we seemed to be no closer to our objective, the low lying Cape Dalhousie which was the start of the run to Cape Bathurst. We couldn't make out the shape of the island marked on the chart, which we discovered later was two small rises joined by a narrow low lying strip of beach. We quarrelled over where to head, how far away the shore was and when we should tack. But I knew everything was OK when Tony suggested we delayed dinner until we got there, "We'll have a morale meal, take our time, have a chat."

We ate at 0130, having grounded twenty-five metres offshore. I was in the drysuit and walked to the beach, occupied by two huge caribou which wandered off down the narrow spit of land. Having climbed to the 'racon' (radar reflector beacon) up a loose sandy cliff about ten feet high, I suddenly realised looking north there was nothing between us and the polar ice cap. How many people come here every year? And of course most yacht crews simply wouldn't have come into shore close to all these shifting sandbanks. Despite the drab scenery of brown sand, it was still exhilarating just being here but then there were the nagging worries. How long would we be here? There was no way we could attempt the crossing in fresh easterly winds and tack all the way. Do we go south and follow the coast all the way round the bay? That would add an extra eighty odd miles. Where do we shelter from a storm? We need to try the inflatable rollers to get the boat up on the beach. This uncertainty might worry me but it also fascinates me. It's why we are here. But I can feel my back aching again.

III

OPEN WATER IN AN OPEN BOAT

K It was fantastic to receive messages from the website that Dan had pasted into one long email. I was amazed at the variety of people who were following our progress. It was obvious from the messages that we were living a story which people wanted to follow. There was real admiration in some of the messages and I felt quite pleased but very aware of the task ahead. We took turns to write the blog for the website, and managed to send and receive messages most days, along with the odd photo that we shrunk down to minimum resolution. Tony sums up our predicament well:

T *30 July, 2009: Thursday morning and I'm lying in my sleeping bag under a damp cloth cover in a space that's just a little too small for two young children but with Kev for company. Cosy, no doubt, but getting a little aromatic. The wind remains the bane of our lives at the moment. Inevitably it's blowing from exactly the direction we wish to go!!!!!! It has been for four days now and is forecast for at least another couple of days. We're not swearing at the sky yet, but if this doesn't let up soon there may be a few choice words being spoken. For those land-lubbers amongst you a word of explanation as to why our progress may seem rather pedestrian. Essentially a sailing yacht cannot sail directly into wind and in order to make any progress at all we must beat to wind. In layman's term one long Zig followed by an equally long Zag, neither of which are in the right direction but put together slowly inch you closer to your destination. It's a constant battle between boat speed and angle on the wind. Coming off the wind increases your speed but means your zig gets just that little bit longer. Pointing closer to the wind means you have less distance to cover but you do it very slowly. Needless to say course selection is a lively source for debate. None of this is helped by the 3-4 foot waves which can easily stop a 17 foot boat dead. Enough excuse-making, we content ourselves that we have indeed sailed about three times the straight line distance on the chart.*

That said, morale is high and we are starting to drop into a routine. Weather and offshore sandbars (everywhere) have kept us on the boat for three days now. Mornings usually consist of waking to the gentle rocking of the boat on its anchor, Kev proclaiming in a moment of optimism that he's sure the wind has moved a few degrees off our nose... and then settling in to make breakfast in a steady easterly! Meals are dehydrated for three days with a 'wet' ration one day in four. Most are surprisingly good but there's the obvious dud one in there and we've resorted to paper-scissors-stone to decide who gets what! Before departure we don layer after layer of clothing. In my case a thermal polypro top and bottoms, a T-shirt, lightweight trousers, aquafleece, micro fleece, gilet, sallopettes, semi-dry top, hat, gloves and 'headover' neck scarf. It's usually just after struggling into all of this that you decide you need a pee.

Normally within an hour of waking we are off and sailing or occasionally pulling on the oars. We both start the day on watch together but as the morning drags on one or the other of us will hunker down in the bow of the boat and either grab some sleep or crack some admin, passage planning, blog writing etc. As the day progresses we will stand alternate watches of usually no more than 3 hours or so. After that the cold and tedium of time on the tiller begins to tell. We have recently set ourselves daily targets to achieve, governed principally by practical considerations of finding shelter for the night. Although we've proved our ability to sail continuously while living on the boat, beating to wind in moderate seas takes its toll on both us and the boat, and a few hours at anchor each night has been a blessing.

Yesterday we started out with the tentative aim of crossing Russell Inlet and making Cape Dalhousie. After a long sail which saw us picking our way through a field of mini-icebergs and then an equally tricky maze of sandbars we finally made our destination at 0130 this morning, tired but content. When we tumbled into our pits last night we had to admit to a little despondency about the continued easterly wind but after reading all the messages from home, today seems very much a different day and just perhaps Kev's southerly tinge to the easterly has finally shown up!!

K   After this message had been sent we received the weather forecast from midday Greenwich Mean Time (Zulu time), on the 30th July until 1200Z on 1st August, in a short email as follows:

DTG WIND(KTS) WAVE(FT) VIS WX
3012Z ESE131823 E0204 NIL Sunny. High 28. UV index 4 or moderate.
3100Z ESE131823 E0204 NIL Clear. Low 13.
3112Z E152025 E0204 NIL Sunny. High 24.
0112Z ENE152000 E0204 NIL A mix of sun and cloud. Low 16. High 20.

With the time difference it was already 1700 Zulu time on 30th July, so the forecast was for eighteen more hours of ESE 13 knots gusting to 18 or 23 knots and then freshening easterly winds. I certainly don't recall the 28 degrees and the sun burn risk, but it wasn't cold. I spoke to Dan back in the UK on the satellite phone to discuss this latest forecast given that we were about to set out east to cross to Cape Bathurst. It was good to hear another voice, and we discussed the slight shift in the wind forecast that might allow us to get across. But of course it was Tony and my decision and this was the first real test of our Go/No Go criteria.

T   I'm not sure if it was imagination or wishful thinking but we both agreed there was a definite southerly element to the wind and were keen to attempt the thirty mile open crossing to the Snowgoose channel and Cape Bathurst. Whilst I do remember thinking thirty miles was a long isolated crossing in our tiny boat I was rapidly becoming seduced by our progress to date and the promise of getting right back on schedule. Kev seemed equally enthusiastic to keep our daily average close to the planning figure so meticulously calculated in the warmth of his London flat. As a result there was little debate that morning.

K   As we prepared to depart, we had noticed a little bit of play in the rudder and saw that the glued cheeks either side of the blade itself were very slightly separating. Having unpacked most of the locker to get the spares and tools, and using my grandfather's brace (hand drill), we strengthened it with a bolt. Sat under the milky but warming sun, carefully tending to our little boat, we were confident and looking forward to Cape Bathurst and what lay beyond. We set off, beating, but able to steer directly in line with the GPS direction arrow set for Cape Bathurst thirty five miles hence. The boat was sailing well, cutting through the two-foot waves with ease. I lay under the flimsy cover while Tony helmed and we talked about the complexities involved in the preparation for and conduct of our journey. With a sense of pride, we listed them and I jotted down in my journal: Logistics of getting the boat to Inuvik, food, fuel and water, navigation, weather and ice, sailing and rowing technique, boat maintenance, blogging and photography, electrical power management, first aid, protection from wildlife, media angles and lastly the potentially stressful interaction between Tony and me. We were confidently looking forward to the milestone of Cape Bathurst.

By mid-afternoon the wind had turned more easterly and we made a series of long tacks with the sea building all the time. We had reefed our mainsail down to its minimum to meet the increasing wind. This is not an easy task at the best of times and the boat was still relatively new to us. The system we had devised involved dropping the curved pole that held up the main canopy forward so you could stand and reach forward to the mast. The helmsman then slackened the mainsheet and headed into wind, bringing the sail towards the crewman who had released the main and peak halyards and lowered the sail. (The peak halyard controls the short curved spar at the head of the sail, which gives it a larger area than the Bermudan triangle, for the same mast height.) He then had to clip the spare mainsheet to a point higher up the sail and then roll, as best he could, the sail around its battens. The reefing lines were permanently attached and consisted of loops with knots which, provided tension remained, would keep the sail rolled away. The loops could only be fastened when within arm's reach, which meant holding the boat close to the wind, and it was a two-handed job so he couldn't hold the sail in as well. Having replaced the original mainsheet, the tension had to be taken up in the main hoist and the gaff hoist, and in high winds this could only be achieved when the pressure was out of the sail, so the boat had to be close to the wind. There then followed the relatively simple task of winding in some of the foresail around itself to reduce its sail area. Sailing lore says that if you have thought about putting in a reef then it is time to do so and often the boat sails faster, and of course always more level after reefing. But our boat was not designed for beating into high winds, and with a reefed sail she did not point into wind very well due to the partially compromised shape of the sails.

Almost halfway across at around 8 p.m. we discussed whether we should turn back. But we were still making progress; four knots through the water and maybe one and a half in the direction of the Cape. Not for the last time, the expected time of arrival at our waypoint at landfall on the Cape started slipping. The boat was pitching up and down but felt very stable and neither of us was overly worried about capsize. It wasn't particularly cold, and as I readied myself to come on watch it wasn't with a sense of dread but I admit to some apprehension. As often happens, the off going helmsman has become confident as the conditions have built up. Even after a few minutes of getting used to helming the boat, I was still somewhat nervous. The boat was pitching around quite violently in the waves and the wind was strong enough to demand concentration to hold the boat close into it. With the sails set as they were, the boat would be driven dangerously fast if the wind came from the side, and this would increase the chances of capsize. In addition to the rudder, the mainsheet had to be played to allow for the gusts, and most importantly you had to read the sea, avoiding the worst waves and those that were breaking.

We decided to don our drysuits. These were a thousand pounds' worth of Gore-Tex borrowed from the military, and of course doubled up as our immersion suits if we were to go into the water. We moved the life raft from its stowed position in the bow into the cockpit—just in case. Tony got into his drysuit, and then had to come back on to the helm while I put mine on. Helming and doing up the other bloke's drysuit zip across the back proved challenging but we felt properly prepared for the weather, which was certainly not abating. I went to return to the helm but Tony resisted, saying he was happy to helm. It briefly went through my mind that he didn't entirely feel happy with me helming, but this was no time to contest it; we needed both of us playing to our strengths and he was a good helm. To be honest I was somewhat relieved. I remained in the cockpit, using my weight to balance the boat, and took the opportunity to do a bit of filming. I had a waterproof video camera which came into its own. The waves seemed huge against the diminutive black hull, and for the size of our boat, they *were* huge.

There are two truths of sailing in heavy weather. The first is that the waves always seem bigger than they are, and the second is that if you try to film them they never look as big. Now while this might seem self-cancelling, it is the perception of the motion of the waves and how it affects the boat that is important. With some experience, but from our position only a few inches above the water surface we agreed these waves were eight to nine feet, and this wasn't just a swell, they were breaking tops. Swell is no problem to any boat as long as the wavelength is significantly longer than the boat length. This wasn't. And my greatest fear, as in any boat, was being caught broadside in a breaking wave. The surf picks the boat up and pushes the boat further over, with the very real prospect of capsize.

The day had started well but with the shifting wind had come a short steep swell that built rapidly, making helming hairy but exhilarating nonetheless. After a long spell on the helm I felt I had the measure of the conditions and could read the next wave before I saw or even felt it. It had taken me hours to build this sense of affinity with the conditions and I found myself strangely reluctant to cede the helm to Kev. The concentration it demanded was immense and was no doubt wearing me down, but it was acting like a drug. Whilst I remained fixed on the helm I barely noticed the hours passing by. I was comparing Kev's handling of the boat having just come on watch with mine having got used to the conditions and knew it was a wholly unfair comparison but nevertheless I think we both felt happier once back in our assumed roles.

Given the size of the waves and the amount of water we were taking into the boat I probably should have been more scared or at least more aware of the risk we were taking. The challenge was all-consuming and I remember the exhilaration of guiding the boat through each set of waves and then pitting myself mentally and physically against the next set rolling in. I became transfixed with the immediate, increasingly at the expense of the bigger picture. *Arctic Mariner* was doing us proud in big seas but she was struggling to point high enough into the wind and again I wondered if the decision to go for a loose footed sail was a wise one. A boom would have given us considerably more control over the shape of the sail and better performance into wind. As it was, despite all our efforts we were making precious little progress towards Cape Bathurst and there was a limit to how long we could sustain this degree of effort in these conditions.

K   I picked up the GPS and the chart but was only concentrating on the numbers on the GPS. We had ten miles to go, but with our tacking angle it would take us about five to six hours. It was going to be a long night, and I longed to be there, in the shelter of the Cape and on land. It wasn't lonely. Tony is usually good company and although we weren't talking much, at least he was there. But we did seem exposed, the wind howling, the grey, cold sea crashing, in the odd light that passes for night at these latitudes in the summer.

   We did talk about the options, and the dangers. We didn't yet fear for our lives, but if we had been in this position thirty or forty years ago we probably would have. Capsizing back then would have meant very little chance of survival. If our boat went over we might not be able to right her, but we at least we had the chance of ending up in the life raft, with a waterproof grab bag containing a satellite phone, GPS, and of course we had our Emergency Position-Indicating Radio Beacons (EPIRBs). These were kept on the body at all times, and in extreme emergency would send a distress signal including our GPS position. It would be an enormous effort for someone to rescue us, involving helicopters flown by cargo plane from South Eastern Canada or maybe an icebreaker could be diverted to come and pick us up. It wouldn't be fun and there would certainly be a few people saying "I told you so," but it stood a reasonable chance of being successful. I thought back over our Go/No Go decision and our thoughts of turning back earlier. I studied the GPS track, our slow painstaking zigzag line. Just after midnight, and having eaten some chocolate and nuts, I finally persuaded Tony to take a break from the helm. We hadn't had a hot drink in eight hours and of course couldn't cook hot food in the well of the cockpit which was awash with icy seawater.

T   Two years earlier at a particularly low point whilst running in the *Marathon de Sables* (a 150-mile run across the Sahara desert), my running partner and I had passed several hours, and many miles, trying to imagine what animal the other most closely resembled. To lighten the mood I decided to try the same approach with Kev. Maybe he wasn't in the mood. After a long pause he said, "I can't think of one but you resemble some kind of dog—loyal, dependable."

   Back in the desert I'd described myself as a wolf so maybe he was close. "Feisty terrier or pet labrador?" I replied.

He didn't commit. I couldn't think of a real animal that Kev resembled so settled for Winnie-the-Poo's partner in crime, Tigger! I think he liked the analogy even if at that moment he didn't feel particularly Tigger-like. His was a wry smile but at least we were still smiling.

K There weren't many jokes, and neither of us was anything but composed and focused. I settled myself into the helming, trying to pinch against the wind to open up our zigzag track. We had no way of knowing if a current was pushing us back as well, but after our latest track it was clear that with the wind now at its greatest intensity so far, probably about 25 knots, and the waves having built to what they now were, we were making almost no progress. We were sailing back down the same track. Where we had been making some progress, it was now impossible to see, and we had no idea how long this wind would last and if it would increase still further. We knew we were on the limit. We never seriously considered beating onwards to aim for a landfall further south, but I think neither of us fancied another few hours beating into this gathering storm to make land that receded from us as we approached on our best angle to the wind.

At 0300 with just five miles to our destination and nearly thirty to run back, it became increasingly obvious to our tired brains that we were not going to make any further progress and reluctantly we made the call to turn around. We knew as soon as we did things would seem better. Running with the wind the apparent wind drops significantly as your speed reduces the feel of the wind where as beating into wind increases it. But running is far from easy in these conditions. The boat wallows with the waves, and too much sail is more likely to over-power the boat and capsize her. Preparing ourselves to change course needed careful planning. As ever Tony talked through it. "We'll run on foresail alone, so I'll drop the mainsail. I'll need to get sail ties round it all and then secure it in the centre of the boat."

"I'll head to wind, release the main a bit and feather us just with the foresail," I replied.

As the mainsail came down the wind caught the peak and main halyards, and started whipping them up. I looked up beyond where Tony was struggling to tie the sail down to prevent it too being caught by the wind. In a mass of dark cloud, spray and flapping rigging I watched helplessly as the loop in the lines from the top of the mast to the base became longer and longer—much longer than they should feasibly be. With a sickening feeling I realised there could be only one explanation. The drag of the howling wind had pulled both lines free of their cleats at the base of the mast. I shouted over the roaring wind at Tony, "We've lost the fucking lines," and pointed at the mast.

Tony looked up, and whilst the black and red main halyard remained flapping just above his head, we both watched as the black and white peak halyard unravelled, slowly at first up to the top of the mast, but then accelerating as the weight of line pulling down overmatched that left hanging in free space. It flicked out of its pulley and into the water, trailing forlornly behind us.

Neither of us blamed the other for the lack of knots in the ends of the lines that would have prevented this. Even if we felt like it, and I didn't at the time, there was no point. We had to deal with the situation as we found it. Tony finished lashing the mainsail and I steered us round on to what was clearly a highly unstable run with the wind and waves. The trick to helming while running is to spend more time looking backwards at the waves that are chasing the boat, than where you are going. It was fortunate that it was extremely unlikely we were going to run into anything else out here. Tony gathered in the now useless peak halyard. "We've got to take the mast down to re-fix that" he said ruefully. "Still, we should be able to run back under foresail alone so we won't need it."

We both eyed the still flailing main halyard, and decided to try and get it. Tony lowered the canvas canopy so he could stand in the boat, and harnessed with our special long line, he ventured on to the deck sides, using the sail for balance. I tried to steer as flat as possible, but at the same time trying to use the wind and the pendulum motion of the swinging line to meet with his hands. The first few attempts were futile, but faced with little alternative we persevered. Again it was dangerous work but we accepted that if Tony went in the water I should be able to get him back in on the harness line. Eventually he grasped the halyard just above his head, and I watched as he ran it back through the cleat by the mast and then deliberately tied an extra-large stopper knot in its end. I still have no idea why that line hadn't run all the way through as the Gaff line had done. There must have been just enough weight in the free end to hold it, even as it flailed about.

T   For the first time I felt the hollow ring in my words. Sailing in these seas without a main should be fine as long as we ran downwind, but our options were narrowing and I distinctly sensed the maw of what sailors and climbers call the 'incident pit' (a potentially fatal accumulation of seemingly minor problems) a little too close for comfort. We were tired, cold and wet, without a mainsail and with nothing but fifty miles of freezing open water between us and the polar ice edge. To top it all I was starting to feel the onset of chronic stomach cramps. We had to be careful we didn't turn a mishap into a disaster.

K   We discussed this, and decided we had to break the chain of events that had led us to where we currently found ourselves, almost thirty miles from our only possible land, in a force 6-7, and nine-foot breaking waves, not having eaten for twelve hours, or slept for eighteen. We were screaming along under a handkerchief of foresail, making over six knots. We checked the GPS, and our track over the last hour since we had turned round was taking us north of our outward route. Re-checking the chart, we realised I had entered the return waypoint incorrectly, and that had set us on to a more northerly route. Having resolved this, I could see Tony wasn't his usual self. I suspected it wouldn't be fear, or worry, and he admitted his stomach cramps. He said he needed to shit. And he was still wearing his drysuit. Over the next twenty minutes, as I steered our beautiful, sturdy boat surfing down the waves on our new course which was almost side on to the wind, Tony stripped off his drysuit, found the bucket, and repeatedly relieved himself three feet in front of me, under the cover of our flimsy canopy. Just when I thought it was over, he would start again.

By now I was struggling, under foresail alone, to hold the course we required to get back to Cape Dalhousie. The further we went off course, the greater the angle we needed on the wind to get back. Tony was finished, and I explained the problem. We tried to hoist a bit of mainsail but without the gaff lifted above the horizontal, the "gooseneck" that slid the gaff up and down the mast just jammed. It even had little wooden balls to help its passage but at the wrong angle these were useless. Our rig was simple and robust but this was a critical point and with the gaff hoist in our hands rather than going up the mast there seemed no solution. Tony was somewhat distracted by clearing up the relatively small amount that hadn't made it into the bucket. I couldn't have cared less if the boat was covered in shit. This was getting serious. The wind must have shifted to come from the south straight out of Liverpool Bay, and we couldn't steer on either tack for either of the landfalls, Cape Dalhousie or Cape Bathurst. Under foresail alone we could only make a course slightly downwind which involved going further offshore. We mulled the consequences. While these winds prevailed, we could only sail, or drift if we deployed the sea anchor, towards the polar ice cap fifty or a hundred miles north. We had to get the mainsail up to seek shelter on land.

Rather than focus on all the hindsights of the day, we concentrated on the problem at hand. There was no swearing, no regrets at our misfortune. We were on our own. Looking at the top of the gaff I suddenly had an idea. If we could fix the gaff hoist to the main hoist, at such an angle that would relieve the pressure on the Gooseneck it would allow us to hoist the mainsail. Tony took over helming and this time I stood on the gunwale with one arm round the mast. I was clipped on and I don't remember feeling any fear, just an intense focus on the sea, the moving boat and the flailing lines. As he kept control of the main halyard I used a karabiner to clip together a loop of rope in the main halyard to a loop of rope in the currently useless gaff hoist. This meant that the curved wooden gaff was held at its mid-way angle to the mast more or less as I had imagined. The angle was far from ideal but I was far from keen on re-doing it. Tony pulled on the halyard and I wriggled the gooseneck up out of my reach to where the mast narrowed marginally and then I pushed up the rings that held the sail to the mast. After several attempts we had a mainsail. Although the gaff swung limply, the sail worked. In fact it wasn't far different from a technique for de-powering the sail where you release the peak halyard, which is called 'scandalizing' the sail. The term has always amused me.

Whilst it was enormously satisfying to feel the change in the boat as we could now head directly for our safe haven, we weren't out of the woods with land still twenty miles away, and the seas showing no sign of abating. I lost count of the number of times we pumped out the boat with the built-in hand bilge pump. It was an essential piece of equipment and we were pleased that we had agreed to the boat builder's suggestion of raising the floor which meant the boat held less water. We could pump out a full cockpit in just over a minute.

Tony slept for a bit in his dry-suit, and that revived him. I willed the miles away, still concentrating hard but every twenty minutes or so I randomly punched the air with alternate hands to keep warm, and to stay awake. The dry-suit was working, and I was still dry, but chilled. The wind had eased, and with Tony back on the helm I lay down and took off my gloves. A horrible sight greeted me. Grey/white wrinkled and flaky skin, peeling off in thin but alarmingly large chunks. I had stupidly worn some close fitting dinghy sailing gloves which sort of kept your hands warm when wet. They had been soaked for over twelve hours when they were probably designed for a two hour dinghy race. I needed to get them dry and warm and quickly realised I was in one of those uncomfortable situations where you have to do something positive to improve things. I took off my drysuit, having been desperate for a pee, and felt warmer. I sorted out the chaos that lay in the front of the boat; waterproof bags, wet clothes, ropes and even the iPod speakers which had been left out and looked decidedly damp. I then put the stove on for a hot drink, after which everything improved. We slept alternately, properly in our sleeping bags, and even had to shake out one reef as the wind had abated.

When I woke, I saw Tony back as his old self, 'goose-winging' the sails, one either side of the boat as the wind was now behind us again. He was concentrating hard, but announced that we only had two miles to go. "What do you think about when you're helming, like last night crashing into the waves?" I asked him.

"I was just concentrating on the helming," he replied. I suppose it was true for both of us, but I spent some time willing away the miles, and on easier watches my mind wandered. It was one of the pleasures, one of the few pleasures, of a long cold watch. I had wondered how I would find the monotony of watch after watch but in reality there was normally something different every day and I was rarely bored. Often tired, normally cold and always glad to stop and at night return to my sleeping bag, but rarely bored.

We tucked the boat into a narrow bay that offered some protection and deliberately ran her aground in the shallow water. We were a hundred yards from where we had started yesterday; it had been a long twenty-six hours. I offered Tony my outstretched hand and he grasped it warmly. "Thanks mate." It was an emotional moment. We were glad to be back on shore but it wasn't as if I feared continuing with the expedition. The thought never entered my head.

T The last twenty-six hours had been something of a coming of age for us. The conditions had taken their toll and I was physically drained by the whole experience, but in taking us so far out of our comfort zone the aborted passage had demonstrated just how far we could push the boat and indeed ourselves. Far from being discouraged by the experience I had a new found confidence in the boat and our capacity to get ourselves out of difficult situations. Perhaps most importantly, as the pressure had come on we found we functioned ever better as a team. We had planned diligently for the trip but there was no way to anticipate every possible scenario and it was inevitable that at times we would be faced with situations we were not prepared for. Despite all our mistakes along the way, successfully meeting the challenge brought with it a very definite sense of achievement and a deeper bond between us. Even if we were only a hundred yards further east after more than a day of hard sailing we were making progress. Perhaps not the kind that could be measured on the chart, but progress nevertheless.

Despite our ordeal the previous night neither of us was ready to sleep, and after an hour or so tidying up the detritus of the night before, putting the boat to bed and erecting the tent for the first time, we set off to explore the tiny island on which we found ourselves temporarily marooned. The boat itself sat in a small bay bounded by sandbars to the north and south and the low island itself to the west. Roughly square and about 400 metres across, the island was dominated by the old 'racon' radar reflector used for navigation in the days before GPS. A twenty-metre-high sand cliff on the extreme western edge dropped down onto a mile long narrow spit of sand that connected to a similar tiny island.

K We walked along the seemingly endless spit of soft sand that joined the two islands, not talking much. The strong wind seemed to leach the moisture from our already dehydrated bodies, leaving us tired and lethargic. We were restless and drawn by an odd-looking red object lying half way along the spit buried in the sand. As we got closer we speculated what it could be, my myopia not helping and I thought it looked like a tent. What would we find in the tent? It was eerie—desolate, deserted, miles from anywhere. There was no boat. I postulated we might find some long dead lone adventurer. In the end a capsule lying one third buried

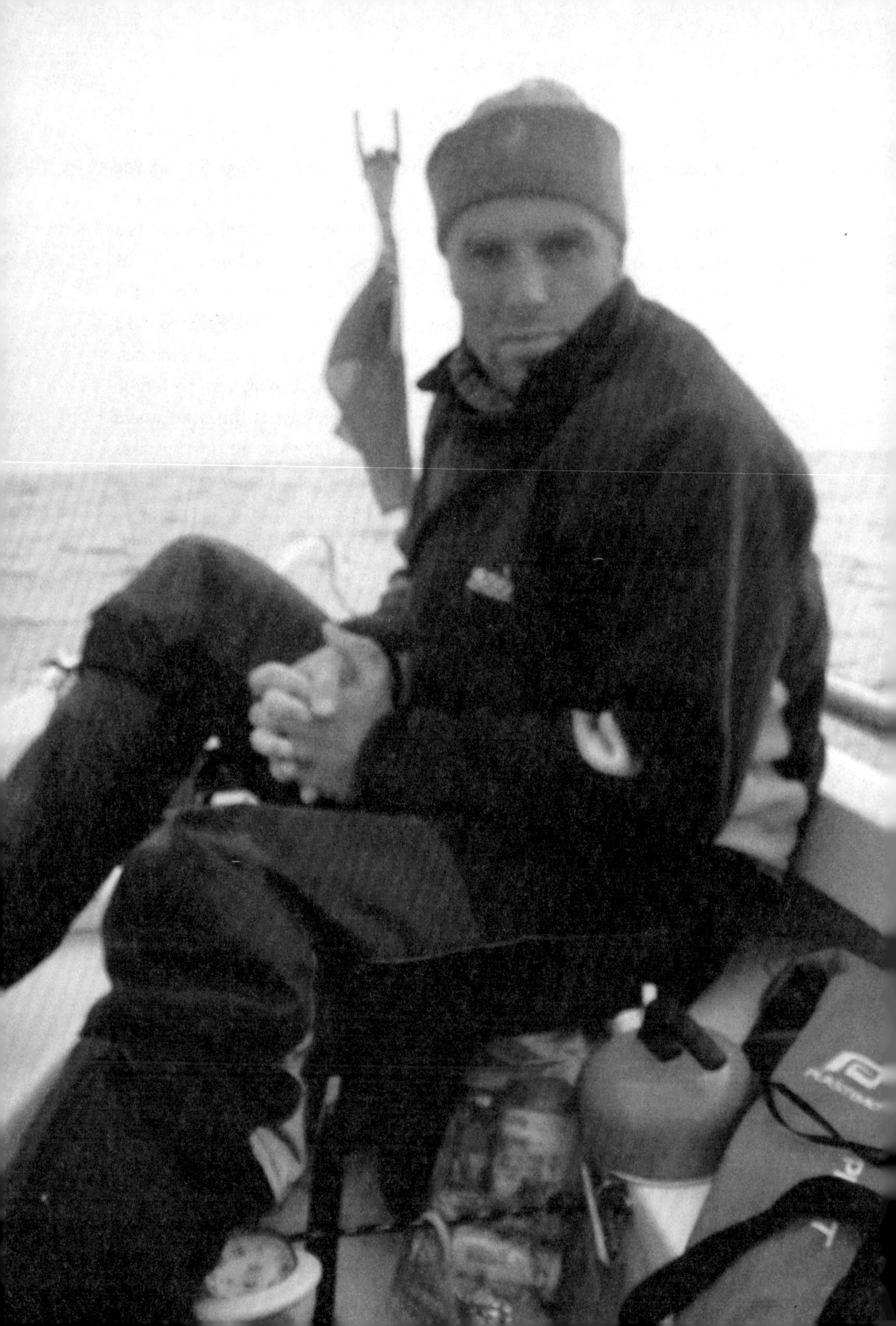

in the sand revealed itself to be an old anchor buoy. It was about ten feet long and five feet across with an identification plate that told us it had been manufactured in Virginia in March 1984. One could only speculate where it had seen its service before breaking loose and drifting to its resting place here.

T   Having walked half the length of the spit we puzzled over the criss-crossing Caribou tracks as we trundled on a further half mile to reach the second island and further signs of human existence in the form of an abandoned Royal Canadian Mounted Police (RCMP) survival cache. These caches are the forlorn remnants of an earlier Canadian attempt to establish sovereignty over the far north. Deposited throughout the Islands in the fifties and sixties they were designed to provide a last refuge for the few mariners the Canadian government managed to coax up into the high north. Almost without exception they now lie empty and broken, often unvisited by humans since they were first established.

K   Having found no water we trudged back along the sand bar, the weariness beginning to bite and our feet increasingly dragging in the sand, back towards the boat. Next to the 'racon' tower we found a shallow, green putrid pool of water which was either evaporating or being drunk by the variety of sea birds in the vicinity. We assumed the caribou were also making use of it, having been marooned on this island after the sea ice had melted a few weeks earlier, and we couldn't see how the tiny pond could sustain them for very long. We assumed therefore that they were likely to die of thirst later in the summer. The naïvety of this assumption was revealed later in the day when we saw these remarkable beasts swimming gracefully between two points of land near our boat. It was obvious they could come and go as they pleased across the half mile straight to the mainland where, unlike us, they presumably had a more reliable source of fresh water. We had ten litres remaining, including our emergency supply which in total was enough for about three days. And of course we had the water maker so we had no real concerns.

We downloaded some messages and a weather forecast before unsuccessfully putting the laptop on to charge. The time lag inherent in sending and receiving messages meant that everyone was oblivious to the trials and tribulations of the

← *The storm had taken its toll*

previous night. But they reaffirmed our belief in ourselves, and lightened the mood. The weather forecast did not, with more easterlies predicted. And after poking about with my multimeter inside the forward compartment where the battery was located it seemed we had let the battery run right down and it didn't have sufficient power to energise the laptop charger. Stupidly I must have shorted something and blew the fuse in my multimeter. Not having a spare, I fixed it with a piece of tin foil, and taped my meter so it was permanently on a high voltage setting. We couldn't mend it out here, and it reminded me of the dependency of the expedition on a few items of equipment. Like the battery, which needed to be nurtured and loved. It needed a long time connected to the solar panels so we retired to the luxury of the tent.

It was the first time we had erected it, and it felt palatial compared to the boat. For the last few days the pair of us had been lying in the cockpit with our legs jammed in under the bow. There wasn't quite enough clearance for our feet to move freely meaning they were immobile and slightly higher than our heads, a situation that wasn't conducive to undisturbed sleep or blood circulation. In the warmth and relative comfort of our tent we had time to reflect on the day. This section of my 30th July journal entry summarises my mood:

> *The weather forecast is a shame, partly because we both want to go and see more of the passage and partly because it looks as if the trip is not working. We have sailed 370 miles in a week but only 170 in the right direction. (My plan had been to make 250 miles a week in ice-free waters.) We continue to take one day at a time. Rest and then see if we can make progress south round Liverpool Bay and up to Cape Bathurst. Am I enjoying it? Hard to say really. It's hard, very hard but there is wonder in where we are and I got some satisfaction from solving our problems yesterday. Five weeks to go and a lot can happen.*

Back in the tent it was a struggle to keep my eyes open. Whilst Kev downloaded some morale messages from home, I made a quick meal and then climbed into my bag intent on some sleep. It had been a hugely demanding day, night and day, and I was physically and mentally drained but feeling surprisingly upbeat. I suspect I was less concerned about the impact on our schedule than Kev. I was keen to get on but not until we had caught up on sleep and properly prepared ourselves for the crossing. I had ten glorious hours in my bag before Kev's enthusiasm kicked in again at 0430. His invitation to get breakfast on was greeted fitfully with a rather curt "Not until I've finished sleeping." I don't recall his exact response but I did notice a distinct lack of protest as we both rolled over and grabbed another couple of hours sleep. At some point during the previous few days my Thermarest had sprung a leak and it was the cold of the ground that finally forced me to abandon sleep at 0730 and launch into a day of maintenance.

K   The following day was taken as rest due to the continued easterlies. So after a late start following a well-earned 16 hours sleep, we set to on a routine of small jobs. Top of the list was watermaking. I set up the system of pipes; one draped over the side and the other into one of our water bottles, and placed the pump across my lap, seated on the rear sliding seat. After pumping to build up pressure and then, sweating profusely having made just three litres, suddenly the pressure dissipated and the system was pumping quite large quantities of what I quickly discovered was salt water into our water bottle. One of the seals inside had clearly blown, and after scanning the manual it quickly became obvious it was irreparable. The machine was almost fifteen years old, and I can only assume had not been serviced correctly. Again, I don't recall any anger, just a sense of acceptance of our situation and a desire to do something about it.

T   It's interesting to note that Kev and I seemed to worry about different things. His focus was firmly on the macro issues of speed, time, distance and overall progress and seemed to oscillate dramatically in response to daily mileage. I was much more agitated by the immediate. On reflection this division probably allowed us to keep perspective but it did mean our priorities didn't always match. My journal for the 1st August:

> *I'm getting a little concerned about our water situation! To be fair I have been mildly concerned about it for a while. I had to obstinately bully Kev into buying a further eight litres of water at Tuk to act as our reserve (We're now drinking it!) Tried the watermaker this morning—All good right up until the point it*

broke. So far it has stubbornly resisted all attempts to fix it hence it was off to the pond with the Katadyne filter, Hmmmmm—Water remains a real concern and we must stock up with a full load of 32 litres over the next couple of days. On a more positive note we managed to get the forecast through over the satphone. Light variable winds in the morning are due to freshen from the NW during the course of the day. The five-day forecast suggests they will stay with us until Wednesday. We should be able to cover over a hundred miles in just one day and get back on schedule if the winds are kind. Even more positively I think I've repaired the leak in my Thermarest and we had a whole packet of Haribo sweets in our rations today (aka Moralibo). Providing we get the forecast winds we should be ok.

K We also had a water purifier that uses a pump, albeit a much less powerful one than used in the watermaker, to force water through a ceramic filter to remove bacteria and amoeba. Although I had used them before, I had never tried it on putrid green water such as we had found the previous day. After pumping hard for a few seconds, the ceramic filter had gone an alarming green colour and the water to be drunk was merely a slightly lighter shade of green. We were not at that stage yet and the risk of becoming ill to the future of the expedition deterred us from tasting any more than a tiny unpleasant sip. Although not yet in a survival situation, we only had six litres and would have to find water within three days. We debated the likelihood of making Cape Bathurst, or heading south into and around Liverpool Bay, although neither left us with any certainty over a source of water, other than some lakes inland marked on the chart that seemed to be on marginally higher ground.

The forecast winds arrived, but we still took some time to pack the boat properly in preparation for the long passage to Cape Bathurst. In the process, I stood in the water for a few minutes barefoot to save getting my boots wet after so thoroughly drying them. We both had Gore-Tex and leather Dubarry boots which although waterproof did hold the water in the leather, which then evaporated in the breeze, providing a cooling effect to the feet. When I got back in the boat to start, I just could not rewarm my numb feet. I eventually placed them in my sleeping bag with my hands covering them, or tucked them in behind the other knee. It must have taken an hour, and even then they didn't feel warm, but at least I had feeling back.

With a following wind, and very light swell, it was hard to believe we were on the same bit of sea as two nights before, but our GPS track eventually told us we were beyond our most easterly point, and soon afterwards we saw land and the Snowgoose Passage, a ten mile long, mile wide channel between the Cape and its outlying island. Forty foot ice walls bedecked the sides of the channel, but beyond that it was again mostly low lying. A flock of what we assumed were snow geese passed low over the boat. There was no sign of human habitation, and it was difficult to judge distances, with no reference points. As usual it was wild, desolate and unwelcoming. With little ceremony we were past the Cape and reaching down the coast of what are known as 'The Smoking Hills.'

T The slow start to the day was a result of my veto of Kev's proposed 0230 departure. The winds had newly turned in our favour and Kev was understandably keen to be away but I feared rushing headlong into a hasty crossing unprepared, and if I'm absolutely honest, fancied another few hours sleep before such a long crossing. When we eventually got away the miles flew by, and rounding Cape Bathurst at 2030 we saw little point in stopping. We turned SE with the wind freshening behind us and the boat flying along at over six knots, and my thoughts turned again to the pressing issue of water. With no clear indication of fresh water lakes we resolved to try what appeared to be a small river flowing just behind the beach. Turning the tiller sharply I picked a wave to run in behind and drove the boat up hard onto a surf beach. Kev disappeared in search of fresh water and I jumped over the side in a full dry-suit to steady the boat. Immediately the flaw in the plan became apparent as I struggled desperately to hold the boat straight in the breaking surf. Each wave pushed the boat sideways forcing me to use all my strength to prevent it broaching on the sand. Alternatively even when I successfully anticipated the wave strike and kept her straight the wave would break violently over the sternboard threatening to swamp us.

As the minutes dragged by I silently cursed Kev for taking so long in his search for water, willing him to return soon. Unbeknownst to me, having discovered the 'river' to be a saltwater overflow, he was frantically searching inland for a freshwater pond. Eventually he returned empty handed and we shoved off into heavy, building surf. Despite the difficulties our need for water was becoming urgent and little more than two miles down the coast we decided to risk the surf again and in a repeat performance of our earlier antics we succeeded in filling up with some of what Kev optimistically described as 'only slightly salty water.'

Having replenished our water stocks we were now in a much better position and making great progress along the coast, but as was rapidly becoming the norm for this expedition, one concern was merely replaced by another. The difficulty was that at no point had we satisfactorily resolved the issue of getting the boat out of the water. Even empty she was far too heavy for the two of us to lift and the inflatable rollers and pulley system was untested. It would require a firm anchor point on the shore close to the waterline, not to mention relatively calm conditions in which to inflate and position the rollers. Our first two landfalls on this long coastline had offered neither and the coastline ahead promised little improvement. In essence, whilst the proximity of the coast offered a potential bolt-hole in bad weather, unless we could find a sheltered anchorage or find a way of getting the boat right out of the water, we faced the unenviable prospect of having to stand off and weather the conditions regardless.

For the moment that was another concern that would have to wait. With the wind behind us every hour's sailing allowed us to tick off more miles. As we sailed SW we alternated watches and as midnight approached Kev slumbered under the canvas cover as I helmed into what I took to be a thick fog. It was already an overcast oppressive twilight with tall dark foreboding cliffs sliding by just 100 yards on my right-hand side when I realised the fog was actually smoke from bitumen in the cliffs which was mentioned in the pilot. It has been burning for centuries deep within these aptly named 'Smoking Hills.' As I put in the blog later:

> *The Arctic continues to be an endless wonder to me. In the early hours of the morning we sailed SW close to shore for around twenty miles in between our two open passages. Such a forbidding coastline I've never seen the like of before. Known as the 'smoking hills' the cliffs here are quite literally alight, and from deep fissures in the rock sulphur-laden smoke pours constantly creating a scene halfway between the Hound of the Baskervilles and Tolkien's cliffs of Mordor.*

More Belugas sighted today and Kev claims also to have seen a big purple whale. Who am I to question him?

K In actual fact, Tony's watch from midnight to 3 a.m. must have been amazing, in the dull misty half-light sailing close to an incendiary shore glowing red hot, and the smell of sulphur adding to the atmosphere. Sadly, I was asleep for most of it, and for weeks afterwards it irritated me that Tony still has it as one of the highlights of the trip. Soon after I came on watch, we turned to cross Franklin Bay, and it was with some regret that I saw the fascinating coastline I had so yearned for in the planning of this trip fade into the distance and quickly disappear from sight, leaving a featureless sea and increasing wind. As for the big purple whale, well, I saw something in the water twenty yards from the boat that seemed to have a spotted dark purple/black skin. I will never know. Certainly we had no hallucinatory drugs, had drunk no alcohol, and were not as tired as one night in Royal Marines officer training when after very little sleep the bloke who shared my trench claimed to see a large tangerine bouncing along the horizon. My journal for Monday 3rd August:

> *It's much colder today (northern element to the wind) and we've got our big mitts on. The watches go quite quickly and I can't say I really enjoy them but it's generally quite serene. The boat sings a song, she hums when going fast and she moans a bit (in lighter airs) when the gaff swivels round the mast. I think about all sorts: Home, distances, or just look at the sea. Made some tea with whitener and it all curdled. Maybe it didn't like the boiling water. I hope it's not the water! Drank it anyway. It was hot, wet and water is precious but it still tasted horrible. Tony's got a bit of a cough and now a sort of cold. Hope he shakes it off soon and I don't get it. We're in pretty close confinement. Apart from a phone call with Amber we haven't spoken to or seen anyone else for eight days now.*

T Throughout the morning the favourable winds held and we made good progress across the wide mouth of Franklin Bay, making our second long open water passage without incident. In sharp contrast to the earlier crossing to Cape Bathurst, my enduring memory is of boredom and fighting to keep my eyes open. As we approached Brook Island on the western edge of the Parry Peninsula I was struggling to maintain a straight course and reluctantly accepted that we needed to stop for some proper rest.

K By mid-afternoon we had completed this 43 nautical mile crossing to reach our next stop, Summers Harbour, which was alleged to be one of the best anchorages in the Northwest Passage. I was surprised by the scale of the charts. I had envisioned a bay opening up the size of Salcombe Harbour, a few hundred metres across but we turned in to find something the size of Plymouth Sound, over a mile across. Whilst large anchorages are important if you are a ten thousand ton container ship, in theory we could stop almost anywhere and it was all rather wasted on us. Still, we had wondered if anyone else would be here. Maybe one of the tiny number of vessels making the passage would have stopped off in need of a safe anchorage We mused how different a transit through the Passage would be in a large steel yacht. There would be lots of time spent far out to sea to avoid the dangers, with landfall made only in a few opportue places. This was clearly one, and I strangely wanted there to be someone else there. The irony of coming all the way up here for the remoteness and then eagerly hoping to meet someone was not lost on us. In a moment of great excitement we saw two large barges anchored in the bay. We presumed that these were the sort of vessel towed through the passage annually to resupply the isolated communities. Tacking up to them, we hoped to find some strange hobo living on board, guarding them! To our great disappointment they were empty and deserted and we turned to run back into the shore and find a landing spot to celebrate our 115 mile non-stop sail, all in the right direction.

I went ashore to secure the boat to a large boulder, then erected the tent and got the stove going while Tony sorted the boat. It was better that way—he was always meticulous in his preparations of the anchor, the lines and the general stowage on board where I would leave things 'as is.' Anyway, it seemed appropriate to our chosen career paths in the Marines; he was a Landing Craft Officer, specialising in small boats where as I was a Mountain Leader Officer, specialising in operating in the Arctic in small teams. Lighting the stove for dessert proved a problem. No matter how I pressurised the fuel bottle, it just would not burn. I've used these stoves for twenty years and quickly dismantled it and removed the jet for cleaning. I tried everything I knew, and was on the point of firstly getting seriously frustrated and pissed off and ultimately getting the spare stove out. Using the spare meant we had no further reserve. At home, I would by now be angry and slightly irrational, but up here knowing that we were self-sufficient I realised I had to remain calm and focused. We had to solve the problem at hand. Tony looked on, but he generally left the technical stuff to my lead. I knew he trusted me to sort it, but this added to my sense of responsibility. Just like I would leave chatting people up to his lead – he's better at that than me. After half an hour, I noticed the fuel bottle was effectively upside down (it lies on its side). This would mean that rather than the pipe getting fuel from the bottom it was sucking air from the top. We had hot dessert and coffee.

We had taken some photographs of us and the boat, complete with our 'Toe in the Water' and Royal Marine flags hoisted up the mast. Our blog references the third member of our crew, 'Commando Joe' still steadfastly strapped to the mast. Also, in the foreground I had strategically placed the other gift from people at work, a three inch long polar bear which stood on a stone that was trying through clever perspective to look like a huge boulder. I was keen to experience all that the Northwest Passage had to offer – bears, scenery and ice. My journal entry for that night, 3rd August, tellingly records my aspirations for the trip:

> Hoping to make Cape Lyon. I know we need to keep moving but I enjoy the stops to see the islands and I hope it doesn't get a bit samey. One third of the way to Cambridge Bay. It's cold on board and I suppose I'm dreading the rain. Looking forward to getting seriously into the ice filled areas at the Eastern end of the Amundsen Gulf.

I was not to be disappointed.

IV

TRAPPED IN THE FREEZER

K   We woke to thick fog, and a total stillness that meant we quickly persuaded ourselves there was little point in rushing off at the crack of dawn. We moved the boat out a bit to account for the ebbing tide and returned to bed. A more leisurely start saw us both feeling a bit guilty, but as Tony rowed out of the bay I was soon mesmerised by the serenity of our world. We were a tiny bubble in the fog, a dot in the vastness of the Arctic, with the gentle lapping of the water against the hull and the tiny splash of the oars after the rolling of the seat on its track. The fog was so thick you could hardly see the ends of the oars initially but it gradually lifted as we meandered out of the sequence of larger bays.

The wind came, just enough to make it hardly worth rowing for an extra half a knot. We had some mellow sailing, round Cape Parry which offered a spectacular rugged coastline of 20-30 metre cliffs bedecked with ice, and even the odd 'island-bridge' where the pounding of the sea in its short season of work had worn a hole right through a rocky outcrop. There were countless islands, even on our route, and I spent some time wondering how many more existed out of sight which we might find if we ventured off into the numerous bays and inlets that we passed, each possessing its own secrets. Helming was very easy, I even managed to read some of my book on watch, there being little danger of collision, especially as the fog had lifted. Breaking all maritime rules, we had decided against using our precious fog horn even in the densest clag; it seemed slightly ridiculous and an affront on the tranquillity of the situation.

T   As the day progressed we tried our hands at fishing. With a long line and a yellow spinner flashing intermittently in the water behind us, we eagerly awaited our first nibble and a supper of fresh pan-fried Arctic char. Neither of us is a natural fisherman and it showed. Or perhaps the fish simply don't like yellow. Either way today marked the start and finish of our fishing attempts for the entire trip, not least because our line would catch on the increasingly common lumps of ice in the water.

The sailing was slow and laborious but finally we rounded the peninsula and turned SE. Almost on cue the wind died completely and the fog thickened. Ahead of us was a thirty mile crossing to the edge of the next peninsula. With no wind we would be relying exclusively on our oars and the prospect of at least fifteen hours rowing was less than appealing. Still the boat was designed to be rowed when required and one of our initial assumptions had been that in light winds we would have to row to make up the distance. Indeed our progress against the predetermined schedule was getting very tight and we couldn't afford to sit out the day awaiting favourable winds. The boat was equipped with oars and sliding thwarts for a reason and here was our chance to prove we knew what to do with them. I took the first sustained watch on the oars at around 1930 in a thick oppressive fog that rapidly swallowed the land and underlined the sense of isolation.

Instantly I discovered the difficulties in holding a straight course in fog. With no external references I relied entirely on the GPS and the wake spreading out behind me. The former had an inevitable lag time that allowed you to drift of course quite significantly before it corrected you whilst the latter made no account for tide or current. To add to it all I seemed to be pulling harder on my right oar than the left. Trying to compensate was both tiring and enormously frustrating but most importantly it prevented me from establishing a rhythm and made prolonged rowing extremely difficult. I focused on trying to relax and counting out an even stroke, making slow corrections over time and not worrying too much about minor course wobbles. By the end of two hours I was more mentally than physically drained and more than happy to hand over to Kev. Almost on cue the wind came up again and within minutes the boat was powering along under full sail at 4.5 knots. After two hours hard work the joke was on me and it seemed Kev's watch would quite literally be a breeze. The joke was short-lived however and it was not long before I heard the grate of Kev's sliding seat and the occasional crab of his oars.

K   The wind died as the light waned fractionally and we adopted a night routine. Rowing for a couple or three hours is more of a mind game than a workout. It's not particularly physically challenging but it is sustained. I struck a balance between every stroke being a hard pull and easing off so that it felt as if the boat was slowing, causing the next few strokes to be a strain. Sometimes I counted in my head, sometimes my mind wandered; sometimes I listened to the seat sliding. Mostly I looked at the end of my right oar; fascinated by the way it entered and left the water. Mercifully my hands didn't hurt; we had special neoprene pad gloves which were fantastic, and stripped down to just undertrousers and a fleece, the fresh night air felt good. She is a heavy boat, and strokes were long and slow, but sometimes the boat seemed to twist and all my energy was put into one side to bring her back on course as the rudder swung pathetically. After a couple of early tweaks, my back settled down and concentrating on looking after it probably helped my technique. Sometimes I would just look at the glassy sea, grey and silver as it stretched out to the reddish horizon, other times the mist would envelope us again, leaving me cocooned.

The complete absence of reference points could be disconcerting. The compass moved slowly so the only useful reference was the arrow on the GPS. There were several times my mind told me I was rowing off course, but like the compass, the GPS never lied. I was never lonely on watch although Tony slept as well as I did when off watch. Sometimes the tranquillity was broken by a failure of rhythm. We had long since stopped using the iPod routinely, in order to conserve power, and my head was full of a bastardisation of Roy Orbison's classic that went "I rowed all night." I thought of home, ate some Haribo sweets and mostly longed for the end of the watch and the return to the snugness of my sleeping bag and some rest. And at the first sniff of wind, up went the sails, ever hopeful, and for a while we perfected a technique of rowing with them up, when the wind was across the beam. It seemed as though the rowing created a bit of apparent wind which then drove the boat and lightened the load on the oars. Or was it just us pulling a bit harder and so maintaining the momentum of our heavy boat?

T My second stint on the oars was different again. I took over just after midnight in a flat calm without even the slightest breath of wind. The sea had an oily quality to it, opening briefly to allow us through and then sealing shut behind us, with little sign of us having passed apart from a double line of mini vortices to mark the strike of the blades. Thick fog obscured all reference points with the exception of the odd piece of floating ice and the occasional seal. For the most part they would appear behind us fleetingly, a dark blob at the limit of visibility. About halfway through my watch one of the seals appeared on the surface much closer than the others. His deep black eyes were fixed on the boat. He could clearly see that I was watching him as intently as he was watching me but unlike his companions he seemed more intrigued than alarmed by our presence. When he surfaced again he was just twenty yards away and then less than ten. Finally he surfaced immediately behind the rudder, his whiskers twitching as he regarded me quizzically from just a few feet away. I woke Kev and we spent the next ten minutes being treated to an underwater swimming display without comparison. It occurred to us that we were probably the first humans or man-made object he had seen but it didn't seem to discourage him as he flashed past underneath the boat spiralling effortlessly through the clear water popping his head out of the water after each pass as if to invite applause. It was a rare treat that ended as suddenly as it began as, show complete, the seal peeled off into the mist in what must have been a fruitless search for other more interactive entertainments.

K   With his human expressions, the seal had partly fulfilled the role of the alternative company that we craved. Tony and I were getting on extremely well, and there was never a cross word despite the difficulties and tiredness. But we both wanted someone else to talk to as well; we are both sociable people, starting to miss varied human interaction.

T   We continued to row alternately throughout the night making slow but steady progress across the open Darnley Bay towards another recognised anchorage known as Pierce Point Harbour. But as dawn approached and I took to the oars once more I found I was pulling almost exclusively on my right oar just to keep the boat on course. Tired by a long night and painfully aware of having a less developed rowing technique than Kev, I became increasingly frustrated with myself and tried everything to streamline the boat, changing my grip, my seat and even waking Kev to ask him to shift his weight to the opposite side of the boat. Nothing worked and even locking the tiller hard over failed to correct my uneven pull. I couldn't escape the inevitable conclusion that I was somehow doing something wrong and needed to work harder to correct it. "Ahhhhhh—What's wrong with me?"

It wasn't until we were both on deck and Kev experienced the same difficulty that we belatedly realised that we were being set to the south in what we estimated to be at least a 2 knot current. With one man on the oars we could just about stem the current and make the tiniest of progress on our intended route. To add to our frustrations the wind which had now picked up with the arrival of the sun was coming from the east and we were back to beating, this time into a strong current. Memories of our earlier crossing to Cape Bathurst sprung to mind as the far side of the bay emerged from the mist—tantalisingly close yet agonisingly unobtainable.

K We closed the coast from about ten miles out, leaving us about six miles south west of our destination. Off watch I checked the Pilot Book, with its vagueness and out-dated single references, only now noticing the bit that talked about a southerly 'set' (current) into Darnley Bay. It was the one useful bit of current information we had seen in the Pilot Book and in the excitement to make use of the winds and get on with the long passages, we hadn't read far enough forward in sufficient detail and had missed it! We debated stopping on the beach but there wasn't much shelter and we wanted to get to our next aiming mark and we were making progress, just. With northerly winds forecast, stopping was merely deferring the struggle to another day. We were in a sluggish boat that didn't point to windward well, having to beat into wind and a 1.5 knot current. Not for the last time I longed for an engine. How easy it would have been to turn it on and nip round this bit of coastline. I think we discussed whether we should or could have brought one, which of course was both completely irrelevant and against the whole philosophy of our journey. We decided that with the exception of the past few days, we were simply unlucky with the winds.

Ice floes became more frequent sights, and the novelty of approaching them soon gave way to annoyance at the way they interfered with the tacking line, and hard fought ground was lost as we had to turn off the wind to avoid them. Tony's journal from later that day:

> *The last thirteen miles to the area off Pierce Point anchorage had taken ten hours of beating against strong winds and current and by the time we begin*

our run in on the huge natural harbour we were both tired, hungry and starting to miss things. Finally the sun emerged and Kev put the computer on charge. After less than five minutes a string of expletives erupt from under the canopy followed by a furious Kev shouting, "Well that's that fucked then—Fuck Fuck Fuck."

It seems the charger for the computer has blown leaving us unable to download the scores of messages we receive each day and putting a rather large dent in morale. Kev's worried about the blog but I'm confident we can get enough stuff out over the sat phone until we can find a way to repair the data link.

The next blow to morale comes just minutes later when in an effort to cheer ourselves up we switch the iPod on. After days of conserving energy for the computer we now have no need of frugality and can start smashing out the tunes. "Bollocks!" the iPod is broken too. To be more specific it won't take any power from the boat. To be honest I've developed a rather laissez-faire view towards things now. If it isn't an immediate threat to safety I try not to get too concerned. Losing a sat phone or the ship's battery system would be much more cause for alarm. Either way we approached Pierce Point harbour in a rather grim silence.

T   Having completed the frustrating ordeal, Kev seemed remarkably upbeat in his journal for 5th August:

K   *The challenge of pure sailing and not being able to rely on an engine is now one of the key things about the trip and I find it vaguely satisfying.*

Pierce Point Harbour is a stunning setting, low hills surround the almost enclosed half mile wide bay, and almost in the middle there is a rocky island with near sheer walls and a tunnel right though the centre. We barely resisted the temptation to sail through the middle and having consulted the Pilot Book, opted for a steep shingle beach with a track that led to a collection of disused buildings. I eagerly awaited the possibility of sleeping ashore amongst the semblance of humanity, albeit long since departed.

T Our brains seemed to be working agonisingly slowly. The pilot book said this was a good anchorage, the chart showed a sheltered beach and yet we couldn't find anywhere to put the boat. Puzzled we ran in on two different sections of steep pebbly beach, unsurprisingly with the same result of no means of securing the boat. Trapped within the problem by tiredness and stubbornness it was a good fifteen minutes before either of us noticed the long sand spit just two hundred yards away and the harbour within a harbour it created.

We sailed round with the water now only a foot or so deep and beached the boat, head into wind on a shallow perfectly sheltered beach just thirty yards from what appeared to be a trappers' hut. With great excitement we went to investigate. My journal continues:

> Surrounded by broken old husky dog pens it looks abandoned and we dare not hope for much. The door is barred by an old bench tied in position with a small piece of rope easy enough for human hands but enough to defeat all but the most determined bears. Stepping inside is like walking in on someone's life in freeze frame. The cabin is basic but well equipped. Winter boots sit under the table and an old fur parka hangs by the door. I cannot escape the feeling that the owner had just stepped out. A dusty note on the desk dated 8th Aug 2008, almost a year ago, dismissed this idea. A small group had used the hut for shelter then, much as we intended to now. It appeared no-one had visited the place in between. It was a surreal and mildly unnerving experience exploring the cabin. On the walls were photos of the trapper 'Nelson Rubin' and some of his trophies. The sheer size of the Polar Bears and Musk Ox he had shot was awe inspiring and a little worrying. The photos taken in the snow reminded me bizarrely of the Star Wars film 'The Empire Strikes Back,' the animals appearing so huge as to be almost alien. To complete the scene the hut also rather incongruously sported a television with a large video collection. Predictably, everything is musty and slightly mangy but to us it is luxury.

K Eager to investigate our surroundings and the cluster of mysterious disused buildings, we set off up the vague track. It was the longest walk we had undertaken, and stretching our legs on up the hills was refreshing if a bit of a struggle.

The pre-fabricated, dilapidated buildings were disappointing, having been painstakingly cleared of anything interesting or useful. Electric cables, old desks and fallen ceiling tiles littered the floors. We assumed that as the Trappers' Hut was called Police Flat in the pilot book, that all of this represented the remnants of a Royal Canadian Mounted Police (RCMP) outpost.

T   Without saying a word we split up and made our way up separate peaks. After so long in a confined space together, just those thirty minutes alone were a real boon. It wasn't that we were not getting on, in fact Kev made a perfect travelling companion, I just craved some time on my own. From the top of my peak I could see a barren yet dramatic coastline carved out by countless years of glacial action. For once the scenery was made up of steep cliffs, crags and valleys that drew the eye into the distance and offered a welcome relief from the low-lying featureless tundra that had been our companion for much of the journey so far. Not for the first time I considered myself fortunate to view such a pristine environment where neither man nor vegetation masked the geographical process that had formed it.

K   The scenery from my peak appeared likewise stunningly wild and forlorn; rocky hills that stretched south as far as the eye could see, resembling more of a moonscape than anything else. I imagined this was the sort of place they could have tested moon vehicles. I looked north at the outline of the near perfect circular harbour in which the boat rested, and then beyond it to a fine white line I estimated at five miles or so offshore. Through the binoculars it was transformed into our first real sighting of the menacing yet strangely enticing edge of the polar pack ice. Later, I had to admit to Tony, "There's something that I just don't like about all this. It feels ominous, foreboding and unwelcoming."

Tony agreed. "The hut makes a nice change but I'll still be glad to be on our way. We're tired. Things will look different in the morning."

Back at the hut, after re-adjusting the position of the almost empty oil drum outside I got a small amount of oil flowing and after priming it with a small paper and wood fire, suddenly, and no one was more surprised than me, we had a burning stove and proper heat for the first time in two weeks. I opened another of 'Amber's treats'—a pot of Wet Wipes! I smiled at the thought of her wrapping it up, thinking how useful they would be and how tight we had been for room and weight. As it was they were perfectly timed. For the first time in two weeks we could undress, wipe ourselves down in relative warmth, and for once felt properly clean. Bizarrely we had both felt uncomfortable about sleeping in the rudimentary beds and instead opted to sleep naked in our sleeping bags by the stove which, without sounding a bit dodgy, felt fantastic. Tony recounts in his journal for 6th August:

T   *In the early hours of the morning I 'awoke' to the gentle rocking of the sea and an alarming close up view of the large rock pillar in the middle of the anchorage bearing down on us. Slowly the dream cleared and I was back in the comfort of the hut, but it illustrated to me how tightly bound up with the fortunes of the boat I had become during our time at sea. The boat was fine and a new day spread before us. The promise of a new day has become a persistent theme throughout the trip and I am learning that each day brings with it a new perspective, new challenges, new opportunities and new experiences.*

We were slow to emerge from our bags this morning, but when we did, we rose full of purpose and immediately set to work on a host of tasks. Mindful still of the huge polar bears depicted around me I cleaned and oiled the shotgun meticulously while Kev busied himself with the electronics. Half an hour of pumping pond water through the Katadyne filter replenished our water supplies and finally we spread the charts out on the floor to assess the route ahead. Up until now the space in the boat had meant we had been limited to looking at just one chart at a time. With several of them spread out in front of us the distance yet to cover looked daunting. For the first time we are both openly considering Cambridge Bay or perhaps Gjoa Haven may be as far as we can get. Will that mean we have failed? What will we do with the boat? How will we get back? Just the thought of stopping short throws up so many questions which I know Kev worries about daily. For my part I try and focus on the immediate challenge of the ice barrier we glimpsed the night before.

K   We discussed the ice in some detail, unconsciously perhaps staying close to the oil stove. It might be that we can weave amongst it, or that it is sitting offshore and we could stay close to shore which was our preferred option anyway. I tried unsuccessfully to fix both the iPod speakers and the netbook charger. Without a soldering iron I had to wrap wires as tightly as possible to try to make a connection, which failed in the speakers. I couldn't see what was wrong with the charger but decided not to dismantle it. We got a weather forecast with the remainder of the battery power in the computer. The prediction was for strong winds early on moderating later but crucially they were forecast to be from the north-west which was perfect. Despite the draw of the warm stove, the lure of more fast miles running downwind after the previous day's labour proved too much, and without having asked for a detailed ice forecast we pushed on, tacking out of the bay in freshening winds to then run downwind at speed amongst the ice.

T   Rounding the point we are immediately accelerated up to five or six knots with the wind on our beam. This is exactly what we've been waiting for and thoughts of an early halt to the expedition at Cambridge Bay were instantly banished. After a short while the ice pack we had glimpsed yesterday began to show itself. It was amazing to see so much ice on the water and exhilarating to power along choosing the right line to take between the bergs without ceding too much speed. So far each day's experience really has outshone the last!

K   Initially the ice was sparse and we concentrated on filming close encounters with floes, sailing fast, enthralled by the clatter as a small chunk of ice rattled down the hull. I thought how often in one's life do you get the chance to sail potentially hundreds of miles downwind weaving amongst ice? Our next target was Bernard Harbour, another natural anchorage 200 miles south east along the Amundsen Gulf, on the south shore of Dolphin and Union Strait. We sailed through some patches of relatively clear water for several miles but gradually these disappeared and the floes ahead merged until it appeared we were sailing straight into a wall of ice. Of course there was no stopping and going back without laboriously beating back upwind so it was like one of those video games which relentlessly pushes your character further up the screen, dodging whatever came our way. As we got closer to the wall, the form of the ice would reveal itself, not as a continuous line, but a series of overlapping large flat ice floes. Standing up in the boat did help, but now I could understand why yachts have someone hoisted up the mast all the time scouting the route. And their engine on!

It was bitterly cold, and getting out of my bag at 2 a.m. had been a real struggle. It was misty and everything had adopted a clammy cold covering of dew. Sailing like this, in the half light of night was not only enormously challenging, requiring a lot of concentration on behalf of the helmsman to steer the boat between progressively narrower squeezes, it also introduced a nagging worry. At least with the preponderance of ice there were no waves and little swell and this helped our speed even more, regularly achieving seven knots on the GPS. With Tony asleep, in the early hours, I would stand up to see what route lay ahead. Of course there was a good deal of luck involved, but also boldness and firm decision-making. Often I would see a potentially better line, after it was too late and we were committed. I longed for clear water and the relative certainty that it would bring. My thought process was something like "It would be nice to have the sense of achievement of getting through this ice band, and then to cover many miles the far side." The longer the ice bands went on, the more we had achieved but then I remembered how long I had considered the feasibility of dragging the boat over the ice before reaching the conclusion it was probably too difficult to drag it far. I remember thinking, "Something will turn up, and after all we are doing what we came for and if we get a fair way through the Northwest Passage without having seen pack ice I would definitely be disappointed." But in the back of my mind lay the big question of what if we can't get through?

Just after 6 a.m. Tony sighted a ship on the port beam, and we contacted them on our handheld VHF. It turned out it was the Canadian Coastguard ship *Sir Wilfred Laurier*, whose captain had left us a message on our website a month or so before we set off. This was fantastic news; surely he would look after us. We would rendezvous, go on board and he'd show us the way out of this maze of ice. We manoeuvred ourselves towards the ship, and attempted to come alongside, which proved harder than we anticipated. The side of the ship effectively stole all our wind, cutting speed and making steering impossible. Rowing was equally difficult simply because we were so close to the ship.

A brief conversation established that they had more pressing needs than two crazy Englishmen in a tiny boat and it was clear that they would shortly be moving on. After most of the crew had appeared on deck and photographed us, they very kindly lowered a bag full of goodies down to us, and wished us well. The Captain said he looked forward to meeting up tomorrow evening off Bexley Bay, fifty miles short of Bernard Harbour, where he offered to take us on board for a meal and a shower. As we bumped along the side of the ship, nearly losing our wind indicator at the top of the mast in the process, it seemed unlikely that we would be seeing the *Sir Wilfred Laurier* again. A quick rummage in the bag revealed an up-to-date ice chart and weather forecast along with a large stash of fresh food. After a cursory look at the ice chart and the weather we tore into the bread, cheese and yogurts. Basic as it was, fresh food tasted fabulous after so long on dried rations. As we made up our sandwiches we reflected upon what the Captain had told us. "The worst ice in this area for ten years." His words were amply borne out by the big block of red depicted on the ice chart, signifying over nine tenths ice covering most of the eastern end of Amundsen Gulf as it lead into Dolphin and Union Strait. His advice had been to head out into the middle of the channel along the route he was planning to take. It would be a different prospect for him, ploughing through relatively thin ice with his massive engines driving him in exactly the direction he wished. In contrast we would have to continue to pick our way through the ice under sail, reliant on the easterly winds that had pushed us so fast down the coast, but which were also driving the pack ice right into the natural bottle neck that was the south east corner of Dolphin and Union Strait before it opened out again as the Coronation Gulf.

We set course to follow in the wake of the huge red ice breaker, but within an hour or so she had disappeared below the horizon leaving us alone to continue our weaving between the floes. The temperature had dived again but I no longer seemed to notice the cold as I concentrated hard on charting the boat through the ice. It became a challenge to be bested and both of us became experts on reading the tiniest clues in the form of the ice ahead. It took nerve to hold the boat on a steady course towards what appeared to be an impenetrable wall of ice with the blind belief a way through it would open up in front of us. On countless occasions I cursed having made the wrong choice only to discover an opening at the last minute. Impossibly small gaps with just inches on either side of the boat regularly led into half mile wide lagoons of open water and a temporary respite. Route finding became a matter of pride and a source of immense satisfaction; unconsciously I suppose we were competing with each other. Unbelievably our good fortune seemed to hold indefinitely and the miles continued to roll by.

K The sailing continued, slower than the previous night, but our awe at sailing in these conditions was coloured by a nagging fear that eventually we would get stuck. I did a watch leaving the ice to the south and then Tony had more difficulty finding a path on his watch. I was hardly asleep, and kept jumping up to see if there was a path ahead. Back on my watch, I was keen to get us out and past the menacing pack ice, so steered further out into the strait which at this point was almost fifty miles across. But then pack ice appeared more frequently to our north as well. I knew it was only a matter of time and with Tony asleep I grabbed the video camera and as I panned around the wall of ice a hundred metres away I simply said, "I have absolutely no idea where I'm going to go in here."

I felt a little bit responsible. Had I taken the right line? Could I have done it differently? I worried that Tony would think that I'd screwed it up, as he had managed to get through what I was now referring to as 'his' ice in my mind. Of course he never said anything of the sort. With Tony up, I squeezed the boat through a narrow gap into an open pool. I saw an escape, and pointed the boat towards it. Tony used the oars to prise two floes apart and we made it through but the reprieve was only temporary, we were now in a small pool about ten yards across with no visible way out. The moment we knew was coming had finally arrived. We were going no further.

I got out of the boat and walked along the flat ice floes, watching the ice move around us. The floes were sturdy, with well-defined edges, not the fragile, thin breaking edges that I had feared. I put an ice screw in to secure the boat but it was largely ornamental, as there was nowhere to go.

But as it was only about four in the afternoon, and although sailing in the confined waters against the wind was no longer an option, we tried to make progress on the oars. We manoeuvred the boat out of its current position as the ice shifted around us and rowed off into a wider open space. The GPS told us exactly where we were on the chart, but in reality that didn't really help much. We had no short term destination to row towards. What we needed was detailed ice information that would literally show us the way out of this maze. Climbing the tallest high point in our world, a broken pressure ridge about three metres high, armed with binoculars, we scoured the near horizon for free water. There seemed to be a black line heading off in one direction, but there was a lot of solid ice blocking our path to it. Even so from our vantage point we could see it led off for a few hundred metres, but then what? There might be a better option over there, or what about behind us? It was fruitless.

I took out the video camera, and suddenly remembered the famous line, and I said into the camera: "The ice was here, the ice was there, the ice was all around. It crack'd and growl'd and roar'd and something'd, like noises of a swound. From *The Rime of the Ancient Mariner*," though I couldn't remember the "howl'd" and inserted "something'd." With the obvious connotations on the name of the expedition, and now the name of our boat being *Arctic Mariner*, we had used that quote alongside a picture of some ice floes in some of our early publicity. The only difference was that in our publicity picture it was clearly easy to weave between the beautiful floes strewn across a mirror like sea. This wasn't the same! Despite our predicament, I was guiltily thinking it was actually quite pleasant to be stopped, treasuring the thought of time in my sleeping bag and not having to get up to go on watch.

When Kev had first woken me I could see the nervousness in his face. He clearly blamed himself for somehow having got us into a position where we could make no further progress and was worried about my response. My interpretation was rather that we had reached the inevitable end to a wild ride that should by rights have ended hours ago. It didn't even enter my head to blame Kev for anything beyond halting us so soon into my 'off watch time' necessitating a premature emergence from my warm bag. Looking around it felt as if we had somehow ceded control of our own destiny to the forces of nature all around us. Gradually it began to dawn on me that we may well be trapped in the ice for some time. Although we had considered how to deal with this eventuality in our planning there is a huge difference between theory and practice.

Just finding somewhere to secure the boat safely was not as simple as we'd naïvely expected. Fortunately solid ice made it possible to attach to large floes without too much difficulty, but we had forgotten that everything is in constant motion relative to everything else and no matter how we positioned her the boat was in constant danger from other ice floes drifting down on to her.

K   It was time to stop, eat and probably rest after thirty hours on the go with little sleep. We manoeuvred the boat into a sort of ice bay that we assumed might offer us some protection from the morass of moving and sometimes alarmingly sharp bits of ice. As we were cooking dinner, we discussed the options.

"We've got three days' supply of fresh water, after that we're in trouble," Tony ventured.

"I hate the thought of having to be rescued, but we do have an ice-breaker nearby," I replied.

"Yes, and he did sort of suggest our route. Surely he'll be happy to use his helicopter to show us a way out."

"Yeah, and land still offers us the best option. But in all the reading I've done, people say patience is the best policy. You can go to sleep all iced in and wake up and it's all moved away."

We were about four miles from land which was largely back the way we had come. Land held a huge draw for us with its familiarity, fresh water and solidity. We discussed the options. "We should be able to drag the boat along the shoreline, and there might be an open lead all the way along the coast," I said hopefully.

We just had to get there. We did try to row back, using the GPS and compass together because with the ice moving it was very easy to become disorientated after not looking up for a few minutes. The wind had died and we had what, in other circumstances, would have been a relatively mellow row of a few hundred metres. As it was, it was tinged with a sense of hopelessness of finding a route and worry if we couldn't. Of course what had been a way back an hour before was now a confusion of opening and more frequently closing leads. We were soon stuck again.

We were treated to a baby seal observing us confidently from a few feet away, with his head raised right out of the water like a cartoon character and then diving

The boat was taking some punishment →

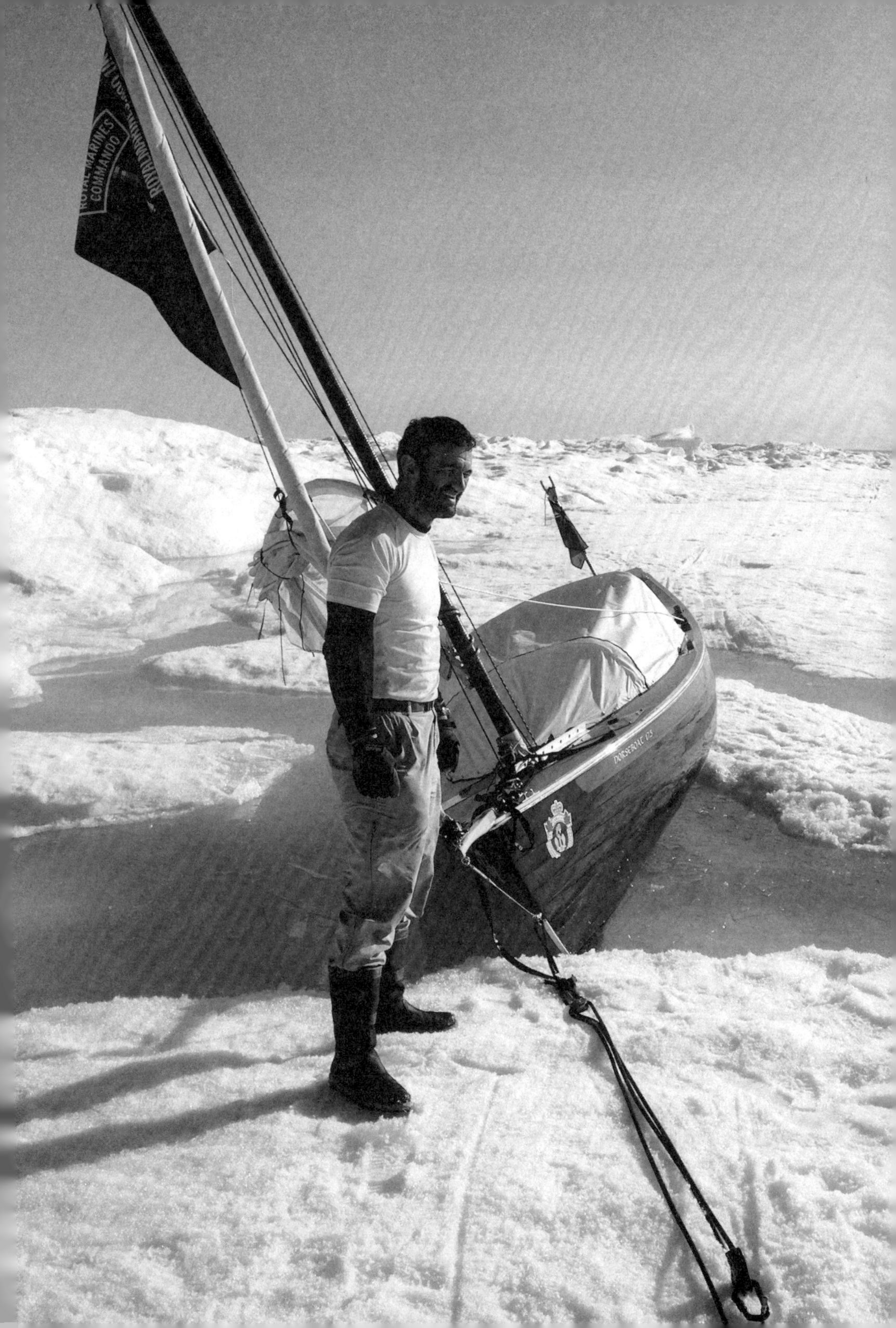
ROYAL MARINES
COMMANDO

under the boat. It lifted our mood, and we both made a short piece for the video diary. First Tony who sanguinely explained how we got stuck before sounding quite upbeat, "With a good wind overnight, perhaps this will start to break out and the ice floes spread out. Either way things will look better with some hot food and a bit of sleep."

I was characteristically more downbeat, wanting to understand where we had gone wrong. "I just can't help wondering how long we are going to be here for. It could be a long wait."

During my last look around before going to sleep I estimated it was about six-tenths ice and ruefully remarked to Tony that there were bits of ice moving near to the boat. We didn't think we would be able to pull the boat out of the water so settled down for the night using the black bin liner that the food from the ice-breaker had been in as a makeshift tent across the opening of our canopy. My journal entry for 7th August, ends with:

> *I thought we'd cracked it—right winds, big distances and Cambridge Bay in a week. But no. I can't work out what we did wrong. We should have stopped sooner and backed out but... Other people negotiate floes. Is it all luck? Will ours change? Feel pretty pissed off but not angry. I'm fed up with the uncertainty. I feel I've done enough. Not that I want to go home, just enough drama. Now a big bit of ice has come in and is grinding against the boat. It's OK it's gone. Tomorrow...?*

As I finally climbed into my bag that night after a difficult day I remembered the first stirrings of concern over the possibility of a nocturnal visitation. We were stuck fast in the ice, slap bang in the middle of prime polar bear hunting ground with just a flimsy canvas cover over our heads. I slept with the loaded shotgun at my hip and a pathetically inadequate air horn by my head wondering just exactly how I was going to discourage the interest of nature's largest land carnivore. I think we would both admit to feeling a little out of our depth but as I wrote at the time, "Tomorrow is another day and we'll start looking at coastguard assistance if the gods are not kind to us" As I drifted off to a fitful night's sleep the snow began to fall steadily around us.

K   Despite everything, I was too tired to lie awake worrying. But when I did awake the following morning I was desperate to look out through the now torn black bin liner at our situation. What greeted my eyes was more like a scene from being in a tent in Norway. The leads had closed, and an almost unbroken white sheet of crumpled, broken ice stretched all the way to the horizon. We were going nowhere by sea.

T   During the night the ice pack had drifted, taking us eight miles to the southwest but most importantly it had consolidated. Apart from the rapidly shrinking pool in which we still floated there was no other open water in any direction. More immediately the grinding of ice against the sides of the boat during the night had woken me with a start on several occasions and was causing me some anxiety. Although in theory the boat should simply 'pop' out of the ice as it closed around us, my worry was that a large sharp floe would hit us hard and either hole us or damage us beyond repair. Tiredness had perhaps made us a little blasé about the need for positive action the night before but we were now convinced that we must do something urgently to improve our position.

K   The awful scraping, crunching sound as the ice either side of the boat squeezed and tilted her alarmingly provided the motivation we required. It was time to attempt what I had been dreading—hauling the boat out onto the ice. We rigged an ice screw as an anchor and worked out the two-in-one pulley system that we had also omitted to practice. With some trepidation we both pulled, and found it surprisingly manageable as the curved bow slipped up on to the firm edge of ice. Once the centre of gravity was over the edge it was possible for just one of us to pull and manipulate the 400 kilogram load with relative ease. We fashioned some ice chocks to level the boat, and with the boat now safe, I 'explored' our tiny ice island.

It was about twenty yards long and five wide. We concluded it was too dangerous to venture onto another floe alone or without the boat, such was the ever changing surrounding ice. We nominated one corner as a toilet and another for sourcing our fresh snow for water. But it was good to walk around a bit and I felt like 'Johnny Castaway,' the cartoon of a little man on a tiny desert island that was a popular computer screensaver about ten years ago. I said to Tony, "This is our very own 'magic carpet,' taking us in the direction we want to go at over a knot. Twelve hours of doing nothing equals twelve normally hard fought miles." But I was deliberately omitting what lay between us and our destination in terms of a barrier of ice.

I remembered reading about the two guys going through the Northwest Passage in their Hobie Cat, erecting their tent over the 'trampoline' between the two hulls of their craft. We knew the dangers of erecting a tent on the ever-changing ice floes and didn't fancy ending up in the water, away from the boat, so there was a certain inevitability of many days and nights on the ice ahead of us, in the boat. We regretted not having asked Kevin Jeffrey to make us a zip down enclosed cover in which we now could have lived quite comfortably. I thought of my stipulation that it had to be an open boat. Tony got the flysheet of the tent out, and improvised a cover over the back end of the open canopy using the elastics that normally hold the tent doors open and the guys, which we fastened into the rowlock holes. There wasn't a lot of headroom but it was cosy.

Despite our difficulties we remained in good spirits, sufficient to set up a couple of staged photographs of us holding up the copy of the *Globe and Laurel*, the Royal Marines' regimental magazine which has a regular feature of 'Where do you read yours?' that we planned to be part of. Unfortunately the photos didn't come out well, and tiredness, anxiety and apprehension are all etched into our faces.

We used the satellite phone to contact the Coastguard in Inuvik, with whom we had been in weekly contact. Although we'd met two delightful people before we set off, we could only get hold of a fairly ineffectual bloke who seemed to be manning the phone every time we called. He failed to grasp our situation, and despite our frustration at not being able to speak to someone who might actually be able to help us with ice information we quickly realised there was little they could do anyway. We needed to speak to the Captain of the *Wilfred Laurier*, Norman Thomas. Norm could use his helicopter, which we had heard overhead, to provide near real time detailed ice information of what lay ahead of us and at least give us an idea of where to focus our efforts. We arranged a time to speak to him on Inmarsat. We weren't going to ask for anything other than his advice, but both of us were secretly hoping that he might offer something.

On an excellent connection, he explained that there was no way he could have foreseen our predicament, the ice in early August was the worst he'd seen in years. He offered assistance if we needed but it would have to wait until after he had gone forward to Kugluktuk, through the ice that lay ahead, changed his crew over there and made his way back all told in about ten days' time . In the meantime, he suggested we should enjoy the 'free miles' by which he meant that the continued ice pack drift in the direction we wanted to go. He explained that south easterly winds would start to dissipate the pack and blow it back towards the open ocean, and that the pack moves at one sixth of the strength of the wind, 12-18 hours after it starts to blow.

The earlier despised but now desired south-easterlies were tentatively forecast for Tuesday, four days from now. And the ice would probably begin to melt in the next two weeks with the barges starting to come through from the third week in August.

We discussed our situation. "We are going to be stuck for at least three or four days and possibly up to two weeks," I ventured.

"At least we are still moving in the right direction, but if the south-easterlies arrive they will blow us back. I can't believe the longed-for westerlies are blowing themselves out around us while we sit here waiting for south-easterlies to break up the ice. How ironic that the very winds we've spent so long cursing are exactly what we need right now," Tony pondered ruefully.

I found some solace in the fact that this was unexpectedly bad ice, and that we weren't simply stuck here through pure naïvety. With a little bit of experimentation we had removed one of our worries. By scraping the snow off the ice floes we could make fresh water. I had studied the way sea ice develops as a potential source of freshwater as part of the planning process. When the sea initially freezes, any melt water from it remains salty, but if the ice survives the summer and becomes second or third year ice, the salt leaches away, and explorers over the centuries have used this as a fresh water source. Unfortunately none of that was any good to us as all the ice around us was clearly first year ice. But of course the snow that had settled on top of the ice floes was just like any other snow, provided it wasn't near an edge that had been lashed by the waves. This was good news and removed the possibility of having to be rescued for lack of water.

T   Much to Kev's chagrin I decided we should cut rations in half, at least until we had a better idea how long we were likely to be trapped in the ice. Given our lack of activity and the warmer temperatures in the sunshine neither of us really needed the huge calorific intake we had scheduled for each day and even on half rations we were taking in far more calories than we would at home. Nuts or beef jerky as a starter, then a soup course, then a main meal, pudding, coffee and maybe one of Amber's treats if the right item came out of the bag that day; we could scarcely claim to be on starvation rations. Fuel was my next concern but it seems we had overestimated the fuel consumption of the little stove we were using and had well over two weeks of fuel remaining. With a good night's sleep behind us and an objective assessment of the situation I found myself somewhat buoyed up with a cautious optimism reflected in my journal entry for that night. "There are no doubt other challenges around the corner but for now we're safe, content and not giving up just yet."

K   I had slept quite a lot that afternoon, catching up and recharging my batteries, and as we chatted after dinner thoughts turned to the very real issue of our recharging our boat battery and the solar panels. We looked again at the netbook charger which we assumed must now be fully dry and plugged it in. Nothing. I took it apart, found the fuse which was intact, and reassembled it as best I could. I plugged it in again. Let's just say there was a bit of smoke; I whipped it out of the socket, and checked the battery with my multimeter. It was reading 20 volts, more than its rating of 12 volts. My euphoria of thinking the battery hadn't been damaged was shattered when I realised that the 20 volts was coming from the solar panel which was plugged into the other charging point. Sure enough when this was removed, the battery was dead. Knowing we had no spare, I had a sinking feeling in my stomach and Tony gave me a look that simply said "Oh fuck, we've blown the battery." And then after a few moments he said "Some sort of fuse?"

Of course. I remembered the fuse container and to my relief we found it had blown, and to much relief, replacing it restored the battery. The whole experience had taught us to be very careful—we only had two spare fuses. But it had also taught us that we could sort of apparently charge the satellite phone directly from the solar panel because when it had been left in, a light remained on after the fuse blew which meant it was receiving power direct from the solar panel. I had an idea; if it could charge the satellite phone charger, would it power the netbook? As ever we took a joint decision, the safer option, which was to only try with one of the solar panels in case anything untoward happened. Cutting the plug from the now useless charger, we taped and wound the wires as best we could on to the solar panel's plug and to our delight the solid orange light that indicated charging was illuminated on the netbook. In a few hours we would have messages.

T   Kev's electrical engineering experience proved invaluable throughout the trip and there were numerous occasions where without his knowledge we would have been in dire straits, but when he very nearly fried the battery I almost let my frustration fly. It wasn't the shorted battery that rattled me but rather the needless risk-taking with a critical system that was a single point of failure for the whole expedition. His enthusiasm and innate inquisitiveness that was to prove so beneficial throughout the trip, on this instance drove him to ignore my repeated advice not to risk the battery unless we absolutely had to. On reflection it was a small thing lost in the relief of discovering a fuse had protected the battery and our sole source of energy, but it was a stark reminder to us both how precarious our position was.

With power restored we downloaded messages and dictated a blog to Dan over the satellite phone. We were both keen not to alarm anyone back home. As with many other ventures, expeditions are often perceived in the way you allow them to be. If we told everyone it had all gone wrong then they would start to look for reasons why. If we remained upbeat and told them everything is under control, they may not fully believe us, but in the absence of any other objective news it's human nature to be reassured. The perception back home was surprisingly important to us, perhaps out of personal pride and the potential embarrassment at being viewed as failing, or maybe the galling thought of all our detractors being proven right. Either way we opted for an outwardly positive approach that perhaps belied some of our inner concerns.

K   We discussed our predicament at length. This could very well be the end of the expedition. After we are finally released from the ice, having been presumably blown back by the winds that break up the pack, we might have to back track to the nearest settlement, Paulatuk. That night I didn't care how far we got. My journal entry of 8th August ends with:

> *I don't know how we will get out of this pack or when, but we're fine. We've got water, food and fuel. The situation is almost comical, proceeding on our track, and we may yet come back this way all while sat in a boat on an ice floe. Awesome photos. It's an adventure. And there could be much more to come. Or not.*

I thought back to my decree, that we needed skill, patience and luck, and that whatever happened this journey would be 80% boredom, 15% frightening and 5% superbly enjoyable. We were in for a long stretch of the 80% part. We read our books. Tony had the biography of Winston Churchill and was avidly absorbing the tribulations of Dunkirk. I was reading *The Great Game* in preparation for my tour in Afghanistan and was equally enthralled by the 19th century adventurers who played for one side or another in the struggle for control of central Asia and the need to protect British India. We were quite content, sat on the bow of the boat in the sunshine, enjoying the sun's radiation and the extreme isolation. Sometimes I would just sit and watch the ice moving. It was as mesmeric as watching fire but more deceptive. With no reference points, depth perception was incredibly difficult. Sometimes I would see a pressure ridge that seemed five or ten meters high maybe a kilometre away. Suddenly it would move and I realised it was actually a meter high and only fifty or a hundred metres away. I was also fascinated by the way the ice horizon often seemed to be a huge wall of ice, maybe fifty metres high akin to the edge of a glacier where it drops into the sea. It was disconcerting, although we knew this was an illusion, called a 'Fata Morgana' caused by the different temperature of the ice and the air just above it, rather like heat haze on a warm day. The temperature difference causes a reflection downwards just above the level of the horizon, creating a wall effect. It all added to our sense of unease as to how we could get the boat over this morass of twisted, buckled ice.

T   The day began with a late rise after a long lie in. It's remarkable how much bag time you can squeeze in up here when there's nowhere to go. Eventually however

Crossing Liverpool Bay, just before the storm

Pierce Point Harbour

Manoeuvring in the ice

Our last mooring before hauling out onto the ice

A break from hauling

No place for a boat

Free of the ice

The view from off watch

A pretty, capable boat

A plug for our employer

An Arctic meadow

The beaching rollers were a boon

Doing the paperwork

The safest view of a Grizzly Bear
Musk Ox

Rock Ptarmigan
Caribou

Our inquisitive seal

Snowy Owl

Polar Bear—when we could finally reach for the camera

A typical camp site

Driftwood for fires was hard to come by

The Smoking Hills

The final pull for Resolute Bay

The serene beauty of the Arctic

Kev

Tony

I got up and made breakfast in bright sunshine and we laid out the tasks for the day. First we must once again improve our living conditions. Kev in particular, being 4 inches taller than me, was suffering from the cramped space inside the boat. To ease our discomfort we attempted to extend the sleeping bay by taking a hacksaw to the fourth deck crossplate that forms our bed. With a little delicate carpentry we managed to fit it snugly behind the second rowing seat and thereby increase the flat sleeping area by about six inches. Next we decided to address the list to port that the boat has taken on during the night. It proved surprisingly easy to slip her off the flow and back into the water and in just half an hour we had her sat on a flatter piece of ice on an even keel. In fact the ease with which she moved did prompt me to consider if we should actively be doing more to break through to open water.

K The laptop had again failed to take a charge, which had ended our promise of messages from home. I presumed this was because whilst the voltage was present the solar panels provided insufficient power. I persuaded Tony to try two solar panels together and although it apparently made no difference to its ability to charge the battery, we found that the laptop would start up and run as long as the sun was out. Inevitably, the satellite phone dial up link, fragile at the best of times, would not connect but after much perseverance we finally downloaded all the messages which was fantastic. We got used to reading them quickly for fear of our power lash-up failing. We even managed to send a highly compressed photo of the boat out on the ice, looking stunning against a blue sky. Pushing our luck, we started to write the blog, but as the sun went behind a cloud, we lost everything. Small successes.

This being Sunday, we allowed ourselves the treat of a short phone-call home. In hindsight I probably shouldn't have called, such was the uncertainty of our situation. My youngest son grasped our predicament and kept asking "What if the ice doesn't melt?"

I couldn't get him to understand over the crackly line about the ice-breaker and a helicopter, probably partly because I didn't want to think about it. I asked myself why I put Amber and the boys through all of this. Lightweight expeditioning always relies to a certain extent on a last resort rescue, because without it an expedition must come prepared for every eventuality, and come equipped with years' worth of food and supplies. I thought we had struck a good balance given that we could survive unaided for up to four weeks. Beyond that we had a shotgun and there were plenty of seals but the weather would have turned by then anyway, and the thought of wintering anywhere here as our forefathers had done was unimaginable. Whatever happened we would be home in just over a month. Yes there were risks, we had seen that in the middle of the crossing to Cape Bathurst, but without risk, adventure is merely travelling.

Despite the tranquillity of our surroundings, both of us were constantly distracted by an inner turmoil of contingencies. This manifested itself as the beginnings of tension between us. It was minor, but with little else to think about Tony would sometimes misread my odd minor criticisms. I had huge respect for his calm, measured demeanour, and I took some solace in that he said whatever happened from here on in, the whole experience had been awesome.

T   Similarly cheered by my phone call home I allowed myself to relax and properly enjoy the surroundings for probably the first time. It was incredibly serene sitting in the bright sunshine listening to the odd growl of the ice moving around us and watching the patterns the sun makes on the ice as it reflected off the small pools of open water. My journal for the day:

> *Relaxing and recharging is good for the moment but I can already feel myself getting restless. We continue to debate if we should be trying harder to get ourselves free of the ice pack, but inevitably I come back to the feeling that without accurate information it would be largely wasted effort. Patience is a virtue of which perhaps we need to make more use. I really want to avoid the ignominy of having to be rescued off the ice but I now recognise that our aspirations will have to be amended. I'm not yet ready to give up, Cambridge Bay or even Gjoa Haven remain firmly within our sights.*

K   I could see no point in trying to pull the boat at the moment; we had nowhere to aim for, and it would be a futile risk for us and the boat. We were still moving, but in a more northerly direction, on this our second full day stuck on the ice. But our position relative to the pack ice around us was what was important and missing. We needed an up-to-date ice chart.

During our third day, after a late start, we started to do some serious joint contingency planning in conjunction with Dan who was orchestrating some sterling work back in the meteorological office in Navy headquarters. Of course it was based on our previously advertised position which was closer to shore, but when we finally downloaded an infra-red satellite image of the ice pack we were confronted with the stark reality. They laid out three main options. Sit and wait for maybe two weeks. Drag the boat back towards the shore and then try to sail or row round the huge mass of ice, or drag the boat across the ice east to the free water channel on the northern side of the Amundsen Gulf. Given that we didn't fancy the huge detour and that we were now half way across the channel we opted to drag the boat further east, the direction we were drifting and needed to go to continue our journey. We knew this was potentially a false economy. Just because we had moved on the GPS didn't mean we had moved relative to the ice that we could see on the photograph. We could still be an awful long way from the free water. We estimated it was anywhere between fifteen and thirty miles!

Once the decision was made just after 3 p.m. we were soon on our way, very aware that this was exactly what we had said we would be unable to continue very far. Dragging the boat was supposed to be an *in extremis* option for a few hundred metres to get over a small ice obstacle. The expedition concept and the boat had not been designed with this in mind. I started to wish we were in kayaks. A few small pools of open water had enticingly opened up just as we were leaving and we dropped the boat into these and began to paddle, one standing on the bow, one standing in the stern. Soon we were dragging her out again, and across some small floes placing the ice screw as far away as possible, just over half the rope length away so the pulley system would work. My 40 metre length of pre-stretched rope, two climbing pulleys and an ice screw were proving to be worth their weight in gold.

T Brilliant! The pulley system worked amazingly well. It was laborious and time consuming and it took a lot of effort to get the boat moving at times but we were at last making progress over the ice and we convinced ourselves we were once more masters of our own destiny. What an extraordinary experience to add to those racked up already on this trip. There can be very few Brits alive today who have man-hauled their boat unaided across the ice pack in this way and somehow it feels special to enjoy membership of that club. It was slow progress but physically not too demanding and I felt we could sustain the effort for a considerable time. The real concern bouncing around at the back of my mind was that progress was relative to the nearest open water and all our advances across the ice pack could count for nothing if the ice pack drifted further away from the elusive band of ice-free water somewhere to our NE. For the moment I took solace in the steadily increasing distance we manage to cover over the ice and enjoyed the sensation of actively taking positive steps to improve our situation.

K   Before long we were established on a large floe that continued unbroken for several hundred metres and contained a pressure ridge from which we could scout the way ahead. Sometimes pushing the boat was enough, but often the rope then became snagged underneath. Most of the way we used the pulley, walking the distance at least three times as we fixed, pulled and ran the icy rope through our gloved fingers. Getting the boat back into the water was easy, but it would often be accompanied by an awful crunch as the very end fell a few inches onto the ice edge. On close inspection we were confident that the boat was strong and didn't seem to be suffering any damage. We soon learned to attach another line to the stern, after sliding the boat back into the water, and just getting a hand to it as it drifted off. The boat was quite literally our lifeline. If we broke it or lost it we were in real trouble. It wasn't ball-breaking work, just sustained. If we had known our destination to be a few miles away it would have been pleasurably challenging, dressed as we were in just thermal tops, enjoying the sunshine. But it was the indeterminate nature of ploughing through this moving maze which, at the time, made it difficult.

After four hours we were halted by a steeper ridge of ice stretching some distance across our path. We pondered if the ice became more rippled how we would fare with our 400 kilograms of boat which slid only over relatively flat ice, thinking back to friends who had pulled pulks to the South Pole. We decided to stop and eat. One look at my hands told me it was the right decision to stop. Under a pair of now soaking sailing gloves, they had adopted that awful white, clammy wrinkled complexion, but I had stopped just before the stage where the skin starts to break and then becomes sore. After a long meal, albeit with better hands, the thought of continuing into the half-light of night didn't appeal, so we slept, hoping the ice would have moved again overnight.

T Pacing ourselves was all-important and rather than pushing on regardless we decided to marshal our strength and wait to see what the ever changing forces within the ice offered up for us in the morning. I climbed into my sleeping bag satisfied with a hard day's hauling and content that another phase of the adventure had opened up for us. Dreams of Shackleton and Franklin stalked my mind all night.

K The morning dawned, in a manner of speaking in twenty-four hour daylight, with clear blue sky and still air. Our latest weather forecast removed the probability of stronger winds that might break up the pack and so the plan remained to continue to haul north. We were disappointed that our GPS reading showed that we had drifted back south most of the distance we had made the previous day but we were continuing to make some easterly progress. It wasn't quite as bad as stopping when you are walking up a down escalator, because there was an end to this escalator of ice, even if we couldn't see it yet. We just had to stick to the plan.

There seemed to be less dragging over solid ice and more manoeuvring between floes, and our technique changed accordingly. We would try to weave the boat through the maze of broken ice, occasionally pulling it up on to a floe, but more frequently jumping off and pushing the small floes out of the way with an oar. With patience, a bit of leverage and sustained pressure, some quite large floes could be manipulated to allow the boat through. Sometimes it required the sort of thought required to solve one of those sliding picture puzzles. "If I move that piece in there, and push the other away, I can move the boat forward just far enough to move another," and so on. I lost count of the times a piece of ice floe broke off and my boots went through into the icy water below, but I usually managed to scrabble out again without getting too wet.

Progress was slow, and inevitably, mid-morning, I applied too much leverage to an oar which snapped. I was furious at my stupidity; Tony was relaxed, simply saying, "I was sort of waiting for that to happen."

Actually, it wasn't the end of the world as we rarely used both rowing stations, but there was a nagging worry that later in the trip we would need the power to get ourselves out of trouble, away from some rocks or round a headland in strong winds. Having decided the oar was irreparable we continued to use it in another way. Often the partially melted ice floes had quite long shallow pools with ice bottoms which ranged from a few feet to a few inches thick. The shallow draft boat could be manoeuvred through these but often "ran aground" on the ice. By using the old oar to take some of the weight of the boat we could sometimes continue, but at other times we reverted to setting up the pulley again. This was more frustrating than pulling the boat along a 'dry' floe.

The prospect of day after day making this slow progress, and the ice moving beneath us, began to take its toll, and despite my trying to remain calm and focussed, I do admit to losing it when the rope dropped into the water. I picked it up and rushed forward, taking out my frustration through sudden exertion, and plunged the ice screw in quickly. I don't recall swearing, but I needed to vent at something, and had no desire to direct it at Tony. He on the other hand, took this outburst at face value, and clearly felt I was blaming him. "Just stop! You've got to consult me before tearing off and doing things, otherwise it gets dangerous."

He was right, but continued, wanting to clear the air on a few other issues. "And I haven't heard you say 'please' once on this whole damn trip, you just assume, and it's pissing me off!"

This really struck a chord, and I told him it was unfair, although on reflection I knew that my manner is to sometimes drop the niceties of conversation when I'm functioning and concentrating on getting something done. But I felt that I had consulted him on most things, and that he was saying that I wasn't sticking to our agreement of joint assessment of difficult decisions. We were working well, I felt I would do things for him, and him for me, and continuous over use of the word 'please' seemed unnecessary in this incredibly isolated and tight association that we inevitably had.

Despite it being an emotive moment, I resolved not to dwell on it, to put his complaints in perspective, but to try to be more as he would wish. It was bound to happen sometime, I was surprised it hadn't happened earlier in the two and a half weeks, and it was bound to happen again. I still felt a sense of responsibility for the success or failure of this expedition, despite his enormous investment, and our stated equal shares. So, at this uncertain time, I probably needed reassurance that he valued my participation as much as I valued his.

T A difficult day today that took its toll both physically and mentally. I was perhaps however more able to lose myself in the immediate challenge of navigating through the ice floes than Kev. For me the mechanics of levering the boat across numerous narrow leads and then hauling her over low pressure ridges distracted me from the nagging worry that all our efforts were being thwarted by the effects of the wind on the ice pack as a whole. Perhaps in reaction to Kev's growing concern, or just a product of my personality, as the day wore on I found myself worrying less and less about our overall progress and focusing more on our personal interaction.

Increasingly I interpreted Kev's requests as demands until finally I took him to task on what I perceived to be unwarranted brusqueness. I've always been one to tackle these kinds of issues head-on and not always in the most subtle manner. I firmly believe that addressing a problem early may bring disagreement but it does at least clear the air and prevents any festering resentment building up over time. I guess I knew at the time that my reaction was a little unfair, and Kev's indignant silence confirmed that I had probably taken the matter a bit too far but I felt better for the release. Neither of us is predisposed to hold a grudge and sulking within yourself this far from anyone else did seem faintly ridiculous—so we simply continued on.

K That night we stopped our haul at 1930 as a headwind had picked up, and this pushed the boat back against the floes we were trying to manoeuvre between, making progress even harder. We were somewhat demoralised but had a good meal, and some much needed swigs on a hip-flask full of whisky. My journal for 11th August:

> *Really looking forward to getting out of this ice maze. But the line of open leads (of which there seem to be more than yesterday) is unfortunately at ninety degrees to our direction of travel. Not that they are very long in either direction. Oh, for them to link together...*

It took a while to motivate ourselves the following morning, so we distracted ourselves with maintenance of the boat, re-fixing the ensign pole and some other small jobs. Although we had a very intermittent connection, the lack of regular use of the netbook and the messages from the website that it delivered, added to our sense of isolation. However we did make fairly liberal use of the satellite phone to speak with the Coastguard in Inuvik and Dan and the meteorological officers back in Northwood. We would look forward to the communication that would hopefully tell us the good news that we were close to free water. After a particularly frustrating ninety minutes of hard pulling through shallow ice pools we stopped for our own sanity to call, to hopefully give us an aim. We watched a seal playing while we abused the Satellite phone. It seemed nobody wanted to tell us, which seemed suspicious. "How hard can it be to plot our position and measure the distance to the edge?"

But they were working on yesterday's chart, and trying their best. The answer came back—probably ten or fifteen miles, all the way to the shore. We couldn't understand how we could still, after two days of frustrating dragging, be the same distance away. And even when we reached the shore we then had to move ten or fifteen miles east to reach the open sea. We had lunch, powered up the netbook and finally cleared the message that had been stuck in the system—a bigger file, sent as part of the ice assessment a few days earlier but which took so long to download that the connection would be lost before it finished, requiring us to start all over again. This frustration, coupled with worries over the size of the Satellite phone bill, was outweighed by the joy of a huge collection of messages which changed the dynamic completely. We set off revived, but prepared for a good few more days of the same laborious, seemingly aimless dragging of our beautiful boat.

We soon realised that we were making steady north-easterly progress as one lead linked to another, with significantly less dragging and more manipulating the floes. Sometimes we used the broken oar to smash the sides of the floes to widen them enough to squeeze through, commenting that our boat was more versatile in this situation than a yacht and also than the twin-hulled Hobie Cat of the late 80s. We spent a peaceful afternoon, suddenly more aware of our incredibly beautiful surroundings. We marvelled at the colour of the deep blue ice under the snow white floes, and the inky blackness of the deep water beneath. There was perfect blue sky, and a true wilderness of ever changing ice, the precise detail of which no other human being had ever witnessed. We mused that we were probably one or two hundred miles from the nearest other living soul. But the nagging doubts remained. Whilst the ice was definitely opening up, would it all close up again?

As the sun dropped lower in the sky, we slipped quietly into a wide basin about two hundred yards square, in which we could see a seal, then five, then twenty seals playfully eyeing us from a distance. They would lift their heads right out of the water and sit apparently motionless, no doubt wondering what strange object had entered their world. We reduced our already leisurely pace and watched and filmed as the seals became braver and investigated further. They were soon swimming right under the boat, and surfacing just a few feet away. The water was so clear and still that we could make out every detail as they swam, as if we were scuba diving. A young one became fascinated with the stern line that had been left trailing in the water. He would bite it, twist around it and even pull it. We wished he would pull us forwards rather than back! As we continued our progress, gently paddling amongst rather than through the ice floes, he stayed with us for most of the next couple of hours apparently enjoying his game.

T   A spectacular day that was marked by ever changing fortunes. After a bright sunny day Kev's spirits were somewhat dampened by a rather pessimistic ice forecast from the Canadian Coastguard. I remained certain however that free water was very near and was convinced that somehow our friendly but rather less than dynamic contact in the coastguard was somehow getting his forecasting confused. Either way our concerns were washed away by a magical two hour display from the seal crèche that accompanied us for most of the afternoon. We both felt privileged to have witnessed upwards of twenty seals cavorting around the boat in progressively braver displays.

K   It was a beautiful evening in so many ways. We felt completely at one with this beautiful wilderness which was finally allowing us to escape. Our method of travel was supremely simple and peaceful, the only sound being the gentle splash of an oar as we paddled or the now pleasantly gentle sound of a piece of ice jostling along the hull. We were still weaving a path but it had led us to the edge of a huge floe that extended as far east as we could see. It had the highest pressure ridge we had yet encountered, and a perfect harbour for our boat just below it. We glided the boat into this ice-bottomed dock and stepped off, securing her with our trusty ice screw. We climbed the ridge and looked north to the welcome sight of land on our horizon. Our GPS told us it was four and a half miles away, but the ice was now taking us westwards at half a knot.

T   Again the highly convincing optical illusions caused us to debate our route. Kev favoured a change in direction to the east to counter the current and to close the 'ice cliff' that stood so solidly just a few miles away. Eventually, like one of those puzzle books where you can see either an old lady or a young woman in the same drawing depending how you stare at it, we managed to discount the existence of the ice cliff and turned our eyes northwards again to the dark smudge on the horizon. The floe we were located on was a perfect spot for the night, it was late and we were weary already. Even if we could find a way through to the distant shore it was still almost five miles away through ice-choked water and only the prospect of an uncertain shore awaited us. We were sorely tempted to stay but the prospect of losing the day's hard fought miles to a night time drift and the almost mesmerising draw of the shore lured us back into the boat.

K   Despite it being nearly 10 p.m. we decided to delay dinner until we made landfall. I took a photograph of our beautiful boat from the pressure ridge which still sums up the expedition for me; her beautiful lines, the ice harbour and the longed-for land in the distance, with many floes apparently blocking our path. I have an oil painting of this scene on the wall of my study.

We could row properly from here, alternating between the oars and standing in the stern steering between floes. It felt good to be able to pull cleanly on the oars for a few strokes, but the plethora of chunks of ice meant that the helmsman would regularly order the raising of oars to skim over them. We changed over every mile to keep warm, and following a glorious fiery sunset we finally touched down on a rocky shore on the stroke of midnight 12th/13th August. It was our first dry land for a week. Our position was 69 degrees 17.8 N, 115 degrees 55.4 W—the northern side of Dolphin and Union Strait, when our plan had been to stick to the southern shore. But we didn't care. After more than a week stuck in the freezer we were finally released.

V

VISITORS ON THE DEW LINE

K   **W**E WERE KEEN TO MAKE USE OF THE SAILS AGAIN despite the steady easterly winds blowing exactly from where we wanted to go. This required us to master beating into wind, tacking amongst the ice floes. For obvious reasons we weren't keen to go too far offshore where the ice looked thicker, so we were limited to relatively short tacks. Sometimes most of the ground we had made on a tack would be lost as we had to steer back across the wind to avoid the ice floe blocking our path. But it was good to be moving again, even if our actual progress along the shore was only one nautical mile per hour.

We chatted about how far we could get now—Cambridge Bay, or Gjoa Haven. We still had lots of time but even Cambridge Bay was over 300 miles away and we still didn't know how much the ice would impede our progress. We had already had an adventure and it wasn't that I was keen to stop, but I found myself doubting how much more we could do. I knew we had to try to continue and get as far as we reasonably could but I couldn't be sure Tony shared this position. Despite our success at escaping from the ice, there was still considerable tension. I sensed Tony thought I was contradicting him when I wanted to discuss an option after reading the pilot. Maybe it was just something to do; after all we simply had to beat into the wind along the coast.

T   Escaping the ice was a momentous event but the realities of our situation soon reasserted themselves. In a biting easterly wind we made only slow progress along the desolate coastline of Victoria Island, a large expanse of rock and tundra significantly bigger than the UK in size but without a single tree to blunt the force of the Arctic wind. Escaping the ice left me confident that given time we could overcome the challenges of the Passage and continue to make progress towards Cambridge Bay. All thoughts of reaching Pond Inlet were abandoned but there was no longer the pervading fear of having to abandon the expedition ignominiously. With little else but repeated tight tacks through the drifting ice to focus on, my mind reflected on our performance on the ice. On the whole we had worked extremely well together, keeping the boat moving forward steadily despite all the challenges. Our decision-making process still caused me some concerns however. We were always open with each other and brutally honest in assessing our options. Indeed Kev's keen analytical mind was invaluable in highlighting 'what-if's' that I had either dismissed or not recognised in the first place. I realised that what irked me was the constant revisiting of our decisions on the basis of a minor change in circumstances. In Kev this would often manifest itself as rapidly alternating bursts of huge enthusiasm followed by equally brief periods of pessimism inevitably accompanied by another proposed change in the plan. Whilst these fluctuations in mood were a source of irritation for me I could not escape the inevitable conclusion that my dogged perseverance with the plan must have been equally infuriating for Kev. Once that was established I felt much better about the whole thing and started to accept the value in Kev's frequent musings. At least by examining the extremes we gained a good idea of where the happy middle of the road course of action lay.

The shoreline was fairly uniform and lacking in any real shelter from the freshening easterly wind, and the beach too steep to attempt dragging the boat up. At about 1630 after a long, slow and demanding sail along the featureless coastline we spotted a sheltered river mouth with a little spit of sand that looked as good a place as any to spend the night. Manoeuvring the boat over the shoals and up into the narrow river channel took longer than anticipated and it was an hour before I finally stepped ashore onto the soft sand with a snow stake to act as our securing point. After just two strides my path crossed that of what was clearly one of our fellow residents on Victoria Island. Running parallel to the shore were a set of rather large bear footprints heading off to the west. We had no way of determining how old the prints were but to my untrained eye they appeared all too fresh. Before we went any further I reached back into the boat and checked the shotgun. Whilst I had no intention to use it I couldn't help but feel reassured by its solid presence.

K   We hadn't ventured far the previous evening after our late arrival and were keen to walk up the rocky steps and explore our new surroundings. Walking was a strange experience, partly because we hadn't walked very far for nearly two weeks, but also because we both had slightly numb feet. We discussed it, and were both probably suffering similarly but I thought back to that morning when I had spent too long barefoot in the cold water. Come to think of it, I had not really had warm feet since. They didn't feel cold, but they didn't feel warm either. In fact they didn't really feel at all. The ball of my left foot was numb, and didn't respond to direct warming by my hand. I knew enough about cold weather injuries to know that we didn't have frostbite, but prolonged exposure to cold had left us with mild 'trench foot.' It was another nagging worry. Had we done permanent damage? Would it get any worse? How long would it take to recover?

We stopped near the brow of a hill, took our boots and socks off and relaxed in the evening sunlight. There were various animal skulls and bones amongst the rocks, probably caribou. We looked north, marvelling at the mile after mile of pure nothingness. It was gentle rolling rocky terrain with no trees or bushes, just tussocks of grass and rocks on shale. So this was Victoria Island, about the size of France with three small settlements and a total population of around 2,000. The wild desolateness was literally breath-taking. We took a different route walking back to the boat, to look into the narrow valley formed by the river.

"I think it's the first day we haven't had any real new experiences" I said Tony as we wandered back. "Just tacking along the coast."

"Well, apart from the bear prints," replied Tony.

We stood and looked at the bend in the river, watching the water cascade over and around boulders and admiring the seagulls, which seemed, and actually were, about three times the size of seagulls in the UK.

Tony shouted "Fuck Me!" and I turned and briefly saw a very large brown bear get up from where he was lying camouflaged on the bracken about fifteen yards away. Instinctively I backed away, going behind Tony who had the shotgun to avoid getting into his line of fire. I can't remember any real fear, just an urge to get my camera out which had been packed away in its case as it was very low on battery power and I was eking out the battery before starting on its only replacement.

T   The opportunity to stretch my legs and doze in the weak sunshine had left me lethargic and contemplative but as one of the large brown boulders in the base of the river transformed itself into a gigantic brown tundra grizzly bear my mind

We were not entirely alone →

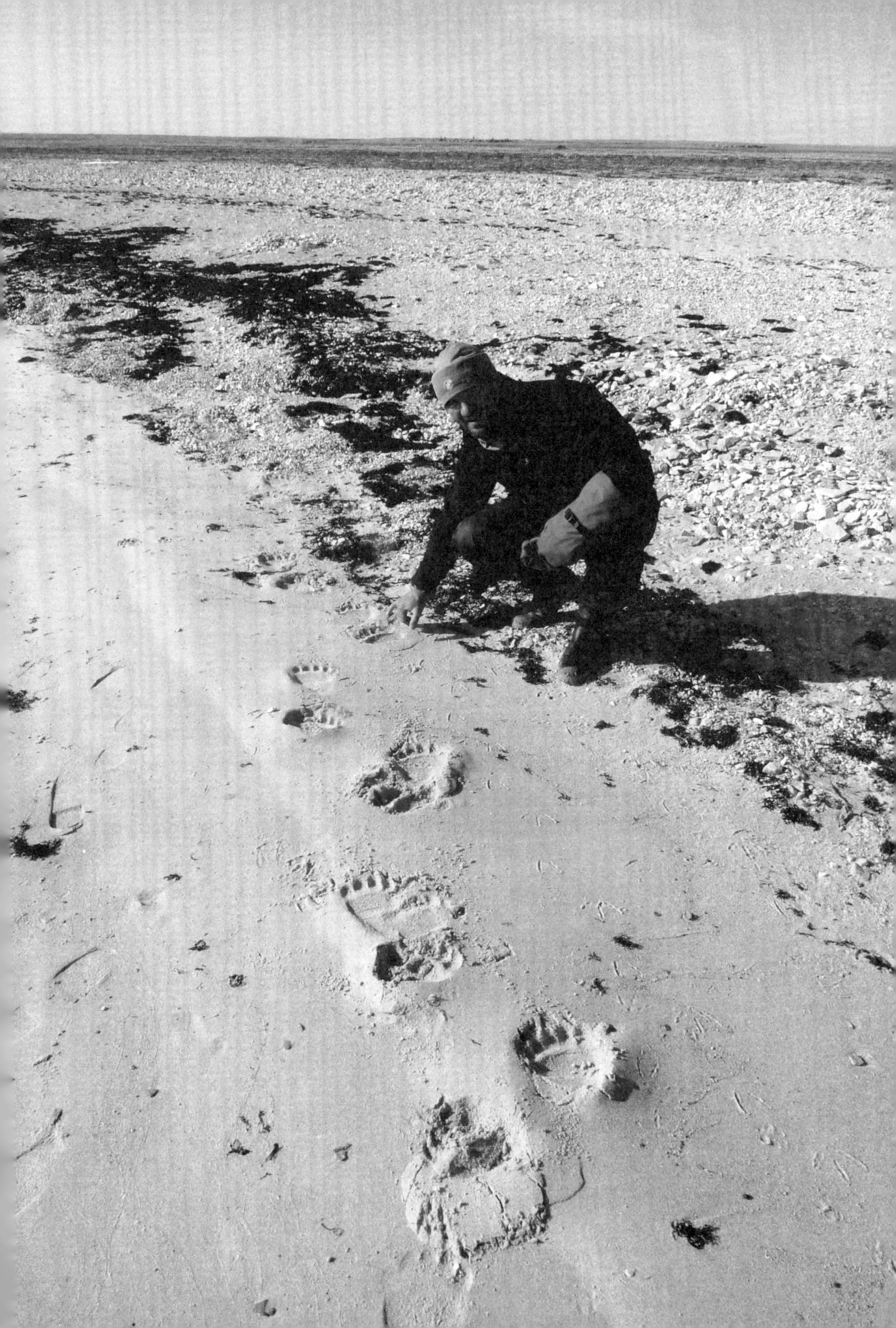

accelerated ahead of my hands in a whirl. The object in the river that the seagulls had swarmed around clarified itself as the half eaten carcass of a large musk ox. It was instantly clear to me that we had disturbed the bear after lunch and where one might expect a grizzly to avoid human contact where possible this one barely paused before opting to charge. With no trees to climb for a thousand miles and our rubber legs having spent too long in a boat, our decision making process was somewhat more limited.

Rapidly realising that there was no way we could outrun a charging bear I instantly raised the shotgun to my shoulder and eased off the safety. With the bear less than ten yards away I squeezed the trigger on the powerful pump action shotgun acutely aware that if the first round of 'buckshot' was not sufficient to bring the charging bear to a halt I'd have to work hard to get the second alternate loaded solid slug off in time. To my horror nothing at all happened. For the briefest of moments I was dumbfounded... I'd checked the load before leaving the boat, the safety was off—But it was not made ready!!!!!! For once my military training had worked against me; I was used to carrying a weapon already made ready with a round in the chamber and had reacted accordingly. In the interests of safety whilst in the boat we'd elected not to have a round chambered and so the firing pin had come down on fresh air. Instinctively I pumped the action chambering a round and bringing the weapon up to aim again. As I pulled the trigger for the second time I knew I would struggle to get another shot off before the bear was upon us. The retort of the shotgun and maybe the sting of the pellets brought the grizzly to a skidding halt barely 5 yards in front of us. Almost certainly more startled than hurt, he spun on his heels and opened up his stride into an easy run in the opposite direction.

K   We watched him go, through the river, down the bank where I managed to take some video until the battery finally died, and then alarmingly, down on to the beach straight for our boat which was just out of sight. Pumped, slightly shaking, but amazed at what we had seen, we set off back to check the boat, discussing what we should do now, passing the half eaten musk ox on which he had been feasting and then probably fallen asleep before we disturbed him. We saw him reappear and then fade out of sight as he ran up into the low hills.

"He's likely to come back and investigate the boat further, and he'll be pretty pissed off," said Tony ruefully.

"We could set sail and continue," I ventured, hating the thought of heading off into the long cold night.

"We've got to move somewhere, but there could be bears all the way along these shores," Tony continued.

I wasn't really frightened, relying on my principle that very few people actually get mauled but I could sense Tony's unease and decided it was wise to be cautious. "Why don't we anchor to an ice floe offshore? After all, he's less likely to swim out, and one bit of shore is much the same as any other."

We agreed. It wasn't as sheltered as our inlet but the floe offered some protection from the choppy seas. Securing the boat proved quite tricky as the water crashed amongst the floes, which incidentally were grounded but of course subject to the tide. I fell in up to my waist when a large piece of floe broke under my weight, but soon the stove was on, and after dinner we decided to open the bottle of Glenmorangie that Amber had tucked into our treats bag, and from which the wrapping paper was now wet and remarkably transparent. 'To calm our nerves.'

T   There had been a surreal quality to the encounter with the grizzly that was hard to define. It certainly raised the heart rate and on reflection it was clear that the bear would have mauled one or both of us if we hadn't managed to get a shot off, but I don't think either of us really felt any fear at the time. More troubling than the immediate threat was possibility of a return encounter when we were not prepared. Early in the planning process we had made the decision not to bring trip flares due to the difficulty of getting them into Canada. On the foreshore we were firmly astride the bear highway in a tiny boat and with just two of us it was impractical to maintain a strict sentry routine. We would have to do what we could to mitigate the risk and ultimately trust to the law of probability and fall back on years of light sleeping. Ironically after Kev's incessant worrying in the ice he was by far the more comfortable with this new threat and I have no doubt he slept easier than me for the duration of the trip.

K   It was warm enough to remove my damp boot, and I sat on the stern, wearing my Crocs, sipping malt whisky when incredibly Tony saw a yacht on the horizon. We had no idea of its size, or how far away it was, but flashed up the VHF radio:

"Yacht travelling west to east, northern side of Dolphin and Union Strait, position 69 degrees North, 116 degrees West, this is small sailboat *Arctic Mariner*, *Arctic Mariner*, over"

"*Arctic Mariner*, *Arctic Mariner*, this is *Ocean Watch*, *Ocean Watch*, where are you? We can't see you, over."

"About a mile on your ten o'clock attached to an ice floe, over."

"OK, we've got you now, Wow, that's a small boat. Would you like to rendezvous and come on board ours?"

"That would be fantastic, yes please."

And so, quickly draining our whisky and packing a few things away, we watched as the small inflatable approached, with three occupants identically dressed in what seemed to us to be pristine Gore-Tex sailing suits.

T   It seems odd how you start to feel house-proud when strangers are coming over, even if your house is only a seventeen foot dinghy and your guests are three fellow Arctic sailors. The three heavily-wrapped Americans were the first people we'd seen since the brief rendezvous with the icebreaker over a week earlier and I was surprised by the excitement the encounter brought with it.

K   After introducing themselves, including the skipper Mark Schrader, and his friend and journalist Herb McCormick, we invited them to look round our boat. They politely declined, laughing that they had already seen round it. With the gentle puttering of the outboard engine in the background, Herb said, "Even for Englishmen, you dudes have got to be out of your minds!"

I instantly swelled inside with a sense of pride and humour at the situation. We had met literally in the middle of nowhere, were about to go on board their beautiful 67 foot steel yacht, and noting that we must have smelled pretty bad having not washed for three weeks, nor changed our underwear for two. Of course, at this stage, as I found out later, all the crew thought we were just a couple of nutcases with a death wish. But we were not hailing them for assistance, just company and curiosity.

They had the kindness in things they wrote and said afterwards that, despite our ragged appearance, we seemed quite sorted and capable. We discovered later that Mark has twice circumnavigated the globe single handed and that Herb used to be the sailing correspondent for the *New York Times*.

Tony and I had a quick check of the mooring, noting the precariousness of our situation—all our worldly possessions attached to an insecure ice floe by one ice screw, and my salopettes drying over the sail, vaguely tied on. "Don't worry, we'll keep an eye on her whilst your on board," said Mark, and with that Tony and I cross-decked into the inflatable wearing open Teva sandals and Crocs respectively. My leather sailing boots were soaked after the earlier incident and were left in the dying sunlight stuffed with the only disposable dry paper we had on board, the old print-outs of weather charts from the ice-breaker.

Settled on board with (another) whisky and some homemade fudge, we made the most of the opportunity to talk to someone other than each other, Tony regaling the incident with the bear and me the tribulations of the ice. Their boat was superb, not new but recently refurbished, and with every feature you could want for their journey, a circumnavigation of the Americas. As I quickly calculated this pretty much equates to a vertical circumnavigation of the globe. The boat had an enclosed wheelhouse on deck, a beautiful saloon with small library, navigation system with live internet, a workshop and even a washing machine and shower. They were six on board, and clearly a happy crew enjoying the adventure. We compared stories of the ice, they had someone permanently half way up the mast looking for leads and it seemed that they had therefore avoided the worst. They were involved in various educational and scientific projects which were part funding the trip. These included a salinity measuring experiment and a camera that was taking the same photo of the ocean every few seconds and storing the results on a hard drive so that this could be cross referenced later with other measurements.

I realised, if I hadn't before, that this was exactly what I wanted to do later in life, admiring their self-contained ability to roam all oceans of the world. But then I realised what our boat was enabling us to do. We could roam the shallows and the beaches with relatively safety, and whilst they could stop and tender ashore, I realised how much more engaged with the raw emotion of the Northwest Passage we were, always in the fresh air, inches from the water, and reliant on the wind and the waves rather than a reliable engine. I started to suspect that our experience on the ice might turn out to be the highlight of our adventure, especially now it looked as though our route was clear to Cambridge Bay. And so, counter to my expectation, I didn't envy their experience.

They were perfect hosts, providing us with a few extra provisions, excellent weather and ice data, but most of all, exceptional company. I sent a blog using their internet and later they sent a photo of us together in the boat. I was dreading leaving the warmth of the saloon and venturing once again into the cold night air, reminded of the start of a long night ski with the Marines in Norway, but when the time came to go, it was surprisingly easy. Our boat had been closely monitored by the watch leader and despite an increasing swell was still firmly attached to the ice floe which itself was still where we had left it. Back on board *Arctic Mariner* after more handshakes, we watched in silence as they tender returned to *Ocean Watch* which then motored off slowly into the distance and out of sight.

Excerpts from their own web diary are reproduced below:

> *What we didn't expect to see late yesterday were two British sailors and their 17-foot sailboat moored to an ice floe close to an otherwise barren and exposed shore. We had heard reports of an 'expedition' attempting to transit the Northwest Passage in a small, open sailboat. Along the way other details emerged. At the hunter's cabin in our last anchorage at Pearce Point Harbor two sailors from a small boat left a note before leaving the harbor a day before our arrival. Their note was confirmation of what then looked to us like an odd, very risky, uncomfortable and wet adventure—from my experience not atypical behaviour for British sailors.*
>
>   *Earlier in the day our radio contact in Cambridge Bay gave us the Brits' latest position and mentioned they seemed to be 'stuck' on an ice floe after hoisting their boat aboard, so to speak, and merrily drifting along atop the floe. We plotted the position—it was just a few miles ahead of our track—made a couple of VHF calls and kept an eye out for their floating encampment. And*

then from their little boat amidst ice floes on an otherwise unremarkable beach they happened to see us go by about a mile offshore. We heard their radio call and immediately made a plan to visit them—by dinghy, ours not theirs. With that, the skipper, David Thoreson and I dropped Ocean Watch's dinghy off its davits, hopped in, and made for shore. Moments later, we were shaking hands with Major Tony Lancashire and Lt. Col. Kevin Oliver of the Royal Marines, square in the midst of what, for them, might be described as a busman's holiday. The former was wearing flip-flops, the latter Crocs, neither in socks. To contrast, the Ocean Watch contingent was swathed in fleece and foul-weather gear from head to toe. Over the next couple of hours or so, it wouldn't be the last time we felt like wimps.

We had a quick look at their boat (it didn't take long!) before ferrying them back to Ocean Watch for a cup of tea and a visit. Tony had purchased the Canadian built Norseboat at last fall's sailboat show in Annapolis, Maryland. They'd reinforced the hull with Kevlar, had a couple of sliding seats installed for rowing, had the boat trucked up to the Inuit village of Inuvik, and shoved off. For shelter, they had a small canvas cover and a couple of sleeping bags. All in all, they were quite happy with their trim little vessel, though as they stepped aboard Ocean Watch and took in our relatively palatial platform, Tony looked at Kevin and said "We're doing this the wrong way."

One thing was clear: If these guys were running the 'British Empire,' there'd still be one. "Sailing the Arctic is about a lot more than a couple of blokes on an open boat," said Kevin, as we shook hands and bid farewell. "It's about the people you meet." We couldn't have agreed more.

In some ways I was content to be back, just the two of us, continuing our adventure. My journal for 13th August:

Really made the evening. They were really interesting, generous and clearly impressed with our efforts. It was great to speak to some other people; it's one of the great things about remoteness that people will always want to meet up. They had been in Summer's Harbour and Pearce Point a day or so after us. Had a bit of a faff repositioning our boat, first on to a bigger floe and then back on shore (having dismissed the bear threat!) I was wading in my boots (which are taller than Tony's) again. We must make sure we make more use of the dry-suits. (Feet still felt numb and clammy). Still OK with it all but could do with some westerly winds to make some progress soon.

When we climbed back on board *Arctic Mariner* it felt claustrophobically small but strangely comforting like returning home at the end of a day. The goodbyes and best wishes from Mark and his team had the feel of sincere concern for fellow adventurers and once again I felt enormously privileged to be here. As *Ocean Watch* disappeared into the twilight we were brought back to the immediate by the condition of our anchorage. Most of the sheltering ice floes had moved off with the tide and we were now very much more exposed. We elected to move to a large floe just a hundred or so metres away and within ten minutes had an ice screw in and the boat sitting nicely. Ten minutes later we were drifting again and reluctantly we accepted that we'd have to beach the boat again. This wasn't easy but within an hour we were firmly aground in the river mouth, anchored to a boulder pile ashore and climbing back into our bags for the night. The air horn and the shotgun (made ready) were the last things I checked before falling asleep. An hour later I sprung upright, the shotgun clenched in my fists, in response to Kev hearing something moving through the water. A quick check outside revealed nothing and whether the grizzly had returned or not we never found out; staving off sleep any longer was too much of a challenge and we rapidly slipped into fitful slumber. It had been an amazing day full of the experiences that seem to make this trip what it is. I pondered the fact that whilst miles covered are always worth it, if we don't take the time to stop and look around, we would be missing out on half the experience.

It was a slow start to the following day with both of us struggling to get going in the cold. Wet boots from the night before meant it was extremely difficult to rewarm our feet. Kev in particular seemed to be having issues with his and my toes had been numb for several days now. Whilst I wasn't particularly worried I was intrigued as to when exactly the feeling might recover. We finally slipped at around 1100 after a breakfast of chilli beef macaroni, my out and out favourite meal so far. It was a mark of our dampened mood that we also dug into the bag of goodies from *Ocean Watch* with the homemade fudge being the first casualty.

My morale seems to correlate closely with what I eat and it is no surprise that my mood rapidly picked up after the morning's feast.

After about four hours of sailing I was on the helm wending my way through one-to-three-tenths ice. Tacking upwind through the ice pack was proving to be doubly difficult, constantly having to 'duck' under ice floes because of *Arctic Mariner*'s by now frustratingly poor pointing ability. It felt like we were consistently giving up hard fought ground (i.e., sea) at every turn. The irritation was starting to show and my mood started to dip again around lunch time. With our progress over the ground limited to 1.5 knots, we considered beaching or even attempting to row close to shore in the lee of the land. As if on cue, in my peripheral vision I caught sight of an aircraft approaching low over the starboard beam. At barely 200 feet with all four engines roaring a Canadian Maritime Patrol aircraft thundered over our heads. We immediately got on the VHF and she circled around for another low pass. It seems they knew all about us and had just spoken to *Ocean Watch* twenty miles ahead of us. They told us that a clear passage through the ice stretched out close to the north shore of the strait as far as Lady Franklin Point! And yes they had got some aerial photos and they would send them to our website. Morale raised and today's new experience ticked.

K   When we asked the military authorities back in Yellowknife much later how they knew where we were, they replied simply that they read our blog every day and noted the Lat and Long! My journal records my mood for 14th August.

> *At least the water is crystal clear, close to the shore it has a lovely green blue colour, like the Caribbean with a rock or sandy bottom. Out to sea it is a deep blue, almost black and not the depressing grey colour of the UK or the brown of the Tuk peninsular. Both of us have had cold feet for a couple of days now. I think it is a combination of the continuing damp cold, the outer layers of the boots being sodden from wading and the wind chilling the feet inside as they dry out. Even in my bag at night they are clammy, and due to the tight space you can't curl up and hold them by hand. Wriggling my toes extensively seems to make little difference. My boots and feet got wet last night so sailing along changing my socks, and actually my feet feel warmer when they are exposed to the air.*

As more ice appeared and the wind died off we contemplated rowing but it seemed a bit pointless into the remaining wind and round the ice coming towards us. We selected a beach, steep shelving, fine gravel and most importantly firewood!

We've got a fire going, and are properly re-warming our boots and feet. If the petrol stove is normally referred to as the 'Commando Television'[1] this is a 48-inch Plasma.

So, three weeks in — I do miss Amber and the boys, but I'm not yearning to come home just yet. We are still under half way to our planned return date but that could come forward. Spending time like on this expedition is pretty mellow. It's wild, remote and I don't feel as though I'm wasting time. Dolphin and Union Strait still blocked in the south-east corner apparently. Better day with Tony today, maybe last night with other people was good for both of us. Have found a way of charging the iPod from the netbook (itself still powered directly by the solar panels), so with the extra penlight batteries from Ocean Watch we may yet have music again. Opened the pistachio treats; perfect by the fire, with Glenmorangie for after dinner. Excellent.

T   Having the luxury of a camp fire I found hugely reassuring and uplifting and it was a genuinely enjoyable couple of hours we spent drying out boots and drinking whisky in its glow. I found myself musing on how the low gravel plains around us had formed and then subsequently been graded and shaped by the environment. They resembled so closely the *jökulhlaup* plains of Iceland but couldn't possibly have the same genesis. At dusk the wheeling of a hawk distracted me from my reverie and once more I marvelled at the animals that make this harsh place their home.

K   It transpired that we had found one of the very few spots in the Northwest Passage that had any driftwood. In the absence of trees, their location is entirely determined by the currents which have carried wood disgorged from the rivers running out of Canada's north coast. The wood had probably travelled thou-

---

[1] A reference to Norway, where all four members of a tent group sit and stare at the stove once it is alight, as if it were a television.

sands of miles to reach us, but now being bone dry it burnt easily and there wasn't much left by the end of the evening. A short walk up the steep escarpment a few hundred metres back from the beach gave us some beautiful but worrying views of the ice which still lingered all along the coast. We weren't in free water by a long shot.

T We woke next morning to the sound of light drizzle on the canopy and westerly winds! We were up, dressed, packed away and off the beach in under thirty minutes, a record for us. After two frustratingly slow days we needed every hour of westerly winds we could get. The Royal Navy weather forecasters had been remarkably accurate in their predictions so far and they did not expect favourable winds to last. Breakfast on the go, and in recognition of our improved moods even the rain stopped for a while. In these conditions we made steady progress at five or six knots until 1800 when the wind finally dropped away.

K We still had to decide between sticking to the shore leads that took us round a long curve and venturing further offshore into potentially closing pack ice on a direct route. We lengthened our journey by remaining within sight of the comforting land, and inevitably by weaving amongst some very large ice floes. Our next target was Lady Franklin Point, marking the constriction at the end of Dolphin and Union Strait and Coronation Gulf. There was still a doubt in our minds that this could still be choked with ice, especially with these westerly winds, but that discovery would have to wait for another day, as the wind died in the early evening and we again sought a beach for the night. We had sailed gently along for a couple of hours almost silently, the boat doing about two knots over a perfectly calm sea and hardly making a ripple. That was until we grounded on a spit of shingle, putting the rudder under some unwelcome pressure.

We reflected that if we had started at Kugluktuk, our original plan, we would probably not be that much further ahead, given the ice conditions, although we would have only sailed fifty miles to reach Lady Franklin Point, and would have missed all our adventures so far, or at least had different ones! The highlight of our evening was watching an Arctic fox wander on and off the ice floes close to shore, presumably looking for food. He kept his distance, but we could clearly make out the slightly bizarre sight of his summer coat. Without his thick white winter fur, he looked almost undressed, with spindly legs and pointed nose and ears. Most interestingly, his brown fur extended up his legs, over his haunches to meet the top of his back, with off white fur on the underside of his body, which blended with the ice behind him. It gave him a ghostly or skeletal appearance in the half light of the late evening as he crept warily along the foreshore, one eye firmly on us.

The beach was shingle and on closer inspection of the various spits of land, we were surprised to see straight grooves and shapes cut into the surface. The stones seemed to have been sorted in size, and it looked as though a giant boat had been dragged through them. It was odd; seemingly human interaction in this desolate place, but we put it down to the exact opposite, it was the pack ice moving in much the same way that a glacier shapes the landscape beneath, and without any human scattering of the stones, the lines remained for us to see.

We had taken to conducting running races on the beaches, to get some blood flowing in our stiff legs. There was no real competition between us, and with partly numb feet, clothed in our usual six layers with heavy boots, and just having finished a big dinner, we flayed across the shingle at maximum effort after I had said, with no warning at all, "Race you to that boulder…"

There was no time or point in Tony asking which boulder was the intended target, he just took off after me and we always ended up breathless and laughing after a minute or so, hoping and wondering if our feet felt any different. Tony usually won, but then as I constantly reminded him, he does have six years on me!

We observed other strange effects, presumably associated with being so far north. There were often aircraft vapour trails in the clear sky, which was unsurprising as we were under the flight path for the shortest (Great Circle) route between Europe and the western USA. But there sometimes seemed to be some sort of reflection of the trail that would precede the aircraft and apparently guide it all the way to the far horizon.

My journal (15th August) reflects the content of the messages we had received:

Thinking a lot about getting to Cambridge Bay. It will be great to have a good sort out and I do genuinely want to do more. Would be nice to be free of the ice though. Strange comment from Dan in the messages, "Have deleted all messages about seal clubbing and bear shooting." I hope he's joking but it worries me. You get some strange messages on the website e.g. Carlo — "Haven't you heard, the Northwest Passage is closed this year, you'll have to walk." — What a tosser!

Of course, apart from the odd crackly satellite phone conversation, and the collated messages, we had no knowledge of what was going on in the world, and couldn't understand the context or how big a following we had on the website, and from where. The power of the internet had spread our followers from a few family and friends into people from all over the world. We discovered later that, for reasons of power management, we had put two photographs on the website on the same day; one of the seal wrapped up in our line, and the other of Tony drinking whisky from a bottle sat by our fire. The implication was obvious, that we had caught a seal and barbecued the poor thing! As for the comment from Carlo, well it amused and incensed me that some couch potato could sit behind his laptop and pontificate like that. At the time, no yachts had yet made it through, but we were soon to meet one who had already come all the way from Greenland.

We now needed to go directly south to round Lady Franklin Point, and predictably woke to a southerly wind! Although we had tide tables for the key settlements in the Passage, we had been unable to truly make sense of them, so predicting tidal streams was impossible. The complexity of the water moving between the narrow channels and islands, let alone the effect of the ice, left us guessing even as to how long it would flow in a certain direction. However, once we got going, we were pleased to observe by our track on the GPS that we had a favourable current as we tacked into the wind.

I was often hungry as we were still on half rations in order to allow for any further delays in reaching Cambridge Bay. That said, I suddenly needed to make use of the bucket, but Tony suggested he dropped me on an ice floe for a "bit of privacy." Without hesitation, given the urgency, I disembarked, and even found a small hole in the floe that proved ideal for the purpose. I took the opportunity to photograph Tony underway as he tacked the boat repeatedly around the floe. He took some photos of me on my tiny floating, melting island and predictably of me squatting! There wasn't a lot of wind, but I did pause to reflect on the incredible trust we had built up. Given the threat of bears on land, we were always together, and this separation of fifty metres or so was the most we had experienced in weeks. I was completely alone (with my Emergency Beacon) on a melting ice floe six metres square in the mist. Once safely back on board, I realised I had become quite attached to the security afforded by being in our beautiful little boat.

T   The thick mist that descended in the afternoon added another dimension to the unrelenting concentration required to make good progress through the broken pack ice. We had both learnt to hold our nerve when approaching seemingly impenetrable ice, but when visibility was reduced to just ten or fifteen meters it made for some sporting last minute course alterations. I consoled myself with the thought that all this was doing wonders for my 'round the cans' yacht racing back home. As the afternoon wore on the winds became increasingly fickle and we were repeatedly forced back onto the oars to maintain surprisingly good progress in the favourable strong current. Kev's little visit to a passing floe not only provided some childish humour to the day but also served to highlight his enthusiasm and attitude to risk. When he leapt onto the ice, it cracked and almost gave way beneath him. Had he fallen in it would have been a serious, and rather chilly, problem but not an insurmountable one. Conditions were calm and we were both trained in ice breaking drills. The point that finally started to sink in as I circled the ice floe alone in the boat was that Kev provided a certain energy to the whole project that went beyond a considered assessment of risk. That is not to say he was reckless rather that once he decided a risk was worth taking he happily went ahead and took it without any hesitation. It was something I went on to ponder over throughout the expedition.

At about 2300 after another stint on the oars Lady Franklin point emerged from the fog just 50 metres ahead of us. Rounding the point was another significant moment on our journey, hopefully marking the end of our troubles with the ice. We stood in the boat and shook hands warmly.

K   As I turned the boat eastwards and ran along the coast looking for the beach that was mentioned in the Pilot Book, we peered at the shoreline which to me looked about 150 yards away. Tony felt we were too close to the shore, and risked hitting the rocks. When I asked him how far away he thought it was he replied, "About 20 yards."

It was another example of the desolate landscape and the light playing tricks on our eyes like it had when we were in the ice. As it turned out, we were about fifty yards away but the sizeable boulder that I had used to help judge the distance turned out to be quite a small rock. It was disorientating and eerie, especially as we knew close by was the Lady Franklin Point Distant Early Warning (DEW) radar station. Built in the late 1950s, over seventy sites were constructed as the northern-most of three defensive lines across Canada to provide early warning of an attack by Soviet bombers. In a massive construction project with 25,000 people involved, it took two years to construct a site every hundred miles or so broadly along the 69th parallel. The relative ease of access afforded by the Northwest Passage meant that in this area they are on the beaches, complete with an airfield and supporting infrastructure. Most have now been decommissioned and those that remain are fully automated, and the sites are being cleaned up.

We anchored the boat amongst some foul-smelling seaweed in a wide bay, and despite it being nearly midnight, we decided to go and investigate. The midnight sun had now ended and it was quite dark, especially with the swirling mist and light drizzle. I was quite uneasy about leaving the boat, not feeling for its safety, but rather for ours.

At 2345 we found ourselves walking along an old deserted cinder track in thick mist heading towards the abandoned radar station. I had more hairs standing up on the back of my neck than the cold really justified and I drew inexplicable comfort from the shotgun clutched tightly in my right hand. It was a strange, spooky and not altogether pleasant feeling walking into the compound of deserted buildings at a fog-shrouded midnight this far from the rest of humanity.

Similar to the deserted buildings at Pearce Point Harbour, it was as though there was a presence, brought about by the fact that other people had been here. We didn't know if there would be anyone here, because some of the stations had clean-up parties working this summer. We approached by a long gravel track, observing the two massive golf balls emerge from the mist. We also found an enormous hangar at the end of the runway, but the whole place was like a moonscape, huge open spaces of endless shingle. It can't have been much fun to be stationed here. The site had been upgraded from the original DEW to a long range capability in 1989 but it had partially burnt down in 2000. It was deserted, so our hopes of a warm welcome, hearty meal and conversation were dashed, though I'm not sure how welcome we would have been at 1 a.m. local time. I was quite happy to get back to the familiarity of the boat and decided there was no way I could have done this trip solo; that would have been seriously unnerving.

The following day in very light airs, and making little discernible progress despite the free water, we decided that we were bored enough to play "Who Am I?" which involves asking a series of questions of the other player who is only allowed to answer Yes or No. There was no point giving up, after all we had nothing else to do, but Tony got particularly stuck on the British entertainer Bruce Forsyth and we had to keep coming back to it, breaking for discussions about how long it would now take us to get to Cambridge Bay if the winds remained coming from the east. We had food remaining, but not enough if we could only make ten or so miles each day. My journal for 17th August:

> *Thoughts of days and days to get to Cambridge Bay returned. We are lucky to be free of the ice and I'd thought we could do it in 2 long days and we can't. It's now getting quite dark between 11 p.m. and 4 a.m. so the long night watches will be hard and difficult. We might have some interesting sailing island to island en route to Edinburgh Island. Got to think of it as a phase rather than a countdown to Cambridge Bay. Pretty miserable in the drizzle and have found out that the spray cover leaks. Quite nice off watch in your bag though.*

We had finally managed to charge Tony's iPod, mine being dead after the storm, by piggy-backing it on to the netbook when it was receiving power directly from the solar panels. Finally it was ready, and we looked forward, albeit with some trepidation to the motley selection of music it contained. With fresh batteries in the speakers, we discovered that all the random shutdowns that had occurred when the sun had gone behind a cloud had violated the classic iPod instruction of "Do not Disconnect." The fully charged iPod had been wiped and contained no songs!

T   It seemed at least 75% of the trip had been spent beating into adverse winds. To make matters worse it rained on and off all day, and the freezing fog sucked all the heat out of the air. We resorted to rowing again in the mid-afternoon heading for the appropriately named Outcast Islands. The day continued and ultimately we both agreed it had been the worst of the entire trip so far. In a fitful mood we decided to push on beyond the island and aim for the less depressing-sounding Nauyan islands, three miles further east and "About an hour away."

K   We ended up tacking to get through the gaps between the Outcasts, and every time we changed course the wind, being channelled was still right on the nose. When we finally reached the Nauyan Islands there was nowhere obvious to beach the boat so we continued to their far side. I rowed for a bit, I said it was to keep warm, but in reality it was frustration and I secretly enjoyed pulling hard against the wind, challenging it to a duel, but progress was still slow and I knew the wind could always win. I was longing for an engine, and for the first time, genuinely ready to call it a day in Cambridge Bay. We were tired, both mentally and physically. But by 2300 with the boat finally on a rocky shore that was exposed to the North West, I knew the feeling of defeat wouldn't last long. If the wind picked up such that it was a danger to the boat then it was the elusive north westerlies and we would sail away quite happily. After all, how many people had pulled up on this shore, well off the standard Northwest Passage route? We looked round our island with some weary satisfaction.

T   After a challenging and dreary day it was good to be able to stretch our legs a little on the island. And with time to reflect it occurred to me that whilst we had rowed along wrapped up in our own world the physical environment around us had changed again. The low featureless limestone had imperceptibly giving way to hard basaltic protrusions worn slick by time and the passage of innumerable ice sheets. It was an impressive sight but a push to call it beautiful. I slept well that night despite the boat being canted over on the rocky beach and my concerns about the wind brewing up from the exposed N or NW while we slept. Bizarrely I dreamt of a towering wall of ice projecting up from a storm-lashed sea.

We awoke still canted over but without any bother from the North and no ice wall in sight. With very little wind we decide to muster our food and make a decision on rationing. Kev wants to go back on full rations but I'm not so sure this makes sense yet. We have three days full rations and 150 miles to go. In the end we agree to compromise. One day's full wet rations now, and then back onto half rations. That should see us into Cambridge Bay by the weekend, and if not we still have some emergency rations we can break into that should give us at least another three very frugal days if we need them.

K   Very light north westerlies eased our departure on the 18th and almost immediately we sailed past a near-perfect beach three hundred metres further on. Sometimes sailing slowly, sometimes rowing, with milky sunshine the day passed easily, reading and reviewing the photos on the cameras, a luxury that we rarely allowed ourselves in order to preserve power. Patience. I thought back to our mantra of Preparation, Discipline and Patience. How long would it take us to reach Cambridge Bay?

T   Dinner was always a treat and we tried to make a social occasion of it if for no other reason than to lift the gloom of a slow day's sailing towards Edinburgh Island. That night we managed to drag it out that much longer, conscious that when we finish it's back on the oars. Darkness was coming a lot earlier now and neither of us relished the long cold watches through the dark hours.

Just as we reluctantly prepared to get on the oars again, in the gloom I spotted another vessel, a large ketch heading west. We called her on the handheld radio and at about the same time she must have spotted us low against the horizon for she altered course in our direction. A very French voice announced over the radio his invitation to "Come and spend some time with us." We were delighted at the prospect and shamelessly hoped for a similar reception to that offered by the team on *Ocean Watch*.

K   The yacht was quietly motoring westward meaning they had probably already made the trip through from Greenland. Again, we were invited on board, now even smellier than when we had been on *Ocean Watch*. It was the world-renowned *Vendée Globe* veteran, Frenchman Phillipe Poupon with his actress wife Géraldine Danon and four children aboard their brand new *Fleur Australe*. He had designed this beautiful yet extremely functional 67 foot yacht himself. They were beginning a four year adventure including Arctic and Antarctic sailing, and travelling and living in the Pacific. The first yacht of the season through from Greenland, he told us about finding shore leads in Franklin strait and about the three yachts, including a steel motor yacht, still stuck fast in the ice there. Again, they were perfect hosts and we tucked into their cognac and chocolate whilst discussing the ice and hearing about their fascinating voyage. We departed, somewhat reluctantly, with a bottle of wine, and some sausage; very French!

T   As we'd seen earlier in the trip, the impact of meeting other folk prepared to chance the ice of the Northwest Passage was galvanising. We were both instantly enthusiastic about the prospect of alternate company. It wasn't that we resented each other, in fact these chance meetings actually tightened the bonds between us, but we craved new voices, opinions and faces. That one of the faces belonged to an accomplished, and rather beautiful, French actress was merely an added bonus. Seeing the couple and their four children so far up here summoned up what one can achieve with the conviction to set your mind to it, to grab opportunities as they present themselves and not to let convention stand in the way of adventure. Kev was more pragmatic; with two kids of his own he recognised the conflict between a life of adventuring and ensuring a settled education for children. Ever the dreamer I'm unconvinced and leave *Fleur Australe* with a new-found conviction that the dream is possible with enough determination.

K   Again, human company lifted our morale and as I rowed my watch through the dark still night I was quite content, wondering if we might be able to continue from Gjoa Haven to Resolute this season... As the wind increased, I experimented with a form of automatic steering. We had already tried to steer the boat by setting the sails, and I found all I needed was a bungee cord to secure the tiller and the boat would happily hold a course while I wrote my journal using my headtorch. So much for maintaining a constant lookout for other boats, but I assessed the risk as manageable given the circumstances. I had the odd seal splashing around the boat for company.

A fantastic pink dawn sky then brought sight of the most dramatic scenery yet, with views of Edinburgh Island with rugged cliffs and green grassy hills; it is so named because it looks like the area south of Edinburgh around Arthur's Seat. We anchored the boat just aground about thirty yards offshore, and embarked on our longest walk so far, to the top of the 100 metre high cliffs so we could look down on the boat properly for the first time. Our tiny boat looked insignificant and strangely vulnerable set amongst the majesty of the deserted bay, with outlying islands sheltering its entrance. So much space!

Ptarmigan inhabited the cliffs and seemed completely unperturbed by our presence. I filmed them to within a few feet before they reluctantly flew off. We walked for a couple of hours, admiring the lakes, escarpments and grassy hills that stretched inland as far as we could see. On finding one side of a set of caribou antlers, Tony decided to see what they would feel like attached to his head. Holding up the four foot long antler and making a suitable facial expression, he decided they would feel very awkward and heavy!

Having literally down-climbed the rocky slopes back to the beach we stumbled across the remnants of an old wooden boat built from very thick old-fashioned timbers and rusted metal pins and bolts. Lying nearby was the wooden ridge-like keel, fashioned from one huge piece of what looked like oak. We estimated that the boat would have been about forty or fifty feet long, and imagined that this might have been from the days of the early pioneers. We did not take the opportunity to have our second bonfire, but did grab a few hours' sleep on the beach before setting off again.

Like other days, we were soon left with the decision to continue to tack laboriously back and forth, into the wind and current, making about one nautical mile per hour in our desired direction, or beach the boat to explore and then rest. When the wind all but died completely leaving us drifting back the way we had come at 0.7 knots we decided against rowing hard into it, and justified the decision to ourselves that this put us in a better position for twenty-four hour sailing when the conditions were more favourable. My journal of 19th August:

> *It seems so pointless to sail in these conditions but the adverse wind and waves make rowing extremely inefficient as well. We said we would have to sit it out on the beach sometimes; it's just frustrating this close to Cambridge Bay. I know I won't remember these boring parts of the trip but I feel a bit as though the trip is running out of steam.*

But it also helped our morale. I really enjoyed the time we spent on land, partly because it was a break from the boat, but also we had come to experience the Northwest Passage, and the land held a fascination due to its wild remoteness. We beached the boat beneath another high escarpment which had one of the current, operational long range DEW line sites, and the huge golf ball was whirring invitingly. Could this one be manned? A long hike up to it revealed some fantastic views but no human habitation. The journal again:

> *I think we are both now craving some other company and I wonder how long we will last in Cambridge Bay before we are keen to get off again. We get on very well considering. There's the odd bit of competition based on paranoia on both sides but it's been a long time on our own. Thinking a lot about what to do with the boat. Given the weather, its pointing ability into the wind and everything else I now feel that I don't want to return next year. Gjoa Haven will be a fine achievement and I know I won't want to 'complete it.'*

T Dinner was taken ashore with the addition of a bottle of red wine from last night's encounter with *Fleur Australe*—extreme sailing the French way. It seemed to raise our spirits and we climbed into our bags a little more confident about the next few days and our prospects of reaching Cambridge Bay soon. It's easy to become despondent when you're tired and nothing seems to be going your way. A hint of home in the bluff cliffs of Edinburgh Island and half a bottle of a decent red wine reminds me that the trick is to recognise the despondency for what it is and accept that tomorrow is another day. A cliché certainly, but clichés are there for a reason. Amazing what a little 'bag time' can do for you.

K My enthusiasm returned when I woke at 0450 to steady westerly winds. We got up to find that the tide, which although not an issue early in the trip, was right out and the boat was firmly on the sand in maybe an inch of water. I just wanted to go, and started kneeling in the water digging a space so that we could insert one of the rollers. We had never really tried the inflatable rollers that we had purchased and I had to admit to some scepticism as to their viability. Tony was more measured. "Kev, let's just stop and think about the viability of this before we get all our gear soaking wet."

I was in what Tony would later call my 'driven mode.' "Come on, we've at least got to try. With these winds we could make some serious distance." I already had Cambridge Bay in my mind with its accompanying rest, shower, real food, and sense of achievement and relief at getting there. To his eternal credit, Tony joined in, rather than doing what some people would have done and stick to his guns. After some effort we had two rollers under, pumped them up and the boat moved easily into deeper water and was soon afloat. We packed up the remaining gear, along with a lot of sand, and soon had the sails up, doing over five knots along the beach towards Cambridge Bay. Tony presented an outstretched hand, celebrating a successful departure. A nice gesture. I was delighted that we had made the rollers work.

T Kev's burst of enthusiasm came in marked contrast to his near-depression of the previous day. It took me a little while to adjust to this 180-degree reversal in approach and I couldn't help but find it a little irritating. The boat was in just an inch of water and deeply embedded in thick sand. Attempting to push her out against all the elements seemed a futile waste of energy when in a matter of two hours the tide would do our work for us and re-float the boat. I could see however that Kev was chomping at the bit to get out and take advantage of the favourable winds and be on our way. Rather churlishly I agreed to try the rollers, secretly hoping they wouldn't work and I would be proven right on my 'more haste - less speed' hypothesis. I was wrong; we got a little wet and cold but the rollers worked and after half an hour the boat was floating freely; enthusiasm and drive go a long way but again I had to curb Kev's enthusiasm to be away and insisted that we put the boat in order first before we sailed off into the Arctic with a cockpit full of half-inflated rollers, the main sheet unattached and no centre board in. It was not a harmonious start to the day but I had to admit that Kev's relentless energy had got us back under way, there was definitely something here for me to think about as my journal for the day indicates:

The whole process was a little tense but on reflection Kev summed it all up nicely: a combination of his drive and enthusiasm and my practical application and measured approach worked out perfectly—The Team Works. [A reference to the recruiting slogan for the Royal Navy]

K   As we skimmed along my mind wandered again to the perennial subject. Maybe we could come back next year. It would be tough on the family after my deployment to Afghanistan but we wouldn't have to come early due to the ice, and if I planned a good family holiday first... Maybe we could finish on Beechey Island in Lancaster Sound where there were two Royal Navy and one Royal Marine graves from the Franklin expedition. I didn't realise until later how fickle I had become and how progress made me reassess future plans for this venture.

As the wind freshened we were once again screaming along the coast with two reefs and a slightly slack main to stop the boat from heeling over dangerously far. The vastness of Victoria Island was hidden from view, and we simply followed a brown line of stony beach separating sea from sky for mile after mile. Day became night and we decided to leave the comfort of the shore and head out into the middle of Dease Strait giving us plenty of sea-room (distance from the shore) which meant that we could continue to make easterly progress without having to tack if the winds changed during the night. The Strait was about twenty miles wide and the wind and waves were very manageable. After supper I reached far inside the bow and retrieved the next chart, carefully folding it so it would fit into our waterproof cover that we used on deck. The old one was packed away less carefully; it is another milestone completed. I entered a few waypoints into the GPS. It calculated the distance to Cambridge Bay at 88 miles. It gave us an expected time of arrival, based on our current speed and direction. "We will be there tomorrow afternoon," I declared triumphantly. But it isn't that simple. Unlike in a motor boat, if the wind dies or changes that time will stretch inexorably to the right.

We were now two months after the summer equinox and the nights were becoming seriously darker. For the first time since before we had been stuck in the ice, almost two weeks previously, we were reminded of the extreme difficulty of changing watches, now in darkness. The new system was a two and a half hour watch, with the last half hour being changeover.

I slowly realise that Tony is calling me, and wake with a start, suddenly more aware than ever of the damp snugness of my sleeping bag and the chill of the dark night air as I shake my head to remove the Gore-Tex bivvi bag that has been covering my face. I just need a minute more. "Right mate, getting up."

After my extra minute or two, I unzip the bag and pull it down, reaching for my damp salopettes which are lying on top of the waterproof bag. In this tiny space I wriggle into them, resenting their clammy feel against my hands. I don't do them up but reach for my boots having turned round to face the other way so I can put them on facing Tony who is staring forwards, clearly looking forward to his bag. I can't sit up under the canvas cover so I lay half down. Boots on, I now stand precariously and then kneel on the seat in order to pee over the side of the boat. The choice of side is influenced by the wind, waves and the amount the boat is heeling. Tony slackens the sails which means I can safely pee not into the wind, off the gunwale closest to the water. As ever, it takes a while to get ready, feeling inside many under layers of clothing, and getting the angle right so I don't further stain the clothes that I haven't changed in four weeks! Then I return to the relative warmth of the shelter, fasten my salopettes properly and add a fleece and then my waterproof smock. I grimace at the feel of the damp neoprene against my neck. My hat has remained on since we were in the tent nearly twenty-four hours before. I retrieve Tony's sleeping bag and lay it out for him. We share the same bivvi bag to save space and packing it away and so the other's warm sleeping bag acts as an extra mattress if you can manipulate it into the right position under your body. Often it ends up like now, pushed down in the end. I add my life jacket and harness, then reach for my thermal mug which contains some luke-warm tea from supper, and grab a chocolate bar from the bag. I'm ready. I precariously step around Tony and clip myself on, reaching for the mainsheet and finally the tiller. "I have."

I settle my backside into the seat and study the sails. Tony briefly talks me through the progress and the all-important GPS which now shows 60 miles to Cambridge Bay. It's 3.15 a.m. and Tony has had a good watch of over ten miles. He unclips, removes his harness and jacket, takes a pee and by reversing all of my steps is soon tucked up in his bag, having wriggled himself into position for a couple of minutes. It's 3.30 and my watch is beginning. I am alone with my thoughts, the dark sky and the sea. There is no artificial light other than the glow from the GPS. But my eyes are accustomed and I can clearly make out the waves, steering the boat instinctively amongst them.

T   Another watch change comes about all too soon and I mentally check off how many minutes I have to dress and ready myself for another spell on the tiller. If I concentrate I can probably climb back into my salopettes and warm clothes a minute or two faster and allow myself that much longer in my bag… It's an enticing prospect but just the act of contemplating it brings a pang of guilt that I'm somehow letting Kev down. Reluctantly I crawl out of my sleeping bag and scramble around in the dark for my clothes. Through the early hours our speed has kept up and the GPS is giving me an ETA 0830 at the Cape and late afternoon at Cambridge Bay.

K   By 0540 we had achieved 95 miles on our desired track towards Cambridge Bay. It was close enough to the target I had set us months ago, of being able to do 100 miles on a really good day's run. As dawn lit the sky our progress continued to exceed six knots and by 0800 the Cape was within sight.

T   With just two ration packs left, we dug them both out with the intention of wolfing down a ration pack each! Scrambled egg—in both!!!! The disappointment was palpable, unequivocally our least favourite meal but with the finish line just 30 miles away we robbed a main meal from the other pack and shared it with the scrambled eggs.

K   The winds held and Cape Alexander passed to starboard, leaving a run across the strait before weaving our way into Cambridge Bay. It was mid-afternoon before we were across, and we had called up Tom Livingstone on the satellite phone. A resident of Cambridge Bay, by a curious quirk of fate he also happened to be a Norseboat owner who knew Kevin Jeffrey. We had been in email contact, and he had kindly received our resupply rations that had been air freighted forward to meet us. He reassured us that he was there waiting, with a trailer to drag the boat up on the beach. This was a huge relief, as we needed a rest, and the thought of having to stay with the boat close to the shore didn't seem very appealing. My journal for 20th August:

So—a great run. We got the winds. The short range forecasts have been very good. Great to have cracked it to here and now after the weekend I think it will be fine to carry on. Tony says he needs to rediscover his mojo.

Studying the detailed charts of the approaches to Cambridge Bay we noticed that we could cut inside an island to save tacking round it, but the chart showed depths in some places as less than six feet. But we were so keen to get there we decided to rely on the steel centreboard to kick up and warn us of any particularly shallow areas. We were through the narrow gap in a few slightly nervous minutes, with only three or four scrapes on the rocks, and just had a mile or so tacking into the northerly wind to reach the settlement at the far end of the narrow elongated bay. The wind was too strong to row, so we laboriously tacked back and forth getting a hundred yards or so closer at every tack. Finally we reached Tom, trailer already in the water, and after one false start of forgetting the centreboard, the boat was rowed on to the trailer and whisked out of the water. We shook hands on the beach and turned to greet Tom and his friend Pete.

T   My first impression of Cambridge Bay was of a ramshackle collection of multi-coloured low buildings tightly hugging a rather desolate shoreline. There seemed little reason for the town's presence here apart from the existence of a rather large bay protected from most sides by low hills and approached via a wide channel branching off the main passage. It was up that channel that we spent two agonising hours fighting our way into the teeth of the wind. We made the best speed we could and finally touched the sand at around 1730 and it seemed our haste to get here was merited. Cambridge Bay has only one bar and it is only open on one night a week. Steak night at the *Elk Club* finishes at 1830. We have just one hour to get the boat back to Tom's, secure it, wash properly for the first time in weeks, change and get in the queue for a steak. Time was tight but steak and beer is a pretty powerful motivator.

K   Tony rode in the boat; I got in the pick-up, and suddenly felt very hot in my five layers. We hadn't finished but we'd already concluded a significant journey of nearly 1000 miles in exactly four weeks. I wasn't elated, but felt very satisfied, especially as I didn't need to think about setting off again. Yet.

VI

FRANKLIN, AMUNDSEN AND GJOA

K   Tom's house was tiny and he shared it with his daughter, but he put everything at our disposal. We had to all but empty the boat into his living room where we were also sleeping and then it was time for a shower. I peeled off layer after layer of what now seemed to be very fragrant clothing and enjoyed the feeling of warm water soaking into my matted hair and month-old beard. Four washes and then my hair felt thin and unnatural. My hands felt a bit tingly but more worrying were my feet which still had very little feeling in the soles and toes. My assumption that warm water would magically rejuvenate them was shattered. I had some lasting damage. Leaving a huge pile of horribly dirty clothes and equipment strewn about Tom's living room, we headed off to the *Elk* Village Hall.

T   The fact that we were now both sporting thick bushy beards and were dressed like refugees in any clean spare clothes we could find drew some attention but critically we made it there inside the golden hour and took our place at the tuck-shop-like bar clutching raffle tickets entitling us to two beers or a shot of spirit.

K   I realised I actually wasn't particularly out of place in the fashion stakes. The room was an eclectic mix of local Inuit and 'whites' from down south, young and old, some dressed to go out, others in greasy overalls. In hindsight this was unsurprising, seeing as it was the only place in Cambridge Bay where one night a week, you could eat out and buy beer, albeit carefully rationed.

    These remote settlements have roads but they don't interconnect to other settlements. In many ways the communications are better in winter when skidoos can be used to travel the long distances over the continuous ice. It is the only settlement within over two hundred miles in any direction and has a population of around a thousand.

    We were clearly minor celebrities and a few people came up to us to ask about the boat and to check if we really had come all the way from Inuvik. Most left shaking their heads. The barbecue was excellent. Steak, chips and salad which was the first fresh food we had tasted in a month. Everyone was incredibly friendly although as the evening developed we could understand why the alcohol was rationed. Liquor sells on the black market for an extortionate amount, although certain trusted individuals are allowed a permit to import liquor for drinking inside their own homes.

T   Conversation was easy and the group ebbed and flowed during the evening. It seemed everyone had their own story of some kind. I'd have loved to know what Tom's was but realised I had to take care not to pry too deeply. There's a reason why people come to live in a remote settlement like this and sometimes it's not something they wish to share. Inevitably we drank a little too much and wandered back to Tom's with beaming grins on our faces and slightly unsteady feet. We finished the evening camped out on Tom's floor surrounded by heaps of boat stores. He seemed happy to have us there and produced a bottle of *Lagavulin* single malt whisky he'd been saving to round the evening off perfectly. For our part we were simply content to have made it this far, to be warm again and not to have to worry about the next watch.

K   Many of the young Inuit cannot find work and live on a generous system of state hand-outs which are a legacy from when they were forcibly moved from their land into these false communities in the fifties and sixties. These generous subsidies have themselves negatively influenced the culture. Traditionally the Inuit would live off the land, communally, making use of every part of the animals they hunted. Very little was wasted, and they lived in balance with their ecosystem, producing very little waste. Now, these communities are littered with rubbish which resides in an ever growing dump a mile or so out of town, partly because the permafrost ground makes landfill impossible. The Inuit have always known this, and traditionally 'bury' their dead wrapped in an animal skin and under a cairn of stones. The area surrounding their modern houses is often littered with rusting skidoos and quadbikes. Of course, the climate is harsh but I couldn't help wondering if these expensive machines might last a bit longer if they were covered or even brought inside for the season that they are not being used. It seemed to us that the welfare culture had sadly eroded their sense of value. I found it hard not to be critical, but I was painfully aware that this ancient culture had been forcibly dragged into the modern age in one generation, and they might have a different perception of value than my own. At least they have retained a sense of communal living, and often if one family member finds work, even away from his home settlement, it will be shared with the family – along will all the subsidies of course.

The whites, referred to in Inuit as *Qabloonas*, all have some kind of wandering, adventurous spirit necessary to exist here, quite literally on the fringes of humanity, during the long winters. Many were initially drawn to the North for the extra salary, or were originally running away from something. Maybe a marriage, relationship or business that failed. Others genuinely see it as their duty to help manage these communities. It is the extreme of small town North America, where everyone knows everyone, and whilst it wouldn't appeal to me, I could understand that some have found a balance of inner peace and challenge amongst the ugly, functional buildings and equipment that keeps the place going.

Certainly the hospitality they afforded us was amazingly generous. We were invited to a meal at Tom's friends Pete and Jean that involved mountains of smoked Arctic char, sausage, steak, ribs, chicken and barbecued fresh Arctic char! Our blog from 22nd August:

> *Tom is the sort of bloke who would quite literally give you the shirt off his back—even in the Arctic! We retired to Tom's flat and he produced a bottle of Tony and my favourite whisky—Lagavulin. Tom only has one rule—My House is Your House—and we've taken him at his word and been made extremely welcome by everyone. We just could not have sorted out our gear without Tom's help.*
>
> *So what next? We are aware that we are a week behind our schedule, and will probably continue on Monday to Gjoa Haven and reassess there. We will not make Pond Inlet, but this trip was never solely about covering distance. It's about the things you see, and the people you meet and it is surpassing my expectations in both respects.*

Tom arranged all sorts of things, lent us some gear, put up with us for five nights in his living room, plied us with another bottle of whisky and cooked us musk ox stew. We sat up late into the evenings putting the world to rights. Tony got his own back, having been given some grizzly bear meat, and we toasted the bear we had met as we tucked into his 'griz' stew. I made a chilli, it being the only thing I can cook.

The few days we spent with Tom and the folk of Cambridge Bay opened up a new perspective on how these isolated communities really work. First impressions are of a simplistic rather dysfunctional community artificially maintained on the very edge of what is viable. Whilst there is certainly some truth in that view the reality is a lot more complex.

One subject was never far from our minds. When to set off again and where we should aim for? The first morning we didn't discuss it. Tom let us lie in, and we simply sat in his living room until 2 p.m. drinking copious cups of strong freshly brewed coffee. We needed to rest, and we enjoyed the luxury of reviewing some photographs without worrying about power. Kevin Jeffrey had sent up a new charging system for the laptop, and a new watermaker. We also got online and were quite surprised to see how many messages were on the website and the number of interested people, which we hadn't been able to comprehend in the limited email traffic.

I sensed that Tom thought we should stop in Cambridge Bay. After all it was almost the end of August, and as he said, "You've achieved a good deal already. I can look after the boat for you."

It was an option, but Tony and I both knew we weren't stopping for long. After forty-eight hours we were getting itchy feet but the wind forecast was awful, persistent easterlies, right on the nose again. We met up with Peter Semoutik, an ice expert who has been relaying information to boats in the Northwest Passage by Short Wave radio for over twenty years. He said that the best time for free ice was the first two weeks in September. This was a genuinely tempting proposal; could we make it all the way to Resolute Bay and finish this year? But then there was the weather which starts to turn at the end of August. Storms become more frequent and of course it gets colder with less daylight. Our forecasters back in Northwood had been pretty accurate, so we might be able to weather the storms on shore but we had to be sensible. My journal for Tuesday 25th August describes our dilemma:

> *I suddenly realised that despite the advice we are the experts on our boat and its capabilities and only we can make the decision. Tom hasn't done that much hard sailing and wants a happy ending, Peter implies that we might be able to push on. I am enthused because we can finish [in Resolute]. Could we really be lucky and do it? We have 240 miles to Gjoa Haven (the Victoria Strait short cut to Resolute is clogged) and then 350 to Resolute. We need to be in Gjoa by 1st Sep to leave on 2nd and so out of the water in Resolute by the 9th. Very tight schedule but if we get the winds… All this has unsettled me a bit—I'd sort of got used to finishing in Gjoa but it's great that Tony wants to push on and take it one day at a time but I just can't think like that.*

T Cambridge Bay was something of a paradox for me. It offered a welcome touch of home, the familiar comforts of civilisation but all wrapped up in a culture entirely alien to us both. The more time we spent there, the more the complex social interactions that governed life in the settlement came to the fore. Viewed from the inside the modern Inuit community is an artificial construct binding an essentially nomadic people together in one place and then adding an alien social structure and expectation. Throw a few free spirited white Canadians into the mix and turn the lights off for 8 months of the year and you have a powder keg waiting to explode. It wasn't until Tom took us out to the nearby Mt Pelly that I began to realise the pressures that threatened to tear the place apart. On the way back I couldn't help but notice the proliferation of ramshackle cabins littering the barren slopes and nestled in depressions in the land. These scattered huts were the community's escape valve. In disappearing off to their own hunting cabins, Inuit and white Canadians alike grasped a degree of privacy, recaptured their independence and escaped the all-consuming goldfish bowl existence of the settlement. It was a sobering discovery underlined by the town cemetery that held the frozen bodies (above ground because of the permafrost) of all those who had ever been a member of the community and who even in death remained a part of it still. My insight perhaps said as much about me as it did about the northern way of life, but it focused my thoughts on the diversity and independence that I have enjoyed throughout my life so far and strangely perhaps left me eager to be on our way again.

Back in Tom's comfortable house we debated our options over a fabulous musk ox stew, Boddington's ale and another bottle of malt. Tom is an intelligent, worldly-wise soul and in stark contrast to my earlier sentiments I felt relaxed in his company and genuinely enjoyed our conversation. Inevitably talk turned to our future intentions. We had much to think about, the approaching return of the ice, longer darker night, heavy weather and the threat of polar bears. Our viewpoint ebbed and flowed in parallel with the whisky; at one point the words of Philippe, the hugely accomplished skipper of *Fleur Australe,* came back to me: "The risks are there for everyone, but sometimes you just have to go out and grab your chance." By morning we had convinced ourselves that Resolute remained a realistic possibility if the winds relented a little, and carried us along at a pace similar to that we'd managed on the run into Cambridge Bay. I went to bed buoyed up with enthusiasm and then dreamt about being sucked underground by an earthquake. Not an auspicious sign.

K Although the preparations for departure went well, there was a last minute rush to get everything sorted, and not leave Tom and Pete hanging around too long. The tension manifested itself in a public disagreement about how to mend the wind indicator that had become slightly damaged during our stopover. We must have sounded like an old married couple, squabbling about how much tape to use so as to not affect its performance. Tony remarked "I think I'm well up on the 'I told you so's."

I was pissed off that we had let ourselves down in front of our hosts, and after a fairly emotional farewell from Tom and Pete, as we rowed out into the bay I was full of pent-up emotion. Stress, anger, embarrassment, fear. Like any relationship, I knew I had to discuss it. Tony was reciprocal which was good because he could have told me to shut up and stop being pathetic. He told me he felt that I ordered him around, that I get my way a lot and that I change my mind often. Of course, I'm more impetuous to find a solution, but I felt that I'd learnt to let him have his way without expressing a preference. But that's probably only when I'm not acting instinctively. We concluded that we had needed the break, needed the alternative company but that it had been a phenomenally intense five weeks and we get on extremely well in the round. I resolved to focus on what lay ahead, recognising that the frustrations of such close proximity would have tested many old married couples! My journal for 26th August:

> *1230 and under sail again and I have mixed feelings. We're beating to windward again and maybe I'm missing home and wishing I was back there. The sun is shining and we're making progress. This afternoon is spent getting back into routine. The new power system charges the iPod so we have music again. Three options. Get to Gjoa in about a week and go home a week early. Push on and have another adventure but then have to get picked up between Gjoa and Resolute or get to Resolute and success!*
>
> *2030 and the sun is about to go down. What a change. It's going to be cold at nights and we'll be glad of the loan of Tom's boots and rabbit skin hat. The weather forecast is not good; south-easterlies all the time with no Friday westerlies. We've sailed 35 miles but the last 7 miles in the right direction has taken us 7 hours. It's soul destroying. The boat gets turned by the waves and at best she makes 130 degrees between tacks, tracked on the ground.*

T   As we left Cambridge Bay I once again felt the rush of being away again, and despite a minor tiff with Kev on the way out of the bay I couldn't help but grin as a seaplane, piloted by one of our *Elk Bar* companions from Friday night, completed a low level fly past over our heads with the promise of the first decent pictures of both of us sailing the boat. Strong south-easterlies carried us out of the channel at an encouraging 4-5 knots and with Kev promising to say 'please' every so often, I felt everything was well in the world again—at least until we turned hard into the wind again!

K   We stopped for the night but the following day was the same. Three hours beating before breakfast put us 3 miles further along the coast. We conducted endless discussion of options. Should we cross Victoria Strait and try our luck on the other side—but it was a long exposed crossing and for what? We still had to go east. Realistically we had 35 miles until we could play meaningful tunes on the routes to get to Jenny Lind Island and beyond. I felt slightly sick but fortunately wasn't off my food, which I put down to the days on shore removing my sea legs coupled with the relentless bouncing around into wind.

There were a couple of highlights. We saw one of the cruise ships (converted icebreakers) that take fifty or so passengers through the Northwest Passage. With much excitement we called them on the radio, assuming given our previous experience that they would want to rendezvous, and having convinced ourselves that the crew would want to show us to the passengers to make their trip more interesting. No such luck. The watch leader merely asked if we were in distress and when we answered no, simply went on his way without further ado.

The second 'highlight' was seeing one of the barges go past carrying supplies to the northern communities. Quite literally barges, the front vessel tows up to three barges filled with stores but I could imagine how difficult it would be to manoeuvre in a big swell. We still wondered whether our boat might be sadly returning to its start point on a barge if we couldn't take it though the passage. It seemed a waste, a failure if it ended like that, but equally I was aware that we needed to sell her to realise funds, and it was unlikely we would sell her up here.

We had no real means of predicting the tidal streams that were probably affecting our progress but it didn't stop the conversation; "If we only do ten miles a day it will take us three weeks to get to Gjoa Haven."

With reasonable winds we could cover in two hours what was taking us a day. But we pushed on, chatting on watches helped pass the time, and if we were going on shore for the night we didn't need the rest.

T Early in the afternoon on a tack close to the shore we sighted a narrow stretch of beach. It was perhaps the only viable landing spot for the next ten hours and we elected to give it a shot. From a hundred metres out the surf rolling up the beach seemed fairly innocuous. As we closed in on the shore it seemed less inviting but still well within the capabilities of the boat and neither of us was unduly worried. The real problem arose when we touched down, as we had to get the boat out of the surf. Kev leapt out with a pre-rigged snowstake and we dropped back into the practiced dragging routine adopted in the ice. Unfortunately for us there is a significant difference between the holding characteristics of an ice screw buried in hard ice and a snow stake thrust into sand. Almost as soon as we put pressure on the system the boat sat down, the stake gave way and Kev was left sprawling on the beach. Whilst amusing for me, it did mean we had some swift rethinking to do. All the time the surf was building up behind us and the boat was becoming increasingly hard to keep straight. Each wave broke hard on the transom and cascaded down into our cockpit. It was manageable for now but it meant one of us had to remain in the freezing surf anticipating the next wave and constantly wrestling to prevent *Arctic Mariner* from broaching sideways on the beach. We came up with a fairly rustic anchor point for our pulley system by piling about half a tonne of rocks on top of the snow stake. More difficult was getting the rollers inflated and seated under the boat with the surf crashing around us and hands frozen by constant immersion in the sea. Eventually after several hasty dashes down the beach to retrieve lost rollers they proved their worth again, and we managed to get the boat high up on the beach beyond the surf line. We were wet and exhausted but the boat was safe and we could explore our surroundings.

K   After failing to see musk ox in Cambridge Bay we had finally sighted one high up on a cliff as we tacked past earlier in the day. Now we thought we could see a small herd a few hundred metres inland, and set off to investigate; Tony carried the rifle and I the cameras. Musk ox have the appearance of prehistoric relics from the last ice age. The size of a cow, but looking a bit like very unkempt buffalo with massive shoulders, huge unruly horns and wild lighter coloured, sometimes white mane, they also reminded me of woolly mammoths from school text books. They seemed to have huge heads but that was probably the fur beard. Most amusing was their small stumpy off-white legs that poked out from beneath the huge hairy torso.

The herd consisted of three to four adults and a couple of calves. They eyed us warily, but allowed us to approach within fifty metres before scurrying off up the hill. I wouldn't describe them as majestic because their movement was ungainly and awkward. It seemed that they spent most of their lives hunched against the incessant wind, looking for any morsel of rough grass. The long winter snows must provide little nourishment nor stimulus for their small brain. It seemed a hard, almost pointless existence but I was still fascinated by their thick coats and stoic demeanour. We tried to cut them off, taking an alternative route up the embankment but even their small brain was ahead of us, protecting their offspring. We walked in a huge arc, and soon came across another group of three, maybe enjoying the sunshine on their backs as they stood rigidly with their faces away from the wind. This group was different, and by approaching very slowly I was able to get within fifteen yards, photographing and filming these magnificent beasts with Tony off to one side ready with the shotgun if they charged. Although how he was going to take on all three neither of us knew. It was exhilarating to be so close but I didn't feel threatened. After a few minutes we left them to continue their monotonous, stoic lives, and returned towards the boat finding the dismembered skeleton of a caribou on the way back. The skull still had both its magnificent horns attached but the legs and spine were spread over a radius of thirty yards or so. We wondered what fate the beast had met, to end up like this, or was it simply that it had died, decayed and the drifting winter snows had spread the bones apart.

Over supper and whilst enjoying some of the bottle of malt whisky that Tom had very kindly given us, we decided that at this pace getting to Resolute was off the menu. We discussed the possibility of resurrecting the trip next year. I thought through in my mind how we had got everything ready and here, how we would now have to return everything except the boat and then start again with funding, flights, shotguns *etcetera* but thought how enjoyable this could be if we weren't chasing every day. I realised that I was ready to go home, and assessed the wind history, as if past performance was ever going to be a predictor of the future! Out of 35 days going east, we had experienced eleven days of favourable westerlies but three of these had been wasted stuck in the ice. Twenty two days had been against us, with two days of calm. The historical records in the pilot said that we could expect over half the days to be westerlies whilst we had enjoyed the use of only a quarter.

T   After the battle to get the boat ashore and the pleasant afternoon with the musk ox, the final acceptance that Resolute was no longer a possibility dampened the mood somewhat. I think we had both independently reached that conclusion some time earlier but had always held onto the possibility that just a few days of favourable winds would make it possible. Now the relentless cold was beginning to take its toll and our enthusiasm was waning to the point where we accepted the literally cold reality that the numbers simply didn't add up. Imperceptibly we shifted our mental goal to Gjoa Haven. Strangely perhaps, once we had an achievable target set in our minds the trip was transformed. Unashamedly my priority was now to get there in time to catch an earlier flight and get home, back to everything and everyone I'd left behind there. The thought of coming back next year was so distant it was hard to frame it properly in my mind. Yes I wanted to finish what we had started but right now I had a lot of other things I wanted to do that had nothing to do with the Arctic or tiny boats.

K Videoing our journey was never going to be an easy task. The size of the boat, the waves, and the effort involved in setting up sailing shots and then having to return to pick up the other person videoing all added to the difficulty. But sometimes we were fortunate. The camera was set in the sand ready to record the smooth re-launch of the boat down the beach. Tony held the bow, and I was to move the rollers from the bow to under the stern as the boat gently glided into the surf. The reality looked more like the launch of a warship as, after the first roller was in place, Tony found he could not hold half a tonne of boat gliding beautifully on the rollers down the steep beach. As I move out of shot, the camera records the boat accelerating away, pulling Tony off his feet, to leave him sprawling in the waves in a reverse of the day before.

The long range weather forecast predicted maybe half a day of westerlies, the rest steady easterly and then gales from the north. We debated whether we could make Jenny Lind Island, slightly bizarrely named after a Swedish opera singer of the mid-19th century. This is a sizeable island in Queen Maud Gulf, named by Amundsen as he unlocked this crucial part of the passage. It offered reasonable shelter and the prospect of some company as we had heard a team were dismantling the DEW station there. But for once the forecast failed us and the wind died altogether, leaving us at the mercy of the unfathomable tidal stream pushing us back the way we had come at 1.5 knots. We rowed, finding it therapeutic to be pulling hard against something, making 2 knots towards our elusive target. We were hopeful that the flaw in the forecast might signify a substantial change, as almost anything would be better than our earlier forecast. Our blog for 28 August:

You can only fight nature up here to a degree. We are both philosophical about our situation. In a small unpowered boat you can only do so much and we always said we needed preparation, skill, patience and luck to make the passage. Our patience is being sorely tested but we remember that some of the apparently unluckiest events have led us to the most memorable parts of the trip. Such is the course of adventure.

T   Kev's frustration with the wind is becoming palpable but I think his time on the oars gradually eases the stress and I've learnt not to comment on it. For a time towards the end of the evening the wind picks up slightly and we take great delight in perfectly balancing the sails and sailing without touching the tiller. It can't last long and indeed it doesn't, and for the final half mile or so we're back on the oars. Again we land on a surf beach, this time steep and rocky. I'm not happy and manage to find a better option just a few hundred metres away. I push off to row around while Kev takes the opportunity to get some video. Two 'takes' and a lot of hard rowing later, *Arctic Mariner* touches down in soft sand. We are still in relatively big surf but experience has made us slicker and it only takes a few minutes this time to construct the rock bollard, rig the pulley and get the boat safe on the shore.

K   As with all days there was a highlight, when a seal came and played, almost touching the boat. However the following day the highlight came in the form of reading a book as we sat out the continuing headwinds in the tent. Tony had brought Robin Knox-Johnston's classic *A World of My Own* about his world first solo circumnavigation of the globe. I lay in the tent, avidly reading his un-dramatic, modest account of equipment failures, and his frustration at the unfavourable winds he experienced in a boat which could barely point into the wind. It put our position into perspective, especially as he had very generously sponsored our expedition. After all he could not get off and sit on the beach; it was a relentless struggle against the elements, and he was on his own. I was glad to be here, almost looking forward to setting off as soon as possible into the cold, wet, dark nights and making progress towards home. I reflected at the time I was effectively wasting sat here, whilst my two sons were enjoying the last few days of their summer holidays—without me. I looked at the photographs of them in my journal; it was nearly six weeks since I had seen them, and I would be going to Afghanistan later in the year. Long days like this are always a chance for reflection, of a different kind than I experienced on the long watches sailing or rowing. I decided it had been worth it, we had already had an adventure, but knew that there would be more to come, and I would always want more. I had to strike a balance between my job, my family and my desire to experience wild, remote places.

At least we had news that we could store the boat in Gjoa Haven for the winter, after a kind offer from a guy we had met in the cargo business in Cambridge Bay, leaving the prospect of returning next year. Late in the afternoon we went to explore some derelict hunting cabins that were dotted along the shoreline. They were simple, functional but very run-down, and surrounded by the mechanical detritus of human habitation at these latitudes, including a rusted skidoo.

We had decided against bringing a mirror, but the prospect of inspecting the product of six weeks beard growing proved too much and I used the camera to take some self-portraits. Mine was never going to be as impressive as Tony's but mine definitely made me look even older, and I knew Amber would insist it was removed the minute I got home. It had long since ceased to be itchy, and I was quite pleased with it, never having achieved more than three weeks growth before returning to work and having to shave.

T   Another frustrating day in the tent stretched into another frustrating night in the tent waiting for the forecast wind shift. Kev was up almost every hour checking the wind while I remained pretty contentedly checking the inside of my eyelids. In general he's the keenest to start out and the keenest to finish early. It makes for an interesting dynamic that I've never felt the compulsion to seriously challenge, although I have on occasion pushed us on longer than Kev might have liked, and undoubtedly caused a later start. By 0730 the wind change had finally arrived and just forty minutes later we were underway making about three knots in the right direction. Breakfast in the boat and ambitious plans to crack a quick forty miles by early evening were frustrated as the wind once again dropped to nothing and we took up the oars in a glassy smooth sea.

K   Sometimes, I decided whilst rowing, you have to make your own highlight of the day. It wasn't hot but the weak sun did provide a small warming effect. The water was flat calm. I was reminded of how I had come to be here, after the prospect of a trans-Atlantic row. There was no sight of land due to the surrounding mist. Mid-Atlantic the rowers bathe naked almost every day, so why not here? I worried about the effect on my still numb feet but decided as long as I dried off and then rowed hard to warm up it would be alright. I roused Tony from his off watch inactivity and asked him what he thought. He agreed to take some photos and video. I removed my clothes, noting the rather unpleasant bits of, I presumed, flaky skin that seemed to inhabit my thermal underwear, and dived off the bow into the inky water.

T   Whilst I can identify with the sentiment and have often done similar things in various parts of the world, this time I'm happy to leave the honour to Kev alone. The video footage however was priceless!

K   Predictably, I hardly got wet, kicking my legs in a frantic breast stroke to keep as much of my body out of the water as possible. After swimming not even the length of the boat, I reached for the gunwale, breathlessly mouthing "Oooh, It's cold."

    Safely back on board, I quickly dried myself on my thermal top, forgetting about the flaky bits, and then decided to row naked to fully dry and warm myself up without getting anything else wet. This might seem odd, but there is nothing more difficult than drying cotton underpants on a small boat in the Arctic, and after all that's what trans-Atlantic rowers do. However I did notice Tony curling himself up as far into the bow of the boat as he could to avoid my arse moving backwards and forwards on the sliding seat. After ten minutes, I was dry, bored of the novelty and getting a bit chilly so redressed in my flaky thermals, trousers, fleece, socks and boots and rowed until the end of my watch feeling fresher in a clean pair of underpants. Small pleasures.

T   An hour later I took my turn on the oars and after an initial struggle to balance the boat I finally got into a rhythm that had the boat flashing along at 3 knots. Absorbed with counting off the miles on the GPS I pulled ever harder, driving the boat onwards and relieving some of the tension in my body through hard physical exercise. Perhaps I got a little carried away or perhaps it was merely the result of six weeks Arctic punishment, but moments before the scheduled end of my watch one of the oarlocks broke loose.

K We took care of our little boat, and hadn't used many spares, but were suddenly reminded of their importance when the screw securing the oarlock sheared. With the minimum of fuss, we dug deep into the bow, retrieved a suitably long bolt and quickly had it repaired just as we were able to put the sails up and tack into the freshening wind and arriving drizzle. The wind was as predicted. We had started in a light north-westerly, then it would be calm with a light south-easterly that we were now experiencing but then it would swing round and bring north-westerly gales. We needed to find a spot where we could shelter from the gales, and as the evening wore on we could see heavy surf just round the headland of Stuart Point. We picked our way between numerous rocks into a small lagoon that offered shelter from all sides and hauled the boat on to the beach, exactly as we had planned if we had a gale warning. The rain hammered down on to the tent in the darkness but the winds remained easterly.

Go/No Go criteria sound great in practice, and we hadn't argued yet over them, or had to deploy our safety principle of going with the most conservative view. The following morning's weather forecast threatened to change that. We had favourable winds, probably for about twelve hours of daylight and then a gale was predicted. We discussed the options, as ever. We could set sail towards the elusive Jenny Lind Island but we would be searching for a safe landing, being blown on to the shore. We had no means of knowing if there were beaches or rocks, or what the surf would be like, though it looked pretty angry just outside our little lagoon. The winds hadn't yet turned to the favourable westerly and we assessed our predicament.

T We had a 37 mile open crossing to contemplate, probably at night and onto an uncertain shore somewhere on Jenny Lind Island. Unfortunately forecasting is an imprecise science and no-one can predict accurately when the storms will arrive. We may just make it before the teeth of the gale hits us. But then again we might not. The risks of getting caught were significant and the benefit was a mere twenty four hours. In the balance I compared it to setting out for France from

Plymouth in heavy seas, rain and fog on a Sunday morning with gales forecast for that evening—in a dinghy! Put that way the choice was simple, we had a lie in and then set off on foot to explore the wildlife.

A small herd of musk ox were happily grazing ten feet from the tent when we emerged. We went for a long walk towards the remains of a DEW station complete with airfield. It was our longest walk for six weeks at five miles there and back, and revealed some beautiful if unexpected wildlife.

The terrain was typically rocky with a series of pools inhabited by a variety of birds. Closer inspection of the water revealed the oddest looking creatures—not really fish but clearly not amphibians either. They sort of resembled fossilised trilobites, about one or two centimetres long, and added to the ambience of this wild, out of this world landscape. Suddenly we spotted a pair of Arctic hares, and watched them, transfixed through the binoculars. One grey and one an off-white colour, they were easily the size of large cats if not medium sized dogs. They sat on their haunches, completely motionless for several minutes apparently themselves transfixed by something. Then, without warning they would do their hop run, at enormous speed, often carving a huge arc as they went in pursuit of what we couldn't see. They came together, faced each other, and then to our delight, boxed each other before setting off again.

Next was a beautiful snow white owl, which sat perched on a rock, master of all it surveyed. We got close enough to make it fly off and re-establish itself with apparent disdain closer to the disused buildings. Lastly, and to our complete surprise we then saw a swan and three cygnets paddling gently round one of the pools. They seemed totally out of place; more at home on a village green back in England. Migratory birds must have some interesting stories to tell. I speculated how my homecoming would pan out. Seeing Amber and the boys, going home and sitting in the kitchen, back to normality, and then, after they had returned to school of just sitting by our pond with our dogs.

Back in the tent, the wind increased steadily to nearly forty knots as the barometer dropped. My last journal entry of 31 August:

Now 2230. Had coffee, scotch and dark chocolate. Excellent. Lying in the dark listening to the wind and the rain I'm dreading the night sailing in the cold and wet. I know I'll be OK when we get to it but I wish it was done, over. We sorted the charts and the route. Long way to go — about 180 miles. Probably at least two nights.

T   So far a combination of accurate forecasting, considered decision-making and good luck had enabled us to avoid the worst of the Arctic weather. By 2100 the pressure was down to 986mb and falling fast with gale force winds building. Outside the wind and rain battering the tent made us doubly aware of the fine line we trod between success and failure, and certainly vindicated our decision to stay put. It was a sobering thought to imagine ourselves out on the open crossing in the dark battling the howling winds towards an unknown rocky shore. Our night's sleep might have been interrupted by repeatedly having to weight the tent's valance with rocks and check on the boat, but we were all the more glad to be weathering out the storm on a beach rather than the open water.

K   Sleep was fitful, as the winds incessantly tore at the tent. We had already double-lashed all the guys to sizeable boulders, and remembering numerous nights in mountain storms I never cease to be surprised at how much punishment these tents can take. But the flysheet was pressed onto the inner and some water was coming through. I had ended up on the uphill side of the tent so it was collecting on Tony's side. At 0230 I ventured to look out of the tent into the half-darkness. To my horror, for the first time on the expedition the boat wasn't as it was when we had left it. The waves and maybe a bit of tide had lifted her, and twisted her round. Miraculously, our canvas cover was still intact but the wind was distending one side. We were up, and out of the tent in seconds to tend to her, finding boulders to hold the bow into the strong wind and minimise its effect. We should have removed the canvas cover, in hindsight, but I suppose we never considered it, now that the wind was going over and round it as if the boat was in a wind tunnel. Satisfied but soaked, and chilled by the gusting winds, we retired to the tent and slept on and re-checked around 0500.

T   It was not the end of labour and at 1030 a further check on the boat revealed that despite our best efforts her stern had been swept round by the waves and she was effectively broached on the rocky beach. One of the rollers essential for moving her was gone and the waves were smashing into her port quarter. After almost two hours of hard work rebuilding rock anchors and painstaking excavation of the beach, we finally managed to swing her through 90 degrees and raise her ten yards further up the beach out of the reach of the surf crashing against her. It was an immensely difficult task that at times seemed destined to fail. Everything we tried was defeated by the power of the waves and it seemed almost futile to be fighting against nature like this but we had no real option, and eventually persistence won out. The sense of satisfaction when we finally had an anchor point that held and the keel started edging up the beach was physical.

K   The surf continued to crash on to the beach ominously and we knew that if the wind abated a bit more, and with it still blowing in the right direction, we could still be trapped on the beach by the surf. We were lodged between two rocky reefs and were concerned that if the surf took the boat out of our control she would be dashed on the rocks. We called Dan who had been watching the storm on the charts pass over us, and he reminded us that we only had two more days of favourable winds. My journal of 1 September:

> *I lay awake plagued by the thought that we haven't moved in these favourable winds, aware of how far we have got to go and if I do sleep, I wake up having dreamt, it is with that realisation that 'I'm still here in this tent in the Northwest Passage.' But we've weathered a storm and overcome another obstacle. We will get there and it will be that much sweeter when we do.*

Playing with the GPS, doing distance speed calculations, it became obvious that if we left the following morning, we would have to navigate a route through the treacherous reefs of Palander Straits in darkness. By 1630 the tide was ebbing and that seemed to reduce the ferocity of the breaking surf. We decided to attempt a departure after a soup lunch.

"We'll be virtually straight into a long cold night, but I suppose we have to make our own luck with these winds," I said to Tony, trying to sound positive.

"Yeah, and we've been waiting for long enough. But if we can't get out, we need to be ready to abandon it and return to the beach and set everything up again," he replied.

We both donned full drysuits, and carefully packed everything away. We gently lowered the boat down the steep slope into the shallow water as the tide receded and then suddenly she was stuck on the sand. But by lifting and pulling we soon had her round, heading into the surf between the ominous looking rocks. We had to avoid her being caught side-on by the waves as we left. And then suddenly, as with all these things, it all happened very quickly. Tony leapt into the boat; fortunately we could make progress running under foresail alone. He tightened the sheet, the sail filled and he was helming whilst I was waist deep then chest deep in water. The boat was picking up speed and making progress directly into the waves which were crashing over the bow. There was nothing more I could do but join Tony in the boat, and he ably compensated for my weight and steered us out past the surf. We were away. It was 1900 and we were making over six knots in a five foot swell.

I sat with my drysuit on until I got cold. It was strange but maybe I didn't have enough clothes on underneath. That night was dark and cold; we had started wearing our thick quilted jackets as a sixth or was it a seventh layer? And that was supposed to be our spare clothing to put on if we fell in. My second watch was more exciting as the wind picked up and we were making good progress but into a broadside swell. I continued to be amazed at how well the boat rose up and then safely slid off even the steepest waves. We passed Jenny Lind Island, our goal for so long, without even a thought of stopping. My journal outlines my indifferent mood:

> *Maybe I've been here too long but I wasn't really enjoying it, more enduring it. I'm pretty certain about next year; I'm not sure it means that much to me. I don't think the scenery will be much better until we reach Bylot Island [near Pond Inlet], it's a lot of effort, there's the boys [my two sons], we've seen ice and we've done a storm... I'll be glad to get to Gjoa.*

T Coming on watch for the midnight to 0200 stint was always going to be hard in the icy-cold Arctic seas, but I don't think I'd realised just how tired I really was. I tried all the usual tricks, singing to myself, shaking my head till I was dizzy and shadow boxing but still my eyes kept closing. Falling asleep here could be dramatic with no other living soul but Kev for over a hundred miles and even he fast asleep in the front of the boat. I checked my harness was attached to the strong point for the fifth time and tried to search for some external reference points. Even the GPS was difficult to see and I had to resort to my red head torch. I was desperately counting down the minutes until I could wake Kev, but even then we had another thirty-minute change over period before I could finally leave the tiller and climb into my sleeping bag. Eventually 0200 and then 0230 came and my eyes could close. Moments later they snapped open as Kev was waking me for my 0430 watch. He looked like he had really felt the last stint hard and I knew I'd got to try something else to stay awake this time. I developed a routine promising myself a dry roasted nut or two every two cables, a slurp of coffee every two miles and a piece of chocolate every 'odd' mile. Somehow it worked and the minutes moved past faster as the sky started to lighten. It had been another hard watch but it was getting better. I was just not sure I wanted to face another night. Getting out of my drysuit helped but the corkscrewing of the boat in a large swell left me feeling woolly-headed. The watch pattern didn't leave much time for talking and we developed a kind of stoic endurance. This was definitely the less appealing side of the trip.

K   There was little to see except the GPS counting down, and I recorded it as a 'funny old day' with little interaction with Tony due to the need to keep going twenty four hours. But looking back, we were making huge progress, larger scale charts were sought, sailed across from west to east and new ones retrieved from under the bow. Working the GPS to navigate between the numerous unmarked reefs reminded me, once again, of the difficulty of navigating without it, or worse still the laborious process of sailing where no charts existed.

Literally just as I was packing my journal away, I looked towards the stern to see a freak wave crash over the side, drenching Tony. He had reacted instinctively, jerking the tiller to steer the boat away from it. He looked at me and simply said "The tiller's broken."

Whether the wave caused the extra strain or whether his inability to steer after it breaking had meant that the wave had then washed over us we will probably

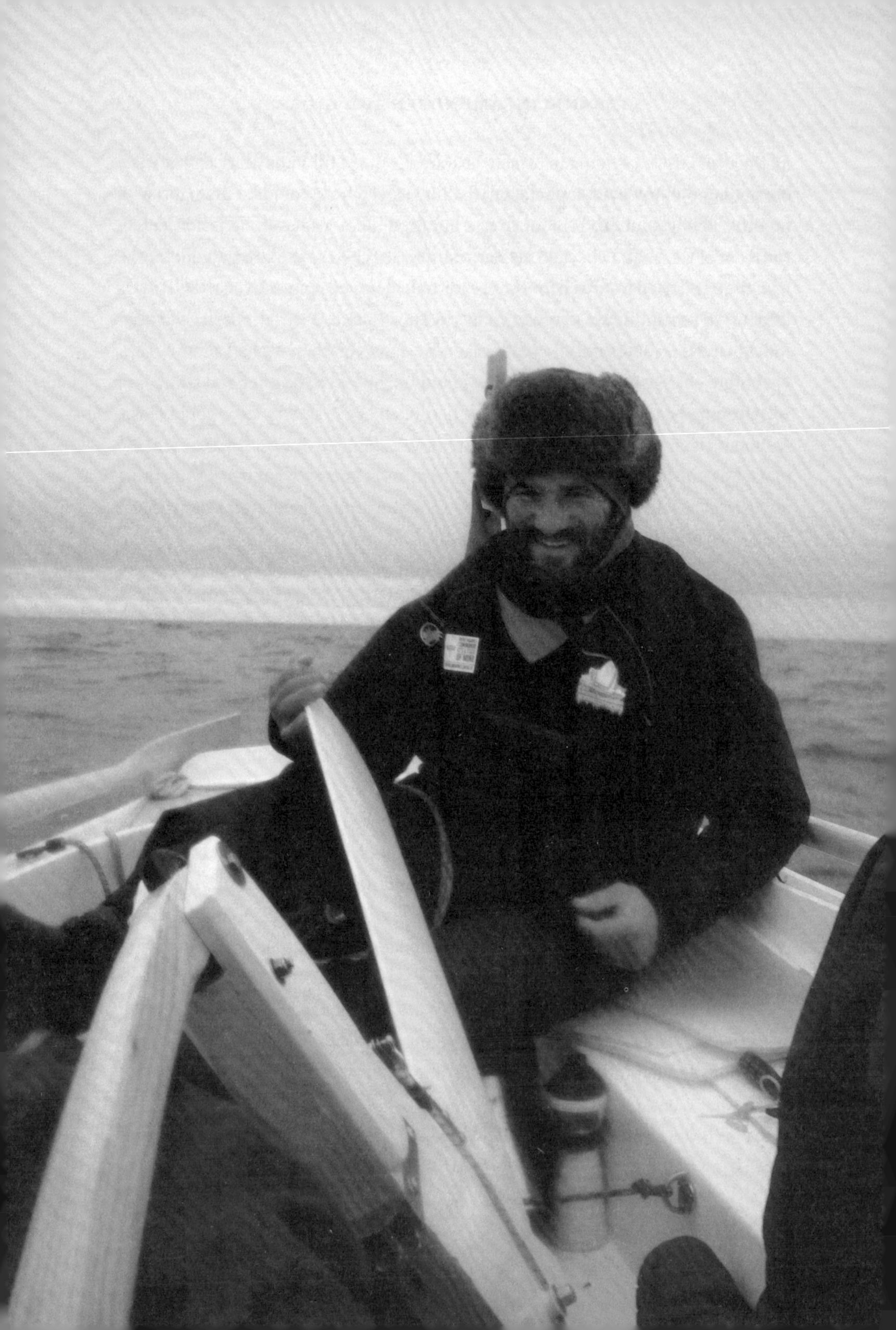

never know, but very calmly and with no swearing, and no flashing through my mind all of the implications, we assessed the damage. There were still a couple of hours of daylight and the wind had eased, and we had plenty of safe water to leeward. In other words we could set the boat on more of a downwind, stable course where she steered herself. For safety we dropped the mainsail and set about clearing the deck space so we could retrieve the tools and spares from under the bow. Tony lifted the rudder off the stern of the boat, being extra careful not to drop it. The tiller had sheared horizontally but thankfully the rudder itself was intact. All we had to do was re-bolt the now somewhat shorter tiller handle and we were back in business, albeit without the ability to lift the tiller. My grandfather's old hand brace was once again deployed. Supper was prepared and consumed, and we were ready for another long night.

T   There had been no choice and we were fortunate the tiller had parted during daylight hours and in manageable conditions, but once again we had proved to ourselves that by dealing with situations as they arose in a deliberate methodical manner they could usually be resolved regardless of how desperate they might first appear. The slight difficulty arose when they came in twos and threes. Not long after the successful repair I noticed a sharp drop in atmospheric pressure, 20 millibars in just two hours. Such a significant change was a sure sign of strong winds ahead, very strong winds. Sailing into the dark hours in big seas with a jury-rigged tiller, I had an especially anxious couple of hours waiting for the gales to strike us. Inevitably we'd be forced to run SE with the wind under a small foresail in an attempt to prevent putting any further pressure on the already weakened tiller. Whilst this it itself would not necessarily be a problem it would mean missing the entrance to the Simpson Strait and another long beat back again. For once we rode our luck and after a fraught night the barometer once again climbed just as quickly as it fell and inexplicably without the usual accompanying gales. The tedious watch routine resumed, nuts were replaced with fruit biscuits, and my mind wandered off planning my return to the UK in a little too vivid detail.

K   I was tired during my watches, thinking of the end. The end of my watch, and then in just another day, the end of the trip. But I was in no mood to reminisce as

← *Pleased with our tiller repair*

the minutes ticked by. After dawn we were into Simpson Strait with its large scale charts and buoys and beacons that aid what limited traffic there is in the Northwest Passage through this narrow gap. Light drizzle didn't dampen my spirits, and for a change we hit the mystifying tidal streams with perfect timing, giving us about two knots in the right direction.

I prepared my thoughts and then spoke to the video camera, about how Amundsen must have been delighted to find a way out of this labyrinth going in the opposite direction. About how Franklin's men were stranded here in the winter and walked across the strait when it was frozen as they desperately searched for a route out to the south and to the forts in northern Canada a few hundred miles through the wilderness to the south. About how the place where they perished, just passing on our starboard side, is now named Starvation Cove. We could only imagine the suffering, both mental as well as physical, they must have endured. I felt guilty, having complained at our lack of luck with the winds, and now longing to reach civilization and a flight home. We had warm dry clothing, satellite navigation, charts, communications and plentiful, enjoyable food.

Still making good progress we calculated that we could make Gjoa Haven by 1900, but surmised that in reality, that would be well after dark. The pilot book told us about the Todd Islands, where they found some remains of Franklin's expedition, eleven miles short of Gjoa Haven. Tony seemed keen to have "A proper last night of the expedition."

With full sails and a freshening wind behind us we were approaching the Todd Islands at over six knots. Our large scale chart showed no detail, but to find shelter we had to pass between the two main islands where it was likely there would be reefs. Both very aware that having come this far, to hole the boat fourteen miles from the end would be extremely careless, we reefed right down and Tony volunteered to don the dry-suit. With barely a clatter of the centreboard on the rocks, I eased the boat on to an idyllic sloping beach sheltered from all sides. There were no boulders to act as an anchor to haul the boat up, but we managed to fashion a 'bollard' out of the grassy vegetation growing on the sand—a technique borrowed from mountaineering to make an anchor out of firm snow.

T Passing through the Simpson Straight within sight of Starvation Cove had a deeply sobering effect on me. With plenty of time for the mind to wander and little or no distractions my imagination took me down into Franklin's chaotic world. As different as our circumstances were it was easy to feel their rising despair as they trekked across the ice doggedly searching for a route south and a route out of their prison. We can only guess at their feelings but it is easy to imagine the enormity of their isolation leaching away their strength as desperation took hold. Todd Island bridged the gap between my imagination and reality. The skeletal remains of what were almost certainly the last of Franklin's crew were found on this tiny lump of rock and earth.

We could have made Gjoa Haven that night but for me it was important we spent the last night of our trial treading the same ground as our predecessors and lying down to sleep in the same place they finally lay down to die. Perhaps we had been alone with our thoughts too long but that night I had the vivid impression that those tortured souls had long since found their peace with the Arctic wilderness and watched over us benevolently. An over-active imagination or not, it was the most peaceful night's sleep of the whole expedition.

K I was glad we had stopped as it gave me time to reflect on our journey. I glanced over to the other island, a low-lying rocky piece of nothingness really, unique but also so similar to thousands of other islands in this part of the Arctic. Forgotten, unkempt and desolate, but to me, strangely inviting. This was it. Our dream trip was almost over. Not entirely successful in that we hadn't gone the full distance, but filled with variety and challenges that had enriched the experience. I wondered if I'd changed. I thought back to those early days, my birthday in Tuktoyuktuk where it had seemed maybe beyond us. A lot had happened in six weeks, but then on the other hand I pondered the variety of what I might have done in six weeks at home. We had focused on one thing; driving the boat forward by whatever means we could. I had learned a lot, particularly an attitude to see how things turned out before getting annoyed at our circumstance—largely from Tony. But apart from that I was pretty much the same, at least in my eyes.

Amber's bag of treats was down to its last few items, and the wrapping paper had long since disintegrated. While dinner was cooking, we had an aperitif of gin

& tonic—a can we had been keeping for just such an occasion. We even had peanuts to accompany the G&T. But no ice! Ironically, just when we needed some, there was none to be found. We drained the Scotch and ate the last of the special chocolates after dinner. Inevitably we looked back over our trip, with a sense of satisfaction:

"Just one thing missing for me," I said to Tony. He raised an eyebrow.

"We didn't get to see a polar bear."

"True, would have been nice—from a distance."

My inflatable sleeping mat seemed to have developed a leak but I lay uncaring on the hard pebbles. We spoke to a friend of Tom Livingstone's, Alan Johnson who lives in Gjoa Haven. He had arranged for us to store the boat and for us to be accommodated in the local hotel. Storing the boat had been the subject of much discussion. Did we want to come back next year? Could we get time out again—from work and from family? Would someone else from the Marines take the boat on? But if not, then it could be taken down south again on one of the empty barges.

But I would really have liked to return the boat to be sold by Kevin Jeffrey who was on the other side of Canada from where it would end up. I wrote in my journal, "I think a full trip to Pond Inlet would last well into September anyway." This was because we would not be able to start from Gjoa Haven until the middle of August due to the ice. It turned out to be prophetic but for a host of reasons which will become clear later.

We woke to a flat calm, and lazily stayed in the tent contemplating rowing the last fourteen miles. But the wind arrived as forecast and we had an exhilarating sail, probably with too much sail up.

The following seas were urging us on, although at one point the boat wallowed in a trough and then headed to wind, heeling right over. I had not the slightest feeling that she would capsize. I suppose we knew her well, unlike during that night over a month ago in the storm. We reefed and then counted down the numbers on the GPS. Having readied the boat for our arrival, found the tiny bottle of champagne we had been keeping, and attaching the Nunavut flag above our red ensign, I made a couple of video diary entries and then just sat and watched Gjoa Haven emerge on the horizon.

T We checked off the minutes as the multi-coloured cluster of dwellings that is Gjoa Haven approached. With 14 miles to run and screaming along at over seven knots it occurred to me how much intuitive understanding had developed between us over the course of the trip. We were slightly overpowered and to prove it the rail buried itself into the swell and several gallons of ice cold water poured into the cockpit. Nonchalantly and with barely a word spoken we reefed down and squeezed yet more speed out of the boat with a confidence unimaginable just six weeks ago. Sailing together over that period had been demanding and we hadn't always agreed on tactics. We came into the venture with subtly different takes on managing risk, but over time we had learnt to appreciate each other's interpretation and critically to moderate our behaviour accordingly. In particular Kev taught me the difference between a considered risk and a reckless gamble, and his raw enthusiasm was infectious.

It was exhilarating to end the journey under full sails with white water breaking over the bow, and as we approached the breakwater neither of us was keen to reduce sail, still making six knots and with the boat heeled right over we picked our way through the jumble of unmarked obstacles and gybed neatly into the sheltered waters beyond it to make an almost perfect landfall on the beach for the last time.

K We were met by a couple of locals clearly bemused by our heartfelt celebrations. Their interest sparked to life miraculously however when our tiny bottle of champagne emerged, and they seemed more interested in sharing its contents than in where we had come from. We shook hands and that was it.

One of the locals said "Why don't you put an engine on your boat like that one," without a hint of irony and gesturing to a metal speedboat with a 115 horsepower outboard on the transom. There seemed little point in trying to explain, and I'm not sure we could anyway.

Alan Johnson arrived, pointing us to the inner harbour (where Amundsen had spent two winters and a summer with his boat Gjoa) half a mile up the estuary. At last we handed the video camera to Alan who then videoed our final approach where we met the Senior Administrator for the hamlet, Don le Blanc.

As promised, we were shown to the hotel where we had a room each! I peeled off layer after layer of rancid clothing and stood in the shower, feet and hands feeling weird, beard feeling soft and body looking decidedly thin. Before long, Don had organized a working party who manhandled the boat on her rollers up the steep ramp and into a container overlooking the bay. We locked it up after a preliminary sort, and retired to the hotel to browse through over nine hundred photographs of the trip and select some for the various media who had picked up on our story. It ended up being a late night once I had Skyped Amber and the boys. My youngest son was still in his pyjamas having just woken up—fantastic to see their faces, and another reminder of how technology has shrunk the world even at this remote outpost of civilization.

Gjoa Haven was similar to Cambridge Bay but smaller and with a 'zero tolerance of alcohol' policy. We discovered a little more about the Inuit's rapid transition into the 21st century and some of the problems therein, having met the local Royal Canadian Mounted Policeman, Pete. In this closed community of under a thousand souls, I was left with a deep sense of admiration for what he was achieving under difficult circumstances. Domestic violence was routine, and he was often called out at unsociable hours. He also offered to loan us a quadbike to explore the local surroundings, and so the last afternoon before our flight we charged around like a couple of kids across what could only be described as quadbike heaven, mile after mile of moonscape, until we arrived at the town dump. Here we saw a huge expanse of waste from the community piled high, there being no possibility of landfill in the permafrost. Driving back into town, again we observed the discarded and apparently un-cared-for quadbikes and skidoos outside most of the houses.

Even though it was only early September there was already a chill, and snow was forecast for the next few days. The short summer was over; the houses would once again revert to being insulated refuges from the ravages of the Arctic winter and it was time for us to return to more normal civilization.

My journal for 9th September 2009, written whilst flying high over the Greenland ice, on my way home:

I feel a certain satisfaction at having done the trip but I find myself wondering what I was really doing there. Did I enjoy it? Hard to say really, perhaps not the actual long distance continuous sailing or rowing, which was more something to be endured. But it was the place, the vastness, the remoteness which I liked, although I cannot describe either the landscape or the settlements as beautiful. Not like a mountain scene or a Norwegian fjord. My feet are not OK by any means—in fact it is hard to detect any progress [over these five days since we re-warmed]. I've just noticed how soft the waterproof bag for my journal is here in the warm, compared to how stiff it was in the cold. [My feet must have suffered the same]—Prolonged exposure to damp and cold with little respite. I look back and marvel at how we managed in that incredibly cramped space and of course how lucky I am with my back. I also look back and remember how I caught myself in the middle of a long passage, at night, looking at our small boat, one other bloke, the remoteness and powerful potential of the Arctic Ocean.

VII

INTERLUDE

K By the end of September the expedition was technically complete with all bills paid, reports written, thank you letters sent, a sizeable donation made to *Toe in the Water* and presentations made to various organisations. There were many legacies from the trip, most of which I was enormously proud of, but one that I wasn't; my feet still felt numb even weeks after we had returned. A bit of research and speaking to a couple of people put it down to effectively Trench Foot, the condition first studied after the First World War, caused by prolonged immersion in cold water. We hadn't suffered full immersion for days on end, but I surmised that the constant exposure to cold, occasional immersion and the cramped conditions that would have led to poor circulation were all contributing factors. Gradually I noticed an improvement, and eventually it became something that I just didn't think about anymore.

I was soon in Afghanistan working as the Military Assistant to General Sir Nick Parker, the senior British General and Deputy Commander of coalition operations in the entire country. I was fortunate enough to travel around Afghanistan a bit, but the majority of my time was spent office-based in Kabul. It was hard work and a fascinating time to be at the centre of things, but ultimately I felt trapped. I was mostly confined to a relatively small base, although I did manage to escape a few times into the mountains around Kabul. More importantly I was trapped by being an assistant. I was fortunate that I was working for a brilliant boss, but it didn't change the fact that I had lost the sense of freedom, self-expression and self-determination. I often found myself long after midnight having just finished work, watching excerpts from our video of the expedition on my laptop. I always took my mind away to a better place.

T When we left the Arctic for the first time I felt an immense sense of achievement in besting a seemingly endless series of challenges to get as far as we did. But nevertheless it was tinged by a lurking sense of disappointment at having not completed the whole crossing. It had been a great adventure; we were both physically and mentally drained and glad to be going home, but neither of us was quite prepared to draw a final line under the expedition.

"Let's give ourselves some time, do something else for a few months and see how we feel at Christmas," I'd suggested to Kev before we left.

"OK, but I'm not coming back up here in a hurry," Kev was less than enthusiastic but agreed to delay the final decision.

We probably should have guessed that time would be an effective and perhaps more pertinently, a subjective, memory filter. The good times became even more spectacular with each mental replay, while the long cold hours of tedious sailing faded into a dim blur. As we regained the lost weight and shed the aches and pains of seven weeks in the boat together, the itch of an unfinished task grew stronger. I accepted fairly quickly that it was an itch that demanded scratching. The problem was, would Kev feel the same way? Even if he did, would I be able to get the time off during a busy tour as a company commander in 45 Commando? We talked about the possibility of returning, but always in the abstract. Christmas came and went and I deployed to Northern Norway with still no decision made, although I could tell Kev was gradually warming to the idea. One evening in early February, having just come in from a demanding exercise in the ice and snow of Norway, I had a message from Kev. He was 'in.'

K   I hadn't spoken to Tony for ages, but soon after Christmas I contacted him to congratulate him on his engagement to Lara. I knew I had very little time to devote to restarting the expedition as I would be in Afghanistan until the end of June. We discussed the options, but ultimately we knew we had to try to get back. For me, it was something to look forward to, but also it was an opportunity to finish what we had started, and there was the draw and mystique of polar bears which we were almost certain to encounter going north from Gjoa Haven. But most of all, there was a picture in my mind of getting back into our boat and setting off north out of the harbour in Gjoa; the ultimate freedom, the possibilities and the potential for more adventures.

"Although we are potentially going to do the most scenic part of the trip at the end, there is always the danger that it won't be as good as last year," I said to Tony on the weak Skype link. "Of course, but it should be reasonably easy to sort out. We know what we're doing, we're a proven concept."

"Yes but we have to find the money, borrow all the gear again, I wonder if the airline will give us discount again. Look I'm stuck here with no time to spare. If we're going to do it you have to take it on completely until I get back, OK?"

"Leave it with me," he replied, characteristically casually.

I talked it through with Amber who simply said that as long as we had a holiday with the boys after I got back from Afghanistan and before I left to go back north she was OK with it. She knows me better than I know myself, but I was still doubtful that we could really do it. I spoke to Tony again:

"Tony, are we definitely going? We need to say here and now—yes or no."

"Let's do it."

Heading off to the Arctic again started with an agonizing soul-search for me. My Company of Marines were starting to gel together well and with a forthcoming tour to Afghanistan looming on the horizon I had to be careful not to take my eye off the ball. A return to the north would inevitably mean taking additional time off on top of my summer leave, at a point when the unit was just starting to prepare for operations.

Long hours studying ice reports and Admiralty charts had given us a potential window of mid August to mid September. Any earlier and the channel around Gjoa Haven would still be choked with winter ice, any later and the autumn storms would make progress extremely hazardous. The upshot was I would need to ask for two weeks additional leave in early September if we were to have any hope of covering the distance. I had to pick my moment carefully and approached the Commanding Officer on the back of a successful exercise in Norway. An insightful supporter of the benefits of adventurous training, he agreed, although not without reservations. As an added bonus shortly afterwards I bumped into the Commandant General of the Royal Marines, General 'Buster' Howes. He too instantly recognized the need to complete the challenge and after a few beers in the wardroom of HMS *Ocean*, he very graciously agreed to be our Patron. We were definitely—on!

INTERLUDE   185

K   I was delighted. We set up some deadlines to sort various things, and I got even busier at work. Frustratingly, I would check my emails most evenings to see whether there was an update from Tony but there was very little. The six months we had left became four, and although he sent only the odd email regarding the expedition, Tony was working in his own way behind the scenes and it was coming together. I got back in late June, and set about sorting the remaining issues before I left to go on holiday. The other issue on my mind was that we must not become complacent. Had we simply been lucky with the weather last year? What would go wrong this year? Would the boat stand another year? We were again in a race with 800 miles to cover in less than four weeks. Tony had a deadline to get back by 10th September. I watched the ice charts develop, hopeful that the area round Gjoa would clear before our intended departure date of 14th August. Although I didn't realize it at the time, we had set off last year on a Friday, against every seaman's superstitions, and the 13th August 2010 would have been Friday the 13th as well!

T   Having made the decision to go back, there was a phenomenal amount to do and very little time to do it in. With Kev in Afghanistan the bulk of it fell firmly to me. But first there was one further delicate issue to work through. On return from the previous year's trip I had proposed to Lara on a Scottish mountain-top. Perhaps mis-hearing my question in the howling gale she had enthusiastically agreed. So far however in 2010 I had spent three months in Norway with another month scheduled in Cyprus, all before June! She had spent a month on a ship in the Atlantic and the result was that we'd been working mutually exclusive timetables. If I was to be sure she'd recognize me again we were going to have to spend some consolidated time together. With summer effectively out I had to do something special with Easter leave. So, before I could get down to any more *Arctic Mariner* planning, an Easter holiday on the Kenyan Island of Lamu needed to be planned and booked.

On my return the mountain of administration had merely grown higher, albeit eased somewhat by the degree of repetition from last year. The first stage was to get acceptance from the Major Expeditions Committee. The usual interrogation by a panel of experts was neatly sidestepped this year as we were the experts. Bids for financial support had to go in, rifle licence applications, kit hire, satellite communications, water-maker, discount fare negotiations, media links, weather and ice support and a host of other details. Establishing a rear link man was another difficult proposition and we had to be sure we had the right person. Dan had done a fabulous job last year but was no longer available. Kev managed to persuade another Marines officer he'd worked and climbed with, Rich Hopkins, to undertake the role. Rich had a love of adventure (and now two small children), but I didn't underestimate the commitment involved and the importance of selecting a cool headed individual.

K I had a superb holiday and returned with four days left before departure. The plan had been that we would be completely packed before I went on holiday and I would have a few days with my two sons before going off and leaving them yet again. Inevitably this had failed and I felt guilty, unprepared and worried. I had a head cold, felt lousy and there were endless lists to work through. We had a spare battery, a new tiller and oar to collect in Canada, a more robust power management system with spares, and a simple robust music system. We hadn't managed to make some of the improvements we wanted, such as a third row of reefing points in the mainsail, which of course was still in the container on the beach in Gjoa Haven. I hate packing at the best of times, I suppose out of fear of leaving something vital behind. And then there was a problem with the satellite telephones, which unlike the previous year we simply could not get to send or receive data. Over the course of the last two days I learnt more about COM ports, ISPs, updating firmware, and installing drivers than I wished to. I was constantly on the phone to the company, and in the end they offered to deliver an alternative system a few hours before we flew to Canada. We didn't take it as it was the size of a briefcase, had no 12 volt charger and couldn't be used on the move. I spent most of those last two days totally pissed off; oblivious to how fortunate I was to be re-embarking on a great adventure.

T I woke to the smell of bacon sandwiches at 0500 and we were soon off to the airport in the back of my father's Volvo estate, with Classic FM calming the worries about how we were going to get over seventy kilos of kit onto a flight with just 20 kilos paid baggage allowance. I decided that another charm offensive at the check-in was worth a try, but perhaps needed a little more to back it up this year. Reverting to a little creative forgery of the previous years' excess baggage permission e-mail worked a treat. The nine-hour flight to Calgary sped past and we seamlessly cleared customs at the far end and collected 20 man days of military rations from a young female corporal who had arrived from the British Army training facility in Suffield, Canada. The blank look we received at the car hire desk for the four hour drive to Edmonton was less encouraging. The schedule was tight and we still needed to pick up some more food, a spare oar and a shotgun in Edmonton, and no other providers had any spare cars. It was an incongruous start that threatened to delay and therefore derail the entire expedition but eventually they found our booking and led us to a 'midsize' Nissan with a chirpy name and a lawnmower engine that looked like it would struggle to accommodate the two of us never mind all our kit. On arrival in Edmonton we located the First Air Cargo depot that had taken receipt of our replacement wooden oar and a speculative bear alarm purchased over the internet. Being eight foot long, the oar fitted in the Nissan so snugly it became impossible to select reverse.

Next stop was our friend from the previous year, Gord McGowan and his gun emporium with everything from WWI handguns to assault rifles and most things in between. We left with a Massberg 580 A1 pump action shotgun and set off for the outdoor shop to buy the rest of the dried rations we needed. Unfortunately for two unlucky campers arriving just moments behind us, we cleaned the shelves of the best flavours of dried rations. Kev seemed a little distracted but after a few beers his mood seemed to lighten and we retired to bed early for the night.

K   Things didn't improve in my mind once we had arrived in Canada and collected some of the essential gear. My journal of 11 August 2010:

> *As I sit here in Edmonton I feel worse than while we were packing—even slightly sick. Worry? Fear? Guilt at leaving the boys, dreading the realities of sailing and rowing long distances, worrying about excess baggage charges or anything else I can find. Although we now have everything we need including bear alarms I do think it is all being done slightly off the cuff and I am concerned that we are*

less engaged than last year—complacency? The ice is free enough to get through but we couldn't have started any earlier. I've just re-read parts of my journal and also 'fear' the inevitable waiting for the winds. I know I wouldn't feel like I do if I was going in a yacht, with an engine…"

T   In the morning we were greeted by torrential rain and our newly purchased bear pepper spray was immediately confiscated at the airport. On the brighter side the First Air staff seemed delighted that we have managed to match exactly our very generous 280lb weight limit for the flight up to Yellowknife. Getting away with a discreet 'toe lift' to bring the weight down was a little victory that kept me smiling away to myself.

The morning flight to Yellowknife lands an hour after the onward flight to Gjoa Haven departs so we are left with 23 hours to kill in Yellowknife, and turn our attention to getting the sat phones to work. Kev's Electrical Engineering degree and latent IT knowledge are indispensable but even he is struggling to establish a data link. It seems as soon as he resolves one issue another presents itself. Finally at about 2300 we think we may have succeeded but need to wait for a better signal to test them out. It's another worry that accompanies us north on the seemingly endless journey just to get to the boat.

K   The flight from Yellowknife to Gjoa Haven was delayed and forecasts told of a temperature of only 4 degrees at our destination. I shivered inwardly and convinced myself that with five layers of clothing we would soon get used to it. Alan Johnson kindly met us at the dirt strip airfield, and took us down to the container on the foreshore in which *Arctic Mariner* had spent the long harsh winter. We had discussed how she might have fared. Would the prolonged cold have damaged any of the fittings? Would the cleats have seized up or rusted? With some trepidation we pulled the doors open and there she was, exactly as we had left her, of course. A quick inspection showed that she was in perfect working order, although one cleat did need a quick spray of lubricant!

T   She'd survived eleven months in an ice box with no ill effects at all and she looked fabulous; perhaps for the first time it began to sink in that we're back in the Arctic

INTERLUDE

and the challenge is back on. Still, the prospect of a night in the container with her did not appeal, particularly given the biting cold wind, so when Alan offered us some floor space in his cabin we jumped at the chance. After some initial preparatory work on the boat I left Kev at the shore side while I disappeared to pen a quick blog for the website and write to Lara. The last few weeks have passed in a blur and now I have some time to think it occurs to me that I have been a little selfish coming out here again. While I'm up here chasing my dreams in the Arctic she's started a new job, moved into a new house, and is having to make new friends at the opposite end of the country, having moved from a hospital in Plymouth to one in Edinburgh. She's a tough independent farmer's daughter from Zimbabwe and can take it all in her stride, but I know I've got to devote some real time to her when I get back.

K   Having found a thick jacket to protect against the piercing wind, I stood for a moment and just looked at the boat. The preparations were over, and we were back to finish what we had started. A lot had happened in ten months, and I wondered what lay ahead as we headed north. We had talked about the possible short cut of navigating the Bellot Strait, a narrow channel about half way with vicious tidal streams that would save us a few hundred miles if we managed a long open crossing on the far side, completely bypassing Resolute Bay. For the first part of our journey north the ice was clear, but the wind forecast was not great with steady northerlies at 20-30 knots for the next couple of days. We were back on familiar territory in all respects.

We removed the dead battery, which by now had been sat for several months in sub-zero temperatures, and back at Alan's place connected it to his high performance 'battery conditioner.' Remarkably it seemed to hold a charge, although we had brought a spare with us from UK, to save the worries from last year when we thought we had killed our only power source. While Tony sourced some tidal information, and sent the last minute safety documents to various authorities in Canada and UK, I had a couple of hours pottering down at the boat. It was sunny but still chilly, and I was very relieved to get back into the warmth of Alan's truck. The inhabitants of these northern communities get so used to driving everywhere and spending the minimum time exposed to the weather in the long winter; they seem to continue in the short summer as well. I assumed I would get used to the penetrating wind once I was again living in the boat with no warm refuge other than my sleeping bag.

After a good night's sleep and a huge north American breakfast of ham, eggs and an inexhaustible supply of pancakes and maple syrup, we treated ourselves to a very expensive pair of insulated rubber waders that came up well over our thighs. We rejected the idea of buying two pairs on the grounds of expense and space in the already cramped boat. A decision we would reflect on repeatedly. Soon afterwards, a fork lift truck arrived to manoeuvre the boat into the water, and the afternoon passed with final preparations. It took six attempts to correctly rig the mast, blocks, sails and sheets, much to the amusement of Alan and Inuk, the Mayor of Gjoa Haven, who observed from inside their truck. It had been over a year since we had last rigged the boat and we had only done it twice in total, once on the Potomac River and once in Inuvik. We had forgotten only one thing—our ensign.

All too quickly the boat was ready in the water and we'd reached the point of no return. It all seemed rather daunting and slightly surreal but we were finally out of excuses to delay and we decided to depart that night. No fanfare just a simple shake of hands and at 1830 on 14th August 2010 we were sailing out of Gjoa Haven, roaring along at over five knots. The scale of what we needed to achieve was a little overwhelming, but at last we were under way and I could feel the excitement rising as the miles dropped away behind us. We rounded Betsold point with ease and headed up along the Gibson peninsula making great progress in a steady NW on the beam. By midnight we'd done 25 miles, heading north, but then the difficulties began.

VIII

HEADING NORTH

K   **D**AY BECAME NIGHT MORE QUICKLY than I had remembered from the previous summer, a reminder that we were already late in the season in order to be free of ice. We attempted to round Cape Matheson, beating into a northerly wind with two reefs in the sail, and sailing up and down the same track on the GPS. We may have been subject to tidal streams but it was an early reminder of last year and the difficulties ahead; we reluctantly made the decision to stop around 0230. We failed to make a safe landfall on a rocky shore but then we saw a small, wrecked motor cabin cruiser through the gloom and decided to tie up alongside it, by which time it was already starting to get light. It was a sandy beach strewn with seaweed, but very different from our first wild landfall on the sandy beach where we saw Caribou and were plagued by sand flies last year. There was a thin covering of windswept snow, clinging to rock, weed or grass which protruded above the sand. Maybe it was the dawn light but it looked foreboding, cold and uninviting. Having tested the shotgun, we slept; Tony in *Arctic Mariner* and me in the sand-filled cabin of the wrecked boat. It seemed an inauspicious start to the trip and I lay awake, albeit for only a few minutes, worrying about the winds and how to make progress.

T   Determined to get around the point of Cape Matheson, we slipped at 1230 after a fitful few hours' sleep and a hot but strangely subdued meal. A long tack out and return almost got us there but it took another long tack out to sea and back before we eventually escaped the tidal rip and rounded the point into an open bay.

K   Sailing on, we found that we needed us both sat out on the rail, and a maximum of one reef to punch into the waves and make progress. It was hard work but exhilarating. The iPod was blasting out a favourite song, and the sun was out. All was well in the world until the iPod suddenly stopped.

"That battery isn't holding a charge; it's just as well we have the spare." Tony remarked. We had been lucky to get the battery on the aeroplane, reassuring the check-in attendant that it was only a big dry cell. Further investigation showed that the battery monitor was just switching from charging (sun out) to powering (sun behind a cloud) which caused the iPod to pause. While helming in the choppy seas, Tony aptly described our the mood to the video diary,

> *"I think we are about 22 hours out of Gjoa Haven now and we seem to have had all four seasons in one day. We've had big seas, but we are now sailing in blue skies and it is amazing the difference having the iPod on makes. We were both sitting here feeling a little sorry for ourselves; it is cold, there is a biting wind but we are both feeling a bit more comfortable about things now I think. But the realities of how far we have got to cover really do bite. Seven hundred miles in a straight line, and we are clearly not going in a straight line. A couple of days of the elusive southerly winds would make all the difference, but if we don't get that we will deal with that on a day to day basis. I think you have to set yourself small targets, one achievable target each day and then move on to the next one. Because the scale of the whole thing is just awe-inspiring, but taking it one piece at a time will get us there."*

Rounding Cape Matheson proved to be a mixed blessing. It exposed us to the full force of the waves and swell that had built up under persistent biting Arctic northerly winds. We were now charging along a lee shore with four-to-six-foot waves taking our tiny 17-foot open boat full on the beam, with both of us hiked out on the rail to keep her level. It was an exhilarating but unnerving sail and we began to ship a lot of water over the side. Maybe we ventured closer to the shore or perhaps the beach gradient changed because suddenly we were amidst huge breaking waves threatening to pick up and roll our small boat. Excitement turned to genuine concern and every ounce of my concentration was focused on trying to anticipate the wave patterns and react before they could wrestle control of the boat away from me. The prospect of being swept up onto the beach in this crashing surf so far from civilization was not something I wanted to imagine. The waters around us were bone-numbingly cold and the beach devoid of shelter. We rode our luck for a while but it couldn't last and inevitably as we dropped down into the deep trough of a wave I read the sequence slightly wrong. As one giant wave rolled under us I was not quite quick enough to get the boat's nose round and through the next one. We looked up to see the water tower above us, curl and then break. The wave took us full on the beam and a torrent of foaming icy water crashed down into the boat. For an agonizing moment I looked vertically down on Kev, convinced that we were going over, but slowly the angle dropped and the wave released us. We were upright and afloat but the boat was full almost to the gunwales with freezing cold water and had lost all headway. We were heavy and beam-on, half submerged and wallowing in the Arctic swell but somehow I managed to get the nose round in time to meet the next wave head on.

K As the boat now bounced head-on into the waves having lost all its speed, Tony handed the tiller to me and took to the highly efficient bilge pump to empty the cockpit. It was a race to empty the boat and get her responding to the helm again, and within a minute the cockpit was clear and we contemplated how we would have fared if we had not requested the design changes to the boat with its raised cockpit floor and the watertight under-floor storage lockers that contained all our food. The boat had remained stoically upright throughout. We were now only a few hundred yards from a wide beach, but the surf crashing onto it made it impossible to land safely and roller the boat up it. We had ten miles to go west to the nearest realistic landfall that would provide shelter from the swell. With a north westerly wind we would be beating all the way, taking the swell broadside.

T The rest of the day was hard, cold and tiring and the enormity of our task started to intrude a little. The iPod helped restore spirits enormously and when the sun briefly broke through we felt our confidence returning. We just needed the right set of winds for seven days and we were there. Still, Pond Inlet was beginning to feel like a very long way. Finally we found a small cove where we could get the boat at least partially ashore, anchored by a long line.

K With the boat secure, we set about mending a three-inch tear in our invaluable canvas cover that had been caused by the weight of water crashing on to it earlier in the afternoon. We took our time, carefully stitching over some sail tape knowing we had only once chance to prevent the tear growing and rendering our cover useless. Over supper, dressed in our thick down jackets (hood up) to keep warm, our conversation turned to progress. We predicted that this was going to be a harder trip than last year, and even contemplated that we might have to return to Gjoa Haven, but it was early days and we just had to take each day as it came. My journal for 15th August 2010:

> *I'm really not sure I wanted to come back, laying here now cooped up in the boat [I must have forgotten how tight it was to sleep in the boat]. Why do I do this? It really is time in my life to be more comfortable. Still we only need 7 days of favourable winds out of 25 — is that too much to ask?*

In a taste of things to come, we spent all the next day tacking north, ticking off headlands and a few islands, both of us up and on the rail. The boat was well balanced but without the extra weight hiked right out, the leeward gunwale was in the water and the boat started to fill up. We needed the sail area to punch into the wind and the waves. It was working, laboriously tacking up the coast. The time didn't drag but it was hard. I watched the grey sea, anticipating the movement of the boat whether I was helming or leaning out trying to balance her. We were harnessed on, and changing over was reasonably easy, provided we didn't change the big green wader boots. Thick Gore-Tex mittens stayed on virtually the whole time. Tony decided to rewarm himself having just finished a long watch and his violent punching of an imaginary bag suspended just below the sail made the boat rock, against the motion of the waves. Lunch consisted of a hot meal, prepared not as last year over an open stove but in a bag containing special chemicals which when wetted warmed the foil container of food. This was excellent and we have brought a good supply for just such occasions. I developed a headache, probably brought on by dehydration, as without using the stove we have not consumed our normal quantity of tea. We were aiming for another point of shelter on the large scale chart five miles away. With three miles to go, Tony said, "How about going on to the next inlet, it's only another eight miles and we would make it by midnight?"

I was not keen but I could see his point, as we started late that morning and I knew we had to make the distance. We decided against it, but I still felt guilty as we beached the boat, having covered only 11 miles on our track today. At least the sunset was quite simply stunning. The orange colour stretched across the horizon, and the few wispy clouds were backlit and almost translucent, fading higher into the sky to a blue, then grey then black. Tony had the good grace to say that it would be hard going having not eaten or drunk properly if we were still out there now. My hands were sore and my salopettes leaked so my underclothes were wet. I was regretting not buying some new ones to bring out that were properly waterproof. The last line from my journal of 16th August:

It's remote, beautiful in a strange sort of way but I am sort of counting the days already! Just need to keep pushing and don't make it any harder than it already is.

The following day again involved a late start but we could just make a course that enabled us to use the tacks into wind to navigate between the Beverley Islands and then into the Wellington Strait, which opened up the next part of the Northwest Passage.

We covered a lot of miles in strong sunshine and blue skies and the slight moderation in conditions allowed us to sail most of the day with just one person on watch. It proved to be little more than a mixed blessing however, with the off watch person wedged against the upper side of the hull at a crazy angle. Unable to climb into a sleeping bag or even get out of full foulies, the inactivity and damp clamminess left you feeling colder than the person on the helm. It did however offer a respite from the mental drain of constantly trying to read the waves, and allowed one or other of us to drift off into fitful daydreams. Somehow I didn't have the same enthusiasm this year. It was beginning to seem like a relentless grind. So much for enjoying the journey; it was now taking on the feel of a race to the finish line so I could get home and spend some quality time with Lara, maybe even make it back in time for her birthday.

At 2030 we sighted the first ice of the year in the form of a series of old ice floes perhaps 30-40 metres across, and as we approached the shore they became ominously more numerous. By midnight we finally completed the open water crossing to the Wellington Strait and as the seas calmed down Kev managed to grab an hour and a half in his sleeping bag. It was the first proper rest either of us had had under sail this year and I remember feeling resentful that any chance of sleep during my 'off watch' had been denied by rough seas and constant tacking. It was a small thing. But then again our world was quite small right now.

We consistently underestimated the amount of time required to identify an appropriate beaching spot and then secure the boat on the shore. Tonight was no exception and having taken to the oars not long after midnight just one mile from our intended landing point it was actually approaching 0400 before we finally climbed wearily into our bags. Shallow reefs frustrated our first attempt to beach and a further three miles of rowing into wind and tide preceded an eventual landing amongst broken ice floes, on a marginal beach that we would have backed off from immediately if we were able to keep our eyes open any longer.

K We had sailed 40 miles, 26 on our intended track. It was a good result but we needed to be doing that day after day. The satellite phone was continuing to make fragile connections, and I just managed to download yesterday's weather and no messages from home. It was annoying, considering how dependent we had become on messages the previous year, but not essential. The next chart was very large scale at 1:500,000 which made predicting night stops nigh on impossible. When we needed to stop, if we were some distance offshore we would have to head inland and search using the binoculars. More worryingly, we noticed that we didn't have the chart for the far side of Bellot Strait through Prince Regent Inlet, so any ideas of a short cut to Pond Inlet, saving us about a hundred miles, were out. At least that decision had been made, we were going via the classic, Amundsen route up Franklin Strait, directly north all the way to Resolute Bay and then east to Pond Inlet.

The ice was getting denser, not really impeding our progress yet but still something to think about. Often we could see free water half a mile or so ahead and had to pick our way, beating into the wind through an ever-changing maze. Each floe was different, and like sitting watching a fire I found watching them pass almost compulsive viewing, accompanied by the occasional sound of small lumps hitting the hull. Occasionally we had to force through a narrow gap and even broke some of the thin connecting layers. It made life more entertaining, and

Colder this time →

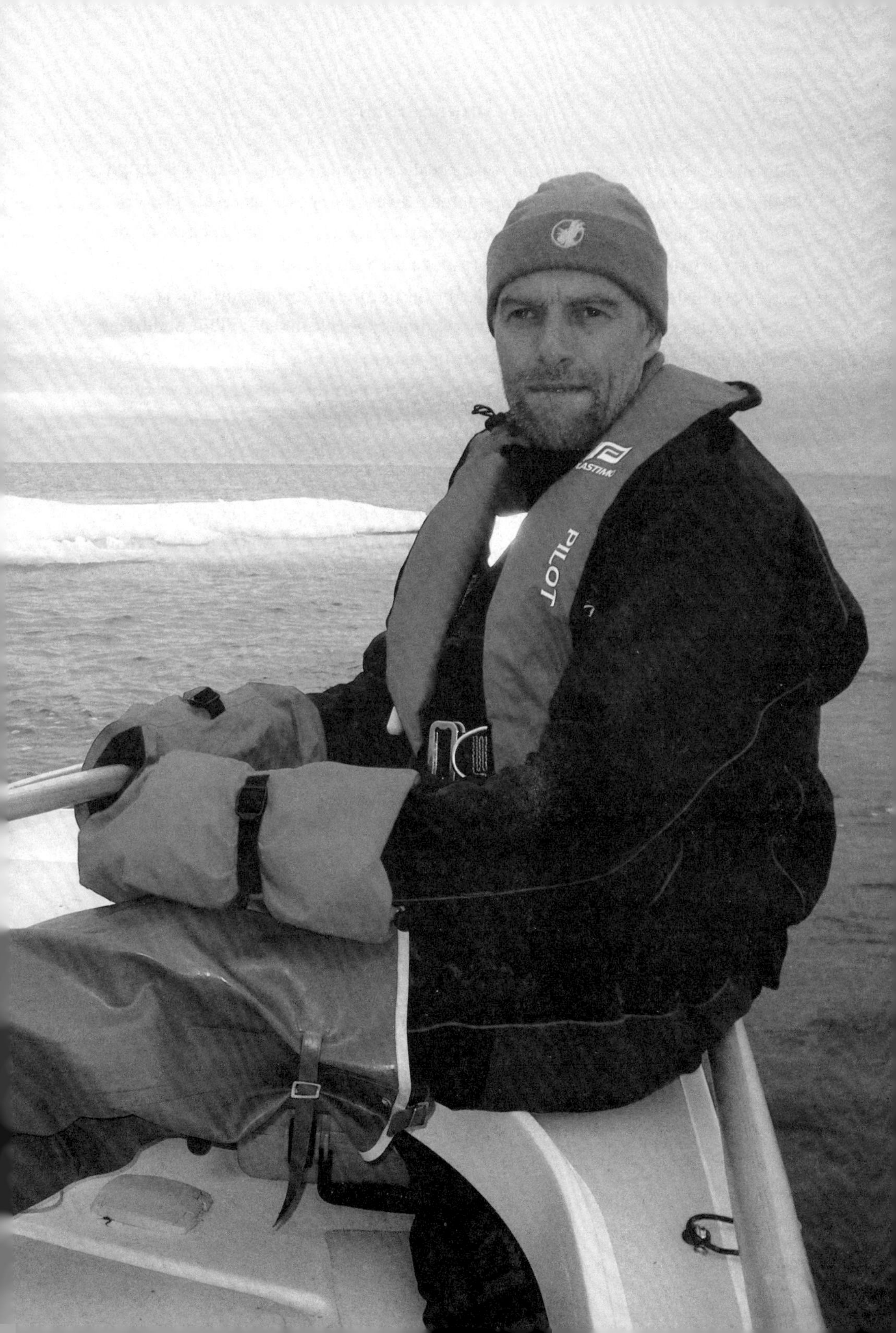
PILOT

I realised that the main reason I wasn't really enjoying the trip so far was simply that we hadn't done anything very interesting yet. I supposed it was all relative!

At our next night stop, the foreshore consisted entirely of sharp rocks so we decided not to use the inflatable rollers to move the boat. We left her a few metres offshore so that we would not be grounded by the tide the following morning. We were trying to keep our feet and leather boots as dry as possible to stave off the numb feet we had suffered the previous year. Getting ashore therefore involved Tony or me wearing the big rubber waders and piggy-backing the other. Once ashore we found some stone cairns that resembled the traditional Inuit stone crosses known as Inukshuk. They were right on the end of a short peninsula, and in the line of a deep red, orange and yellow sunset. The obligatory photos included a silhouette of each of our frames, casually sporting the shotgun resting on one shoulder. When we looked back towards the boat, a large musk ox was eyeing us inquisitively, and his huge horns could have done considerable damage. We skirted round and returned to the false security of our fibreglass boat. We never really worried that a musk ox might pierce the hull with a horn because they seemed to like to stay away from anything unusual, but it was another potential threat never the less.

Half the morning was spent on electrical maintenance, as the solder joint inside the plug that connected one of the solar panels to the boat and the battery had broken. I wrapped the wire as tightly as I could to make a connection, wishing we had made more thorough checks of everything back in Gjoa Haven.

Sailing across James Ross Strait, that separates Matty Island from the Boothia Peninsular, in the early morning sunshine was a joy. Beating hard, just able to maintain the course in the easterly wind and enjoying battling the waves and surf tops, I was sat on the stern, leaning out while Tony rested. Those five miles reinvigorated me, and I began to believe that we could make considerable distance up the coast of the Boothia Peninsular towards Bellot Strait. We ventured offshore to avoid the ice which clung to the rocky coastline. Tony's blog, albeit written much, much later that day (19th August) continues:

T   *No sooner had we left the coast thick fog surrounded us on all sides, the eerie sound of waves crashing on unseen ice echoing across the still water. The fog cleared and the ice revealed itself and we were pitched into an exhilarating high speed slalom through big ice floes reliant on a questionable combination of fine judgment and good luck to see us through. Still the miles passed under the keel as we made rapid progress in the desired direction and we managed to work a full watch routine with the off watch getting a decent amount of bag time. It just so happened that Kev was off watch when the next change in weather struck and it was three and a half hours of helming in driving rain for me. Finally the winds dropped and the cold drove us to seek shelter on the shore.*

K   We did not routinely check the atmospheric pressure, though we noted it every day to send back to the weather forecasters to assist with their predictions. However the GPS was silently logging not only our steady progress but also a significant and sudden drop in this invisible commodity.

T   After fifteen hours sailing, with dusk approaching and a hard driving rain lashing into us, we quickly opted to seek shelter on the shore. Turning the helm in towards the beach I started to scan the shore for an appropriate landing with a big enough anchor point against which we could winch the boat out of the swell. Squinting through the rain my eyes settled on a large, white boulder about five yards back from the shore and I turned the bow towards it and began our run into the beach. Large white 'boulders' were not unusual as bits of ice floes were often left on the beach. It was difficult to hold a course in the squalls but all appeared to be going well as we edged slowly in towards our chosen anchor point and what we hoped would be a good few hours respite from the cold and wet conditions. At just over fifty yards from the shore the curtain of rain parted slightly and simultaneously we both realized that the large white 'boulder' we were rapidly approaching was not made of stone, nor ice for that matter; it was staring right back at us through two dark round eyes.

K   This was part of what we had come back for. We were observing the greatest carnivore on the planet, truly in the wilderness, from a small open sailing boat. It was just the three of us. He looked up at the sky, lay down, then got up and stretched all of his powerful limbs. He wandered off down the beach, as if he owned it. Which of course he did.

"Where the fuck are we supposed to land now?," Tony whispered, to me, but it might as well have been to himself.

"Not here," I replied, rather stating the obvious.

I took a couple of slightly blurred grainy photographs on maximum zoom, and suggested we rowed a bit closer.

"He might get nervous and swim out. I don't think it's a good idea." Tony's counsel was wise but I was a bit disappointed.

Instead we rowed on up the coast, putting some sensible distance between us and the bear, but of course oblivious to his movements or indeed those of any other bears that might be conducting their own lonely wanderings, using the beach as a natural highway in their search for food. This predicament wasn't entirely unexpected. We had brought bear-scarers, which were a heat sensitive alarm system, to act as early warning, and we had our shotgun but unfortunately our bear spray had unhelpfully been taken away from us before the flight north, and for some reason you can't buy it in the northern communities! We had to find somewhere away from the beach to rest. Perversely we decided that while bears can swim, and hunt for seals from the ice floes, we would be safer attached to a floe.

By now there was a fresh breeze blowing offshore and it took a while to select a solid-looking floe that offered some shelter about 100 yards offshore. I secured the boat with an ice screw and after dinner we settled into our bags just before midnight. The wind kept catching the boat and slewing it round before the rope attached to the trusty ice screw would jerk it back into position. Despite this, we were secure if not very comfortable and I was just about asleep, listening to the wind howling the other side of the thin canvas cover close to my face. As usual we were unsure of the exact state of tide, and had assessed that our floe was parked for the remainder of the season because we had experienced quite strong easterly winds for most of the last twelve hours of the tidal cycle. But the winds were stronger now.

We couldn't sleep and pondered our next move. During the evening the wind had continued to build to a steady force 7, occasionally gale 8, coming straight from the shore which we couldn't see any easy way of reaching. All our concerns about bears were now overtaken by a more imminent threat. We had set the anchor watch on the GPS just in case the floe moved, and at 0130 the GPS alarmed to tell us that we were drifting offshore at 0.75 knots. Looking out from under our feeble shelter, we realised we were rapidly approaching another large floe still grounded just fifty metres away. The boat was about to be crushed between the two floes. I leapt off the bow and disconnected the ice screw as Tony set about rowing and we found we could just hold station but could make no further progress towards the shore.

The main was lowered, gathered and tied up tight but in the howling wind it still providing enough windage to push us back offshore. Tony was pulling hard, and whenever he eased off we slipped further offshore. Of course we had no idea how long the storm would last, but definitely didn't fancy the night at sea, sat on our untested sea anchor, or alternatively running with the waves fifty miles to the other side of the wide channel. That way lay the notoriously ice-choked Victoria Strait, where it is believed that Franklin lost his two ships *Erebus* and *Terror*. Neither option appealed. Somehow we had to get to the beach.

"There's too much wind for the mainsail," I shouted to Tony.

"Maybe with just the foresail and one of us rowing, we can make some progress." He unfurled the jib and instantly the boat started to move forward but making only a little progress towards the shore. He was helming, keeping the boat as close to the wind as possible, 'feathering' the sail, and I was pulling hard on the oars. Frustratingly our way was blocked by a large floe meaning we had to steer off the wind, losing all we had gained. Manoeuvring out into free water, we tacked the boat, and begun again inching our way towards the shore. Apart from having to pull much harder on one side to fight the effects of the wind, I felt like I was back on the rowing machine, pulling hard for those last few metres to beat my best time; my strength draining away. We knew we would lose ground if we changed over so Tony counted down the metres until we touched the beach. Even landing presented problems, we had to do four things simultaneously; sail, row, raise the centreboard and jump overboard to secure the boat. I was wearing the waders and jumped overboard before the wind could blow us off, but not quite in time and the water poured over the top of one of the waders. But we were back on dry land, and I sat for a few minutes having secured the boat, breathing hard to recover.

T We were still in a howling gale on an ice-choked steeply shelving beach and less than a mile from where we'd sighted the huge polar bear. It was by no means the ideal spot for the night, and sleep was fitful despite our fatigue. We did manage to grab a few hours' sleep with the boat slewing around alarmingly in the weather, and as soon as the wind moderated enough to attempt to move off we ate a rapid breakfast and set off again.

K With just the foresail up it was possible to make some progress paralleling the beach, but with the wind still at over force 6 we were putting too much stress on the boat and her fittings and after just half a mile we decided it was too dangerous and retired back to the safety of the beach. Unfortunately it shelved much more steeply than before and this time I got both the waders and two pairs of socks absolutely soaked. An excerpt from our blog for 20th August:

> *Out of the frying pan and into the fire applies well here, but after all the excitement we now face something of an anticlimax as we wait once more for the wind. This time it's just too strong to sail or row.*

IX

POLAR HIGHS AND POLAR BEARS

K ALTHOUGH WE LONGED FOR SOUTHERLY WINDS, our weather forecasters explained in a short email that there was a large area of high pressure around 80 degrees north and slightly west of us, known as a polar high. These are notoriously slow-moving and although we were experiencing weather from a sequence of low pressure systems south of it, the predominant airflow was from the north and was likely to stay that way. It was typical. This area does get southerly winds in the summer, but the position of the polar high was preventing them for the foreseeable future. Understanding all this made it doubly frustrating that we were missing these rare easterlies, as we were confined to the beach in winds that I measured at over 27 knots.

Properly testing the bear-scarers was long overdue, especially given the very obvious bear prints just a few feet from where the boat was beached. With Tony acting as a very small polar bear approaching from different angles, we reassured ourselves that they might give us early warning, and probably cause a curious bear to back off. The high pitched siren certainly seemed a strange noise to hear in this stark, empty wilderness. I had never really been that frightened of a bear encounter, probably because I tend to play the odds with dangers that I cannot directly influence. If you parachute jump out of an aeroplane, which is a choice you have made, then there is a very small chance that something will fail. But I always assumed it wouldn't happen to me so went for it without any further thought. I took enormous care packing my parachute but after that it was literally in the lap of the gods. The same logic sort of applied here. We had made a deliberate choice to enter bear country, and not many people do, but the incidence of mauling is extremely rare. The polar bear absolutely fascinated me, more so than the grizzly that had charged us the previous year. Some say they kill for fun, and as with most things the most dangerous ones are those that have become accustomed to, and are then threatened by, human existence. The chances were that these bears had never seen people or if they had it was a pretty rare and I assumed that they would seek to avoid contact. Despite all this, it occupied our minds, and despite my curiosity and desire to observe and film them up close, I agreed with Tony that we had to do our utmost to avoid a chance encounter. Our solution was to find small islands which could be thoroughly searched, and which a bear had no apparent reason to swim to.

Amber's next treat to be unwrapped—and she seemed to have doubled up on last year—was a bag of her favourite sweets, Gummy Bears. Commenting to Tony on the impeccable timing as I reached into the bag to pull out a handful, it occurred to me that probably the only thing she would have enjoyed about this trip so far was the fact that I wouldn't attempt to ration her to eating them one at a time!

T   After a hilarious hour testing the bear-scarers I was perhaps less convinced than Kev about their effectiveness. Far from being scared by the high pitched warble, polar bears might be just as likely to investigate further. That said, bears were now becoming significantly more of a worry for me and I could never fully reconcile myself with Kev's rather laid-back approach to the prospect of a nocturnal visit. Not being in control of the degree of risk worried me, and whilst logically I took comfort in the low probability of an attack it didn't stop me hearing imaginary bear approaches on several nights.

Eventually the wind moved round to the north and *Arctic Mariner* started to be pushed broadside on the beach. We were faced with little choice but to brave the seas again. With just a reduced foresail and no mainsail and both of us on deck, the boat was taking on significant amounts of water, but after an hour or so the stresses on the boat seemed less and we were able to raise the mainsail and settle down into a watch routine again

K   Crossing Pasley Bay, with Tony off watch, I had one of the most exhilarating sails of the entire trip. The sea was a confusion of waves from several directions interacting with a tidal stream. The wind was whipping up white horses and spray, occasionally straight into my face but it didn't matter. I was guiding *Arctic Mariner,* hardly heeling over but bucking violently in the waves, consistently close to her maximum hull speed of just over seven knots. The Norseboat is certainly not an agile racing dinghy, more the equivalent of a steady robust four-wheel-drive, but with exquisitely beautiful lines. I would have had enormous fun sailing her for hours in these conditions in Plymouth Sound, but here I could add the satisfaction of being the only boat, one tiny spec moving across our large scale chart through the words *Magnetic Compass Useless*. Maybe we were beating the Passage at last. It was one of the few times I genuinely didn't want to hand the helm over to Tony.

T   Most of my watch was spent weaving between a tangle of small ice floes being tossed about in a chaotic sea. As the sun dipped towards the horizon and the gloom gathered around us I spotted a shape hunched on one of the floes watching our approach. When we were within fifty yards it seemed to trigger this large adult male polar bear to slip impossibly gracefully into the water. We were moving swiftly but I remember pondering on just how fast those enormous paws could propel him through the water. I had little doubt he could easily flip us into the water if he so chose. Fortunately he seemed far more intent on other things and set off swimming hard out into the frozen seas.

K   Bears number three and four were a mother and cub on the beach playfully rolling about, but it was almost dark and I couldn't get any decent photographs. I realized what an enormous privilege it was to observe these magnificent animals, on our own, completely self-sufficient. I considered the effort we had made, and the hardships and worry we were putting ourselves through. Of course it wasn't all fun but it was definitely worth the effort. I will never forget some of these experiences and therefore maybe the photographs are irrelevant.

T   We sailed on through the night in difficult conditions, but making steady progress while the wind held, but as the early hours stretched on the wind deserted us and by 0300 I was back on the oars fighting to make headway. At 0430 I handed over to Kev and over the next three hours we were able to make just five frustrating miles. Again on handover we discussed what to do. In light airs we were making little progress and getting colder, wetter and more tired. Balanced against this was the very real threat of polar bears on the beach, or attaching to an ice flow and risking a repeat of the previous night's difficulties. I suggested an island, and on cue:

"What, like that one?" Looking over the top of my head Kev had sighted a small islet perhaps 400 metres across lying directly en route and less than a mile away. Back on the oars I rowed us into a pebbly beach and we secured the boat before setting off on a 'clearance patrol.' It did nothing to prevent the possibility of a bear swimming out to join us, but it was enough to reassure us that we weren't setting up camp right next to any of our large white friends. A few hours' sleep, with Kev in his sleeping bag on the beach and me in the boat, was followed by some much-needed time on the satellite phone and some encouraging words from home. Lara, when I finally got hold of her, was house-sitting at Kev's place studying hard for exams and making a dent in his wine cellar. The contrast in our positions could not have been more obvious.

My journal for 21st August:

> *I chatted to Tony about how I feel. It's colder, wetter and has a more endurance feel than last year. We're both philosophical about not getting all the way to Pond Inlet. It will feel incomplete but it's hard enough already. It might get better but it's hard to see how it could get any less enjoyable, but then there are the highlights of bear sightings.*
>
> *Boots still not dry. After lunch felt steady wind from ESE and set off to make the shortcut through the Shortland Channel. Found it full of ice and anyway the wind died. Tony on watch; Wine Gums and listening to The Corrs on the iPod makes everything better but we are now beating into wind again. By 1930 we were tacking, albeit going with a current but do we tack all through the night [when the current will be against us]. There may be a bay at the Western end of the main Tasmania Island. I suggested it (as usual) and we decided to head in but I always seem to suggest going in.*

The ice-choked Shortland Channel was a surprise and retracing our steps we were able to skirt around the western edge of Tasmania Island, but again after just 5 or 6 miles we found ourselves tacking across the face of a weak and variable wind in a sea state that made rowing untenable. A short debate followed, around the relative merits of thrashing ourselves for hour after hour for little gain. I was naturally predisposed to carry on regardless but there comes a time when you have to pick the battles you can win. Kev was clearly reluctant to again be the one suggesting we went in but the logic in his choice was sound. The deciding point for me however was our lack of knowledge of ice conditions ahead. Over the last 10 miles of so we had started to see a substantial change in geography and the rocky bluffs on the island to our right rose several hundred meters above sea level. From the top we should be able to get a better idea of the challenges ahead.

K   Before we reached the intended large bay marked on the chart, we discovered a tiny rocky cove about thirty metres across with a sandy beach at its head, flanked by steep rocky escarpments. Its mouth was south-facing given it perfect protection from the persistent northerlies, and it became our home for the next two days while we waited for the weather.

After conducting some realistic analysis of the charts, we concluded that we had to make the northerly tip of Peel Sound within the next four days if we were stand any chance of making Pond Inlet, with the onset of winter and more ice forming in early September. Our progress had been steady but slow, and if the forecast was to be believed we would probably have to be content with Resolute Bay or perhaps even Beechey Island, where the three Royal Navy and Royal Marine graves from the Franklin expedition stood on their desolate spot. I had lots of time to think, and even recorded a long soliloquy into the video camera sat on my own overlooking the bay. I felt a bit depressed, partly a symptom of being static on this island, but more through realising that the summer holidays were slipping away back home. I was missing Amber and the boys as I had in Afghanistan but this time it was my choice to be away from them. I could only console myself with the fact that we would have completed the heart of the passage when this ended. I sound miserable on the tape, but I finished with the words, "It's not necessarily enjoyable but it is still quite special and I know I'll look back on it with some fondness."

My journal of 22nd and 23rd August:

Just re-read my journal from last year travelling from Cambridge Bay to Gjoa Haven. It is about the same distance that we have done already and there are very similar frustrations. Amazing that the mind forgets the bad bits. If I'd re-

read them carefully around Christmas time in Afghanistan would I still be here now? I spoke to Amber on the satellite phone and told her I was regretting coming back. Characteristically she said there is no point—you are there. As ever, she is right. Quite inspired by the book I am reading about Nansen's crossing of Greenland. They had weeks of uncertainty and delays and got through it by sheer bloody-mindedness. They had to build a boat out of wood and a tent flysheet to reach the settlements after skiing across Greenland. He said it didn't go well to windward but they still rowed it 20 kilometres per day! We need to re-establish a system to get us moving steadily into wind. We have got to rise to the challenge and fight it.

Some would say cruelly at this point, we received the following forecast albeit with some very welcome messages of support:

5 day winds outlook for Arctic Mariner's area as at 23 Aug 10:
Tue 24: N to NE 10kt
Wed 25: N 10-15kt
Thu 26: N 15-20kt
Fri 27: N to NW 20kt
Sat 28: N to NW 20kt
Sun 29: N to NW 15-20kt
No significant change in wind direction. Synoptically the area continues to lie to the south of a large area of high pressure sitting around 80N and a series of low pressure centres which move to the southeast, maintaining the northerly airflow through the area.

We tried to make the most of our time on the islands, trying to dodge the rain. We had a long walk the first day, the entire length of the island, overlooking the ice in the channel. It reminded me of Scotland, plus the ice of course. The weather was dank, clammy and with a piercing northerly wind. It didn't feel anything like a crisp winter's day. The scenery was impressive, rocky, barren, and clearly blasted by the elements. When I thought where we were and what we were observing it was awesome. It was good to stretch our legs properly, and on the way back we even did some easy climbing up a granite slab. We took turns at carrying the unslung shotgun, passing it between ourselves when two hands were required. The island may not have been unexplored, but it certainly wasn't well explored with no sign of there ever being any habitation. We notionally put our climb down as a first ascent but I suspect it will be a while before the route is repeated and anyway we left it un-named. Equally pointlessly, on our second day on the island we entertained ourselves moving a curious looking boulder that had been left in a precarious position by a retreating glacier. It was balanced on another boulder on a sizeable slab and we could rock it but not displace it. We found a piece of driftwood, and being cautious of receiving an entirely unnecessary crush injury we levered it, chocked it, rocked it and heaved it for about an hour before we finally moved it from its perch. Bizarrely we were pleased that we had given the rock its first move in probably ten thousand years! I was fascinated to think all that had happened in the world while this boulder had been perched there. We must have been bored!

T The 48 hours on the island recharged my batteries and allowed me a little time to reassess long term objectives. Pond Inlet was almost certainly out but mentally I softened the blow by proposing Beechey Island. It seemed fitting to close out our trip at the only known grave site of any of Franklin's men. On that tiny barren island two Royal Navy ratings and a Royal Marine lie eternally gazing out over the straits into which the rest of their crew disappeared. After a very cramped night on board, waking to find the boat canted over heavily and Kev squashing me against the port side, we determined to get the tent up. A long grassy slope led up to the interior of the island and we pitched the tent at its base, still within easy reach of the boat and sheltered by mini ridges on either side. The poor weather forecast was disappointing but the messages from home and some uninterrupted sleep raised my spirits and left me keen to explore the rest of the island. So far I felt we had got the balance wrong, with too much emphasis on the end point. It had become an endurance event, and we had perhaps stopped taking in and appreciating the little dramas happening around us every day.

Maybe two miles long and rising to over a thousand feet, the island was a weather-blasted collection of complex rock formations offering a fantastic view of the passage ahead. There was a lot of ice out there but there seemed to be a way through if we were lucky. Either way it was a problem for another day. The mini engineering project to move a large boulder from its millennia-old resting point was a welcome distraction from the adverse winds and persistent drizzle. Kev had appeared a little melancholy of late but this little challenge seemed to raise a spark of enthusiasm. I know it was mainly the frustration of being locked on the island and the cumulative effect of consistent exposure to the unrelenting hardships of the environment, but I could tell he was also missing Amber and the boys. Whilst I also miss home and those waiting for me, ironically the decision to opt for Beechey Island meant we'd probably be able to depart the Arctic a day or two early, and raised the possibility of getting home for Lara's birthday in mid-September, which gave me something positive to aim for.

Dinner and an early night with the wind howling outside but a new sense of purpose and a strong desire to be off in the morning . I had enjoyed the last 48 hours on the island and caught up on some much-needed sleep but I was constantly aware of the clock ticking away and the relentless advance of the ice.

We slipped early and tacked out into the bay in relatively clear but bitterly cold skies. Whilst we managed good speed through the water a strong current with its confused back eddies made progress hard to detect. After clearing the Tasmania Islands we needed to sail NE up the coast for around 50 miles towards the Bellot Strait and inevitably the wind was blowing hard from the NE. Instantly frustrated, Kev immediately proposed a new plan. His ability to change his mind at short notice on the basis of scant evidence has become a genuine source of amusement to me. He does however have a point and it perhaps serves more to illustrate my tendency to stick rigidly with a plan for too long. Either way I decided the new plan had some merit but called for us to head west of north, towards the west of the passage. This had the added advantage of allowing us to make use of the forecast northerlies later in the week to bring us back again to the east side. The drawback however was a thirty mile open crossing. It was a serious undertaking and required careful consideration before we commited. After a brief discussion we both agreed to attempt the crossing and set off initially making a respectable 4-5 knots. Eleven miles in, the wind momentarily dropped away and Kev wanted to change the plan again. In the interests of maintaining progress I agreed but it amused me how the figures used just two hours before to convince me of the merits of an open crossing were now just as passionately presented in favour of a return to hug the coast. Last year the inconsistency would have annoyed me and no doubt resulted in a vigorous debate but interestingly this year it merely made me smile. We had both learned so much about each other and played off each other's strengths. It seemed we made a pretty effective team. Maybe, just maybe, having the last word wasn't all that important.

K   It was interesting sailing with a wind-over-tide effect that picked the small waves up into points that darted around in between isolated chunks of ice a few cubic feet in size. We settled on a heading aimed at Cape Sir Frank Nicholson. I loved all these names, and wondered what it must have been like to not know what lay ahead, drawing the chart yourself and naming prominent features and islands after important crew members or sponsors as you went. We thought we had made good use of the wind available, and despite the cold we sailed and rowed on into the night, supper being the only real highlight. Around midnight I was 'power sailing,' trying to use what little wind there was to assist me on the oars as I moved through the fog, when a quick positional check on the GPS revealed we were going southwest at 1.6 knots. With a compass virtually useless at these latitudes I had absolutely no reference points apart from the GPS. It was enormously frustrating to be working hard in the dark, and going backwards towards Gjoa Haven, but at least we knew. I could only presume that in similarly foggy conditions before the advent of GPS, boats would have just drifted, unaware of their course. I woke Tony and we decided to row to land, blindly following the arrow on the GPS and aware that there were no islands to aim for. Tony could sense my frustration and offered to row. I steered and scoured the horizon with binoculars for any break in the fog. When it finally cleared, to my amazement and this time a touch of annoyance, there was another large white shape on the beach less than a hundred yards from our intended landfall!

T   The fog clung to us leaching any heat away and left us shivering through each three hour watch. A laborious half hour handover extended the misery further before three blessed hours buried in the depths of sleeping bags. The imperceptible progress seemed to be denting Kev's morale and in an attempt to cheer him up I lent him my iPod Shuffle with Simon Sharma's *History of Britain* to help pass the lonely hours on watch. The frustration of the errant winds, adverse currents and lack of all reference points cannot possibly be overestimated. Compasses didn't work at all here so even if the GPS did offer a track, in the thick fog we'd little idea which way we were pointing. Put simply, it was cold, hard, unrelenting sailing.

K   Rowing and then sailing back out to sea in light northerly winds we felt trapped in our tiny craft. Never before had we had the feeling of not being able to get off. Was this trip, finally, now going to become something more akin to rowing the Atlantic, where it had all started? I shuddered at the thought of spending day after day cooped up afloat, unable to stretch our legs and experience the wild landscapes first hand. Long, slow, boring tacks interspersed with short rows when the GPS track told us we were going round in circles finished what left of the night, and at 6 a.m. we were a mere 2.5 nautical miles from where we had seen the last bear. The currents were not being kind. Before breakfast I made another video diary entry; thick black down jacket on, with hood up, looking and sounding miserable:

> *"It's desperately cold in this mist which is all around, and I think we are both pretty hacked off with the amount of progress, but we have to accept that our latest weather forecast is for three or four more days of northerly winds, exactly what we don't want. I think we are going to have to just keep plugging away and try to make Resolute in small steps, slow beating against the wind. It's not a lot of fun, but then I guess nobody said it had to be."*

Later, we made the call to stop on one of the small Gibson Islands having travelled over 60 miles, 38 on track. It had taken 31 hours. We had travelled 230 miles on track from Gjoa Haven with 200 still to go, and we had been going for eleven days. The small island offered a sheltered beach and surprisingly a small flat grassy patch just the size of our tent a few yards from the boat. There was a rusting chain attached to some sort of animal trap attached to one of the boulders, a remnant from the early days of exploration. Despite this being one of the most perfect landfalls of the expedition, my mood made me decide that I was getting slightly bored by small rocky islands. I dreamt of arriving in Resolute which I portrayed as a large ordinary British town, and then unpacking the boat with my kids at home in Devon. I interpreted this as that I was looking forward to the end, but clearly so in love with our beautiful craft that I would have liked to keep her.

T   I was more tired than I thought but despite the temptation to just flop down into my bag and sleep I still managed the obligatory bear patrol round the small island with gun in hand. It seemed we were not sharing the island with any big furry friends and the tent went up quickly. To lighten the mood we played a little cards while waiting for dinner to heat up. Kev lost tonight's little clash becoming the day's 'Shit-head.' I was starting to will the miles away now with my mind set on an earlier flight home and a reunion with Lara who was moving her life up to Edinburgh without me there to help. I felt guilty but recognized there was little to be done about it now and banished the thought. The evening concluded with coffee liberally laced with Connamara Irish whiskey, stood on top of our tiny island gazing out over the ice we had yet to fight our way through in the morning.

K   Good weather always lifts my mood, and in the Arctic it was no exception. The following morning dawned crisp, still and sunny. The view from the small rocky outcrop above the beach was serenely striking. Large pebbles arranged improbably due to the striations of glaciation led past our bright red tent down to the boat, elegantly poised ready for departure on a deep blue Arctic sea devoid of even the tiniest ripple. Random chunks of pure white ice were loosely scattered on this canvas which lost its blueness as it approached the thin brown mainland shore, undulating to account for low rocky hills. Above, a hint of high altitude cirrus cloud in the distance that was affecting the colour of the sea, but above again a perfectly clear light blue that despite the sun's warmth gave the entire scene a polar chill.

I filmed Tony rowing the length of the island; despite us not being trained rowers, it looked good, the oars cutting into the blue surface but from my range hardly leaving a disturbance. We both probably place the oars slightly too deep, but it couldn't ruin the scene. Of course we had discussed the pick-up at the far end of the island, but I was again aware how reliant we are on each other. I felt in my pocket for my emergency beacon but didn't fancy my chances on this speck of an island for very long. Reunited on the boat, Tony wrote the blog for 26th August whilst we were underway:

T   *With the iPod blasting out some tunes and the sunglasses making their first appearance, morale was suitably restored and Kev chanced a bit of his Eighties disco. [Billy Joel – My Life] Clearly the wind god didn't appreciate his devotee's dancing because soon enough we were again being blown backwards by a combination of heavy swell and adverse winds. Kev kept control of his morale outbreak and stayed firmly in his seat this time and the gods relented. Despite limited progress we both have today down as one of the most enjoyable days of the trip. Threading our way through the ice-encased islands and weaving past ice floes to the sounds of the Rolling Stones takes some beating. Now tied up to a small rocky island about to tuck into a well-deserved dinner and then get some sleep before tackling the mass of ice just ahead. Messages from home have been fantastic, please keep sending as the only certainty here is that the sun won't last and our morale will need more buoying up before this adventure is over.*

K   Now only 15 miles from Bellot Strait, we became aware of the huge tide which rushes back and forth along its narrow length. We needed to be careful of going too close to the entrance at the wrong point of the tide for fear of being sucked in and dragged down the channel at a maximum speed of seven knots. We sailed through an ice band heading north only to find that the GPS was telling us we were actually going south-west. We had assumed we were making good progress against the obvious reference points of chunks of ice — but which themselves were heading south. Strangely inside the ice band the current was less. With the sun out, music on and only wearing four instead of our customary seven layers it was the perfect contrast to yesterday.

   Another day, another island; today was the southern-most of the Arcedeckne Islands and our night stop was forced on to us by the amount of ice between the mainland and the island. We were now spending considerable time scouting whenever we could climb a short rocky outcrop, scanning ahead to find the best course through the ice. Of course on a normal-sized yacht we would have one of us hoisted up the mast to achieve the same effect. But what a place to sail and row a small open boat! Exploring our current island led us to find two almost mirror-image ice floe-choked bays on either side of the island separated by a narrow shingle ridge, providing the identical beaches. The evening light contrasted the brown rock, deep blue-black water and the bright white ice. It was pretty, but no place to moor up a small boat that would be crushed in the incessant gradual movement of ice.

T   We lingered over breakfast in thick fog as neither us relished shoving off. The air was bitterly cold and we seemed to be rowing through a bizarre slush-puppy like ice surface that flattened the surface of the sea but made each pull on the oars that bit more draining. Almost between one stroke and the next we burst out of the fog into bright sunshine and the ice porridge was replaced by a steadily increasing swell. Looking back we could clearly see a sharp delineation where the fog sat above the colder island and the ice that surrounded it. Free of the ice, the swell grew to five or six feet and progress on the oars was increasingly tricky. We switched to full foulies to cope with the big seas coming over the bow and resigned ourselves to a difficult day on the oars. About mid-afternoon an hour or two of favourable winds helped take us past the ice-choked maw of the Bellot Strait and out of the powerful tidal currents threatening to suck us down onto the jagged ice.

K   Bellot Strait was completely choked with ice which made me feel better about our earlier decision not to use it. It was hard to see how that ice could ever clear even with the strong tidal stream. Once past the strait there was a steep orangey rock escarpment which climbed a couple of hundred feet above the crashing waves. As we tacked we regularly got a close view, and were soon rewarded by the magnificent sight of another bear clambering from rock to rock. He was so obvious, possessing a sort of reverse camouflage, but I suppose a polar bear only needs to be camouflaged when he is hunting prey. His coat seemed extra white, not the dirty yellowish colour that we had seen earlier. Through my telephoto lens we could see his face clearly; he really did look like a toy with a friendly, almost comic persona. He eyed us carefully while sniffing the air and I managed some bouncy video before he set off up the hill and we returned to sailing the boat hard trying to make progress against the wind.

When the wind died and the current started pulling us inexorably back towards Bellot Strait we headed for shore but this time there were no small offshore islands, just the huge expanse of Somerset Island separated from the Boothia Peninsula by the strait. We would have to just trust in the bear-scarers and although they weren't false-alarming as much as we had predicted we mulled over the flaw in our plan, which was that a polar bear's fur insulates him so well it might not be enough to set them off. Each of a Polar Bear's hairs is a tiny cylinder containing warm air. My journal of 27 August:

> We are like a tortoise in that we carry everything we need in our shell (boat)—and our progress up this coast has been tortoise-like. Rest assured if we get almost any consistent wind from anywhere but the north we will turn into the hare. Got met report through—light southerlies from 31 August predicted. Could be hard tomorrow into the strong northerlies but long day-sailing is bearable. We had a great message from Lara encouraging us on, in response to the blog from our darkest times. We also managed to speak on the satphone to the lone Frenchman Mathieu Bonnier [who had set off from Greenland in a rowing boat with his Alaskan Husky called Tico and got stuck in Resolute because of ice.] Unfortunately he's past us now on his way to Cambridge Bay, no doubt enjoying letting the wind carry him and his boat south while he sleeps but as he says he needs to get off to walk the dog. Not for me, doing it alone. Looking forward to finishing but I have the trip in perspective now.

We woke up to the piercing siren of the bear-scarers. Both sat bolt upright, Tony holding the shotgun, and then looking at each other as if to say, "OK, what do we do now?"

The problem with being in a tent is that you can't see your assailant or indeed whether there is one. You can only wait so long, and in the absence of any sound, we opened the tent just a fraction and peered out. It was as if we were opening a front door with a chain and the thin canvas would offer the same protection as a door against the supposed threat. There was no bear outside or anywhere near the tent. No musk ox, nothing. It must have been a bird. The sun was out and it was quite hot, or was I just sweating? We decided to pack up despite the wind still being northerly. I was keen to get going and breakfast en route but Tony wanted to ensure everything was properly prepared. He was right and I felt a bit guilty as we set off, only to find the centreboard was jammed up inside the hull. Of course without it deployed we could make no progress at all into wind, as what wind there was pushed us backwards, and rapidly offshore. We rowed frantically back to the beach.

I tried reaching under the boat, exposing my whole arm to the freezing water, having partially stripped off. I could only just reach the slot, and could not feel any stones jammed inside. We concluded that as the boat had twisted round in the surf during the night before the tide went out, something must have been washed up inside. We resigned ourselves to emptying the boat completely, tipping her on her side and working on freeing the centreboard. We could find no anchor points on the beach to use to haul her out, and there was a nagging fear that even if we could get her up and over on her side we still might not be able to clear the jam. I tried pulling one more time on the rope we used to raise and lower the heavy steel blade and it with a great sense of relief it eventually slid free.

T   Pleased to have survived the night without any special visitations, I was even more upbeat about the successful struggle with the centreboard, although that may have more to do with escaping the need to get half naked under the boat. With the latest difficulty resolved we set off under glorious blue skies in a substantial swell that tested us both as sailors. It tested our patience too as the wind see-sawed between 25 knots and nothing in a matter of seconds. Rowing cross swell through eight-foot waves was difficult enough to force us to eventually admit defeat and head in again for a difficult landing on a heavily surfed beach.

K   The little bay was our only choice, and we came in at speed on to the shallow sand. I readied myself to jump over the side in the waders only to be brought up short, as I was still connected to the boat via my safety harness. I stumbled, getting slightly wet, and swore loudly. The tide was well out and coming in fast but there was a steep bank up and down the beach as far as we could see, just beyond the high tide mark. There was no way to drag the boat beyond it and so we set about digging a slot in it to act as a bespoke mooring for the boat, hoping that the stern would be high enough to prevent her being swamped by the surf, and the bow tight enough in the slot to stop her twisting. We were now very protective of the centreboard slot. In the process of hauling the boat up, one of our remaining inflatable rollers exploded leaving an un-repairable eighteen inch long split. "I'm wondering if the equipment is telling us it's time to finish, but we could do without losing anymore rollers" I remarked to Tony.

T   The weather forecast showed more of the same for the next few days but seemed to indicate a potential three-day window of southerlies towards the end of the week. If we sailed non-stop, three days of favourable winds could take us almost to our new end-point. We were two weeks into the expedition and dropping into a daily routine but I was also missing the comforts of home and mentally started imagining the coastline slipping by. It was important to be fully rested and ready for a hard sail north when the winds did eventually change, so we pitched the tent just above the high tide mark any perhaps ten feet from the bow of the boat in its improvised dry dock, and settled down for some sleep. Despite being back on the mainland, possibly due to tiredness or complacency we neglected to place out the bear-scarers.

At around 0100 I woke from a deep sleep to the gentle rocking of the tent. In my sleep fuddled state I could think of only one explanation. Somehow the tide had risen above the bank and the surf was now striking the tent directly. Water must have been pressing down hard on the tent above Kev's feet bending the poles inwards and pressing down hard on the flimsy material on his side of the tent. The bit I was struggling with was, I was the one sleeping closest to the water and far from rushing to help, Kev seemed to be making an awful snorting sound; Or at least his feet were.

"Kev, Wake up, there're waves hitting the tent, Wake up."

K   I had all the draw-cords closed on my sleeping bag with just my face exposed and was deeply asleep when I became aware of Tony muttering, half awake. Very briefly, in the gloom, I thought how fortunate I was to be on the land rather than the sea side of the tent. It was then that I looked down the length of the tent and noticed that the normal perfect symmetry of the red material supported by the flexible poles was distorted. In fact the material was pressed down to within only twelve inches above my feet. Something was pressing on the tent from outside and it wasn't the waves. It could only mean one thing. I wriggled my shoulders free from the sleeping bag, parting the draw-cord and fumbled for the air horn. Tony, now fully awake, sat up grasping the shotgun and shouted "Fuck Off!" just before I managed a lengthy blast on the air horn. The tent sprang back to its normal position. There followed a few seconds of indecision. Both of us sat perfectly still in the semi-darkness, unable to speak, waiting for something to happen. I remember feeling my heart beating fast, but no feeling of real fear, more a sense of nervous anticipation. Whether that was ignorance, confidence in the shotgun and Tony's ability to use it, or just a feeling that on a balance of probability, nothing would happen, I'm really not sure. I wanted to see the bear, partly out of curiosity but also to discover where he was and the danger he posed. I think Tony was happy to be prepared for any consequences.

I whispered to Tony, "I'm just going to have a look outside."

Using nothing more than balance of probability I decided to look out of the other end of the tent than where it had been pressed down. I peered out, and could see nothing. Emboldened, I stuck my head out gingerly and twisted it round to look past the feet end of the tent and there, about ten yards away, I saw two huge bears gently ambling down the beach away from us. Everything was in slow motion; partly due to my increased sense of awareness and partly because that seems to be how bears move when idling along. They periodically stopped and sniffed the air but I don't think they saw me. Excited and feeling somewhat safer I returned to the tent and grabbed my camera, whispering to Tony what I'd seen and unzipping the other end of the tent. He pushed the shotgun out first and I took a very grainy photo which was blurred, probably because my hands were shaking, it was semi-dark and there was no time to fiddle with the camera settings. We watched them silently until we could no longer make out their huge forms far down the beach. Returning our heads to the tent, we both started laughing. Relief, awe, and a realization of the ridiculousness of what had just happened.

I pictured in my mind two polar bears walking down a beach (sounds a bit like a joke) coming across a boat on their beach. They may have looked over it, and then (in the joke) one says to the other, "What's this large red dome shaped object? I'm going to investigate," and then standing next to each other, one touches it and presses down with his huge paw. Suddenly it shouts, and makes a loud horn noise. They are shocked, but still not aggressive. They clearly didn't run off, but may simply have said the equivalent of "Let's just leave it alone, not worth the bother at this time of night."

There followed the dilemma as to what to do next. Would they return? Might there be others? Should we organise a two-hourly sentry? We placed out the previously neglected bear-scarers and returned to the tent where we quickly found it easier to lie down than sit up. I was delighted we had 'seen' bears close up and got away with it and despite the initial shock I don't remember lying there worrying for very long. In fact we both returned to dreamless sleep after about half an hour.

The nocturnal visitation left me feeling deeply privileged to have been close enough to these incredible creatures to hear the air expelled through their nostrils. It can be hard to see past the popular images of polar bears as either lovable cuddly toys or man-hunting predators. Neither bear seemed the least bit interested in attacking us or, for that matter, cuddling up to have their fur rubbed. I came away from the experience possibly over-confident about our ability to co-exist in their domain and have to purposefully remind myself how differently our encounter might have gone had either one of us reacted differently or if the bears had been in need of a meal. Good fortune had favoured us, rather than anything else, and fortune is frequently the most transient of companions.

The following morning we woke to a howling northern wind that precluded any further movement that day, but also discovered the action of the surf was progressively digging the boat into the beach giving rise to concerns about our ability to get her off when we eventually did decide to move on. Opinions differed regarding the need to move the boat immediately, but we had long since agreed on a strategy for resolving these differences of opinion and both got stuck in.

K   We had a roller stuck under the boat in the sand. It was unpleasant work digging with bare hands and whilst I couldn't feel the coarse particles cutting into my numb hands I was aware of the potential damage they were doing. Finally we freed the roller and released the boat from the suction effect of the soaking sand. A few moments later the boat was floating again, but we couldn't leave it exposed to the surf and soon winched it back up again admittedly having achieved very little. This time we held it in place with a large rock padded with spare equipment, and on the other side our exploded roller filled with sand as a makeshift fender.

T   Our morning fun and games left me with hands so cold it took twenty minutes to rewarm them to merely painful. However, the boat seemed to be relatively stable again after its brief sojourn in the surf so all was well... I thought. Lying in my bag listening to the horrendous sound of the hull grinding against the rocks was not good for my soul and it took considerable self-control not to get up every few minutes to check on her. A dull and rather listless day followed with us both constrained largely to the tent, the only highlight being a successful satellite phone call home to Lara. I caught her just minutes before she boarded a plane back from a weekend with the girls in Dublin, and more than anything it emphasized the contrast between our simple day-to-day existence and the complex social interactions back home. Still, it made me smile to think with any luck we'd be back home soon enough. The weather forecast when it came through seemed to indicate the winds veering round to the south with the potential for us to get away sometime around midnight. In preparation for the off we decided to go for a brief walk after dinner to assess conditions. Kev was first up and before he was even fully outside I was surprised to hear him ask quietly for his camera.

K   I looked round, and just beyond the other end of the tent was another polar bear casually observing me. I didn't feel threatened but made a point of not making any sudden movements. Tony asked what I could see, and I replied it was another bear, at which he grabbed the shotgun and poked his head out. By this time the bear was moving off down the beach, not running but moving purposefully. I took some photographs and even a thirty-second video clip, by which time he was well over a hundred yards away. He looked back at us, sniffed the air and turned left, inland. We continued to watch, debating whether he would come back towards us. He climbed the rocky moonscape inland, apparently carefully keeping the same distance of about a hundred yards between him and us, the tent and the boat. Tony said "He's circling round, he's not going on."

We moved slightly, trying to appear unthreatening so we could observe his eventual direction of travel. He finally reached the beach over a hundred yards past us having skipped a small peninsula and turned right, continuing his listless, wandering journey. It was as if we had been a mild impediment which he had neatly bypassed. I still wonder how many other bears had walked past us without stopping.

X

JOURNEYS, NOT DESTINATIONS

K   Despite copious amounts of rest, the tension showed in our blog from 30 August:

> *The rest of the night was spent waiting for some abatement in the northerly wind and big swell. Waking this morning the wind finally dropped away and we made the call to get off the polar bear highway and try and get under way again [with the tide out]. Easier said than done and before we could go anywhere we had a two hour engineering task to dig the boat out of the sand get her up on rollers and re-float her. As we packed up we cracked the ice that caked all the lines and exposed surfaces on the boat and broke out the oars. We can make 2-2.5 knots into light swells and thick freezing mist. Slow but steady and if we can maintain it for at least 24 hours that's a third of the remaining distance done.*

Resolute was still 153 miles away as the crow flies, and the conversation soon turned to our destination. Beechey Island was fifty miles beyond Resolute, and then we had to get back as well. We asked ourselves why we were going to Beechey? For the graves, to see the desolate spot or to finish the journey somewhere meaningful? Our original destination, Pond Inlet wasn't really an end either, as it was another thirty miles beyond it to the opening into Baffin Bay. Unlike the Hobie Cat expedition in 1988 we didn't have a father and media crew with hired boats that would meet us and tow us back. As usual, and very much by design, we were completely on our own. We had arranged to sell the boat to a resident of Cambridge Bay who had arranged to collect it in Pond Inlet, but was now having to recast those plans to move it from Resolute. In a quiet moment I looked through the photographs on the camera. We had seen so much on this journey and where we stopped seemed less relevant. I didn't want to make the call to not go to Beechey Island but I suspected it might be anticlimactic if we didn't. It seemed lazy not to go, as we had the time but then we could easily get stuck in adverse or high winds and not be able to get back. Or was I making excuses? I knew I was ready to stop.

T Late morning the wind picked up and we were soon screaming along at seven knots in big following seas. It made such a difference to be able to tick the landmarks off as we went along, morale buoyed by the sense that finally we were making real progress. iPod tunes helped the miles roll by as we sailed, and rowed intermittently, and as evening approached and the conditions eased we settled into our two-and-a-half hour watches. In freezing cold conditions we agreed to complete watches sat at the tiller half in a sleeping bag, and it wasn't until midway through my first watch that the error of our ways became fully apparent.

Out of nowhere the wind and seas rose up and suddenly we were once again surfing along at over seven knots, overpowered and with me unable to escape my sleeping bag whilst keeping it dry. After a precarious second hour pushing my luck yet unwilling to prematurely wake Kev, we were finally able to reef down at changeover. In these seas it was a difficult procedure involving dropping the canvas cover and balancing precariously at the mast to change reefing hooks before swapping over mainsheets in order to allow the primary to be moved to the next reefing point. Finally the excess sail needed securing with three hook and loop fastenings, essential in a loose footed mainsail. The process was well-rehearsed but nevertheless in heavy seas and darkness it was an uneasy evolution with a substantial but considered risk. In addition every second the canvas cover was down increased the possibility of our kit getting soaked. By the time we'd finished it was fifteen minutes trying to rewarm hands and then another fifteen minutes for the off-watch person to get back into their hopefully still dry sleeping bag.

K We continued into the night and the wind picked up and we had some superb sailing, surfing down waves at over eight knots in an unstable swell. The cooker had blocked earlier but we simply pulled out the reserve and I remember thinking I would probably be fixing it back at home. My journal of 30th August:

> *The forecast is for more steady southerlies tomorrow then light and variable then maybe a bit of northerly before southerly to take us in to Resolute and I started to believe we could do the same as arriving into Gjoa Haven a year ago — a long sprint finish. Went over in my mind the pleasure of stopping, a shower and being warm and going home — so close. It really feels like the end of the expedition and*

I'm so ready for it. While Tony was peeing over the side I accidentally gybed [sail swung across the boat] and he fell back into the boat, fortunately not overboard. He wasn't tied on. We must avoid complacency! I was haunted by how I would get back to him in the darkness. Would probably have to reef the boat down to tack back to him—on my own. Awful.

T   We sailed on through the night, probably overpowered but making fabulous progress and reluctant to shorten sail. Around dawn the winds dropped away and we settled back into routine. With memories of Kev's inadvertent attempt to pitch me overboard fresh in my mind, I was sorely tempted to return the favour as he tried the 'Long drop' off the stern. In the end the thought of the potential mess in the boat was enough to stem my mischief-making and he completed his ablutions blissfully unaware of how close he'd been to an early morning dip.

K   The day wore on as we ticked off the miles and by mid-afternoon I was manoeuvring inside the Wadworth Islands in light winds. The islands were nothing more than meaningless shapes of piled shingle but at least it provided some variety. I wasn't bored but there was an element of over-familiarity with our surroundings. However, the narrow channel was magnifying the current and, as a result, I was having to row quite hard just to make half a knot. Tony was asleep and I was tiring, watching the land inch past, unable to ease the pressure on the oars. I steered the boat out of the central channel to within six feet of the shore and my speed increased to two and a half knots. I was pleased. It was a small but invaluable victory. We rowed on towards the evening, but with little wind and after 36 hours and over eighty miles we decided to stop, having covered nearly half of the remaining distance to Resolute.

    The ice had returned as if to remind us that it would be September in just a few hours, and as we headed into a sheltered spot in McClure Bay I took the opportunity to drop Tony on a floe to take some rare footage of the boat from a distance. It showed that despite the distance and the time, my rowing technique had not improved, I was digging too deep with the oars, but it seemed to work and the boat looked elegant and graceful slipping past the blue and white ice. It looks like a single-handed boat when rowed like this and I was reminded as ever that the sliding seat travel was about an inch and a half too short for my height. It wasn't perfect but it didn't matter anymore even if, as the weather predicted, we had to row all of the remaining eighty miles to Resolute.

T   Inevitably as we approached our chosen beach I sighted our tenth polar bear of the trip. He was a full-grown male bear about 400 metres further north and heading away from us. It is perhaps a mark of our fatigue or perhaps complacency but neither of us considered altering our plans and we duly hauled the boat up on the shore regardless and settled down for the evening. Over the last day and a half at sea we had covered 86 miles leaving just 70 miles to Resolute, and perhaps another hundred to Beechey Island and back. With light winds forecast much of it would have to be under oars, but surely we could maintain 30 miles a day. Kev's eyes seemed firmly fixed on Resolute but I couldn't yet escape the poetic pull of Beechey Island and wondered how to convince him that the extra effort would be worth it. Getting there, even under oars, shouldn't be too difficult but I was concerned about the mental and physical effort of turning around and battling back again a further 50 miles to Resolute Bay. The weather forecast was inconclusive but without favourable winds a detour to Beechey Island could add up to an extra week on to the trip. If I'm honest the prospect of another week in the boat held little appeal to me either and I determined to delay the decision until the last safe moment.

K   Our evening walk gave us a clear view of the ice ahead and no further bear sightings. As the sun was setting it made the sky turn a fleshy brown colour instead of red, and this was reflected in the calm water amongst the blue ice. The grey shingle of the beach completed this lifeless yet striking scene. It was to be our last night on the beach and it passed uneventfully.

    The ice wouldn't quite release us and we weaved and backtracked a few times before we were out into Lancaster Sound, committed to the forty-mile crossing of Barrow Strait to Griffiths' Island and then Resolute. My journal of 1st September:

> *The wind held steadily and we talked about Beechey. I think Tony was quite keen as he said it would make 'the perfect end' but we resolved to make the crossing and get a weather forecast before finally deciding. I stated that I wasn't keen but*

would of course go. I wondered if Tony was really trying just to not talk ourselves out of it, and force an informed decision. We even played cards around 1700 whilst making about 2 knots of progress. Limestone Island [off the northern tip of Somerset Island] looked magnificent with its cliffs — would there have been more sights like that all the way to Pond Inlet? — Irrelevant. The wind died as I came on watch and while we made dinner, then literally as we were packing it away it came up. I had a fantastic 'last watch' on my own [Tony asleep] working around and through random floes in the gloom and mist at up to six knots, maybe slightly overpowered. I felt the boat scything through the light swell. Fantastic. I could sense the end, at this rate 0400 into Resolute! No more night watches!

I enjoyed that watch partly because it was the end, and partly because I felt totally confident in the boat in those extreme remote conditions. I was truly living the final part of my dream which had begun over two years previously. There was a tinge of sadness that it was all over, but this was out-weighed by wanting to stop. Most importantly, unlike last year I felt less attachment to *Arctic Mariner*. I had done everything I had wanted to do in her; the project was complete as a journey. I sat on the side of the boat grinning for a host of reasons, concentrating through one of the fastest two-and-a-half hour watches in which I covered nearly fifteen miles.

T Crossing Lancaster Sound at speed under full sail in the early hours of the morning offered some picture-postcard views of the cliffs that lined it, and not for the first time I wondered if we would miss the most dramatic scenery of the whole passage. Even now we still had the option to turn east for Beechey Island and a finish on the high rocky shores of the deserted island rather than the cluttered Arctic staging post at Resolute. Once again I felt the pull of the 'perfect ending' and perhaps at any other time I would have been more prepared to push for it, but no, just before dawn, damp, cold and tired and with less than fifteen miles to go to Resolute, I couldn't quite stump up the conviction. It seemed somehow contrived to push on to Beechey for little more than a photo opportunity before having to turn back again for Resolute and an exit from the Arctic. I determined that when Kev awoke I would not resist if he wished to conclude our adventure in Resolute. A few minutes later when the wind died away and I wearily took up my position on the oars once more, I was even more content with the prospect of a final landfall in just a matter of hours.

K   I climbed into my bag for the last time only four miles from Griffiths' Island but woke again when Tony started to row, in a final sting in the tail of no wind and adverse currents. A thick layer of fog lay over the top of the escarpment that seemed to cover almost the whole of Griffiths' Island. It looked like an ice topping, a sort of mini-Greenland. The wind eventually re-appeared and we made slow progress in the mist the last eleven miles towards Resolute. I saw a shape emerging from the mist a few miles off, and through the binoculars it looked like a patrol boat, I assumed left over from the Canadian Navy exercise that had taken place around Resolute recently. I called them on the radio, "Small Patrol Boat, three miles south east of Resolute, this is small sailing dinghy *Arctic Mariner*, over."

"*Arctic Mariner* this is *Octopus*, *Octopus*, we are a 139 metre long private motor yacht" came the slightly indignant reply.

We chatted for a while and he did not reveal who they were but explained that it was not possible to invite us on board. Disappointing, as we found out later the yacht belonged to Paul Allen of Microsoft. It would have been fun to see inside the very antithesis of the boat in which we had navigated the central Northwest Passage. They were continuing south to attempt the Passage with every technical aid that money could buy, not the least of which being two hugely powerful diesel engines and a strengthened bow that gave limited ice-breaking capabilities. We consoled ourselves with the fact that we had probably had more fun than they would!

The weather forecast was for consistent light south-westerlies and we finally decided against going on and then tacking back from Beechey Island. Our reasons were simple. We had had enough. But the irony was that if Pond Inlet had been a realistic possibility with the time available we would have continued on cheerfully. As I rowed the last mile to shore I tried to convey the significance of what it meant to finish to the video diary.

"Just after seven o'clock on 2nd September and journey's end, Resolute Bay. We always said it's not about the destination it's about the journey and I think looking at the crap that is behind me on the shore, that's probably just as well.

[Tony laughs]. Thinking of the 139-metre yacht moored offshore, I think they will have a very different journey from us. When I think that this boat has brought us over fifteen hundred miles on a fascinating journey, with many more hundreds of miles that we have sailed and rowed to make that fifteen hundred. But yeah, this is the end of the trip, the end of the expedition and I'm ready to finish. I've been ready to finish for a while actually. We had a good sail over Barrow Strait and then the wind died and we're now rowing in the last bit which of course is exactly how we started, rowing down the Mackenzie river back in July last year."

We glided in to a dark grey scrappy piece of beach next to a rusty old trailer that was half submerged. Tony laughed at the ignominy of the ending. There was no welcoming party, no media, just a couple of men moving some containers in a large yard a hundred yards up the beach. They were trying to spend the minimum time out in the open, moving from truck to fork-lift cabs and they paid us no attention. We didn't even bother to drop the sails, just stood by the bow and opened the tiny bottle of champagne. "Thanks mate." It said it all.

We were as cold and damp as the day which had dawned a few hours earlier but still, the ice-cold champagne felt good. "It's probably the only booze in this town," remarked Tony, referring to the strict no-alcohol policy.

We were soon accommodated in the settlement's only hostel, that plays host to most expeditions to the North Pole. The shower felt as good as last year and lunch was a long event, before we turned our attention to sorting the boat. We had arranged her sale, along with all the accessories, and carefully cleaned and packed everything neatly for her new owner. As we turned our backs and closed the container we didn't feel as much sadness as last year.

T   As with many things the culmination of such an epic journey came as something of an anti-climax and I couldn't quite let go of the nagging wish that we'd pushed on to Beechey Island and the graves of our forerunners. Logically it didn't make any sense to go so far out of our way and yet—The weary ache spreading through my body and the promise of an early return home did much to counter my disappointment and soon enough I was happily enjoying the luxuries of what passes for civilisation this far north.

Even as the adventure drew to a close we continued to ride our luck. Instead of departing on one of the tiny scheduled supply planes that serve the northern communities, we soon discovered the Canadian Special Forces had just concluded their annual Arctic exercise nearby and would be flying some of their kit out via a huge C17 transport aircraft. A little more liberal use of the charm that was now beginning to sound a lot like pleading resulted in the two of us stowing away on the huge aircraft as it roared off the frozen dirt strip heading south. As we sat perched on the piles of kit strapped to the floor of the aircraft I mused over the expedition as a whole. It would be a while before I could fully appreciate the entirety of our journey and just how much it had affected me. Despite many years of travelling and an appetite for adventure the experiences of the past two summers have been unique beyond comparison. The unadulterated nature of the physical environment, with so very little sign of human impact, appealed to me immensely. Conversely evidence of the raw power of nature was carved everywhere in the landscape, uncluttered by the complex physical systems that mask her work elsewhere in the world. I shared my trip with the most amazing host of animals but above all I lived it all alongside a fellow adventurous soul with a genuine desire to squeeze the most from the experience. Kev was my ideal foil and I will be eternally grateful for his enthusiasm and drive, without which the expedition would no doubt have foundered. I learnt an immense amount about myself during the course of our time away and yet, like the icebergs cluttering the eastern entrance to the NW passage revealing just a fraction of themselves, I suspect it might just be like that for me, the beginning of that journey.

K   Waiting for the flight to touch down we had some time to reminisce and ponder the possibilities of what might have been. We could have had minimal ice conditions like 2007 and we may have got to Pond Inlet in one season. It would have been hard, relentless rowing and sailing, and frankly quite boring. If we had started in Pond Inlet we may have become stuck in Resolute early in 2009 and achieved very little. If the winds had been kinder we would easily have made Pond Inlet this year, but for some reason all of these questions didn't seem to matter anymore. Was it worth coming back? It had been a huge effort and we both had to admit that it wasn't as good as 2009. But it probably was never going to be. We had enjoyed the remote islands and our experiences with the bears were simply magical; we discussed how fortunate we had been to have such close encounters. Maybe we were just lucky, but our experience was that they were curious but generally wanted to stay away, and they did not live up to their reputation as ferocious carnivores who kill for pleasure. For me, they were just another facet of a wonderfully serene wilderness that we had immersed ourselves in.

We were enormously fortunate to have made the trip, but to an extent we had made our own luck. I don't feel that the expedition changed me fundamentally as a person, and I will undoubtedly return to the high latitudes in the future. In the months that followed I realised how much I missed the project that was the *Arctic Mariner* Expedition. In terms of records, I am very careful. We had not navigated the whole of the Northwest Passage but we did the majority of it, and I think in the smallest boat. I think we went further in one season than any other un-powered open boat. But at the end of the day, none of this matters. We had completed a journey in unique style. We weren't explorers in the true sense of the word but our mode of travel means we visited places that had never been visited before, such is the vast expanse of nondescript beaches and coves. We had the same desires as those early explorers but the world has shrunk such that maybe true exploration above sea level is no longer possible. Perhaps most importantly we had explored our own minds during ten weeks of isolation and adventure, and made some interesting discoveries. In hindsight I was categorically unsuited to rowing the Atlantic, but I like to think I could have made it through sheer bloody-mindedness. Our trip was very much more suited to me, and Tony was the perfect partner. He sent me an email on our return:

T
> *I just wanted to thank you for making the whole trip possible and two months of boys own adventure in the Arctic. It's easy to get lost in the tale somewhere when describing our trip but I genuinely enjoyed the journey and have a host of experiences to draw on as a stepping stone to further things. We certainly put the Adventure back into Adventure Training and learnt an independence and self-reliance that hopefully would not have shamed our predecessors in the frozen North.*

K I replied:

> *It was an extraordinary trip looking back—and I guess most satisfying of all is that I stand by what I said at the start of the Ice Road in Inuvik. There are always two successes to any trip—doing it, and staying on speaking terms with the other(s) on the trip. We certainly achieved both. Thanks for your company, humour, stoicism, grace under pressure and calm consideration of the problems. I've learnt a lot.*

The last word I will leave to Tony in this, the final blog of the expedition.

T *Location: Resolute Bay*
3 September, 2010

Sometimes you wish an experience will go on for ever and never end. This isn't one of those occasions, but there is a sense of something missing to be ashore in Resolute, sat in the town inn with no need to worry about wind or tides and little chance of a polar bear joining us for dinner...... Still warm beds and real food fill that hole fairly well.

    On the final leg of the trip we spent long periods surrounded by thick sea fog, but on occasion the veil would part treating us to a rare glimpse of the imposing cliff faces that line Lancaster Sound and emphasize the scale of the geography. The latterly-arrived southerly winds held to within ten miles of Resolute, then as a final reminder of the Arctic's power to confound all forecasts, they dropped away to nothing, leaving us with an energy-sapping 12 miles to row through thick fog and pack ice to journey's end. Whilst perhaps not the dramatic picturesque end to our adventure that we might have hoped, the cluttered shore of Resolute Bay offered welcome relief from hour after hour crammed into our tiny boat, and the little isolated bay from which so many expeditions have departed on Arctic adventures makes for a fitting conclusion to our own adventure.

    Looking back over the two consecutive summers spent in the Arctic, we can reflect on a truly unique experience that will remain with us for the rest of our lives. Together we've faced an almost endless list of challenges ranging from bro-

ken tillers and failed electronics to charging bears, impenetrable ice floes and persistently adverse winds. One way or another we've bested each difficulty in turn and managed to sail, row and drag ourselves and our ½-tonne, 17ft boat over 2,000 miles through some of the most isolated seas anywhere on the globe. Travelling in such a small boat and without any engine has undoubtedly shaped and enriched the experience immeasurably. Weather and sometimes sheer fatigue have necessitated frequent landfalls, offering us the unique opportunity to walk through strikingly remote landscapes, some of which have never been visited by man. During that time we've had the privilege to watch musk ox, caribou, beluga whales and polar bears in their natural habitat.

We have now agreed the sale of the boat, the proceeds of which, along with other sponsorship, will go to our charity Toe in the Water. Whilst we were sad to finally pack her up for the last time and put the cover on, we both feel we have had our time in her, and we wish the new owner every success with her in the future. Having lived out of the boat for over ten weeks together Kev and I have developed into an effective self-reliant team, our strengths complementing each other neatly; but we could not have got past the start line without the help and encouragement of all of you at home who have supported us throughout the expedition. I cannot overestimate the importance of receiving our daily weather forecast from the Fleet Met team or the eagerness with which we downloaded support messages from the website every evening. You have all played an integral role in completing this adventure and for that you have both my and Kev's sincerest thanks. Two years from early planning, the Arctic Mariner *Expedition* is now complete and has more than surpassed our expectations.

THE NORSEBOAT 17.5

NorseBoat founder and president Kevin Jeffrey, a design engineer and entrepreneur with over 30 years of experience in the sailing industry, developed the concept for the NorseBoat in 2002. His idea was simple: a seaworthy, high-performance sailing and rowing boat with classic lines that could be sailed and rowed equally well, and used as a comfortable camp-cruiser or motorized launch.

Kevin Oliver on NorseBoat: "Arctic Mariner has been our home for six weeks, and she has been superb. She has been out in big seas…on, into and off the ice, beached on rocks, and there are no dents in her hull, just the odd scratch. Her rig is simple and robust, and she can be rowed at over 3 knots by one person. And everywhere we go, people say how pretty her lines are."

A team of Australians took another NorseBoat 17.5 from Inuvik to Gjoa Haven in the summer of 2013.

LOA	17ft 6in	5.33m
LWL	16ft 0in	4.57m
Beam	5ft 2in	1.57m
Draft (board up)	9in	0.2m
Draft (board down)	3ft 1in	0.94m
Mainsail area	105 sq ft	9.76 sq m
Optional jib area	34 sq ft	3.16 sq m
Optional drifter area	65 sq ft	6.04 sq m
Mast height	17ft 6in	5.33m
Mast weight	8kg	
Rowing stations	2	
Storage compartments	4	
Motor min/max	2hp/4hp	
CE design category	D	
Positive flotation	yes	
Max persons	6	
Loaded displacement	495kg	
Lightship displacement	240kg	
Max load (person + gear + outboard)	735kg	

1

NORSEBOAT

KIT LIST AND STOWAGE PLAN

Forward compartment (under sleeping area)
Sea Anchor / drogue
Standing water pump
Multimeter
Charts
Waterproof chart canister
Pilot book - relevant pages only
2 Satellite Telephones + Charger
Netbook for web updates
Deep Cycle Battery
Battery Tester
Life Jacket
Spare gas for life jkts
Safety Harnesses
Waterproof torches
Trip Flares
Flares Box
Rifle + ammunition
Very Pistol
Block and tackle + ice screws + karabiners
Tent
Trekking poles
Articulated crampons
Snow Stakes
Sail sewing kit
Spares Kit
Tool Box
Seals for drysuits
Climbing tape for lifelines
Black Marlow rope
Sail repair tape
Gaffer tape
First aid kit

Ready use waterproof bags
2 x GPS and power cable - from 12v battery
Video camera
Camera, battery and charger
Handheld VHF + Charger
Anemometer
Survival kits and blankets
Signal mirror / heliograph
Waterproof chart case - for current charts
Binoculars
24 hrs food + water
Handheld reverse osmosis watermaker

Underseat compartments
Waterproof log book
Passport, ticket, wallet
Sleeping bag, Gore-tex bivvi bag
Gore-tex Musto dry suit
Tevas / Crocs
Rucsac liner
Thermarest
Headtorch
Toothbrush etc
Light Gore-tex pile jkt, pertex, fleece
Shorts, Ron Hill
Thermal top, T-shirt
Underpants, socks (2)
Hat, cap
Paramo trousers
Softy suit—military
Expedition Gilet
Mitts, thin gloves, rowing gloves
Sunglasses
Lighter x 4
2 x stoves
Water tabs
Mosquito repellent
Sailing Boots
Books to read - 4 each
AA Batteries

On person
EPIRB
Strobe light
Knife

Aft Locker
Fog Horn
Buckets x 2
Anchor—5lb
Air Pump (for inflatable rollers—stored under gunwale for extra stability)
Warps
Throwing Line
Cooking pot, mugs spoons
Hanging system for cooking underway
Fuel containers
Fishing kit
Fire extinguisher (fixed under transom)

FURTHER READING

Admiralty Mariners Handbook — UK Hydrographic Office, 2012
Comprehensive guide to seamanship and key aspects of navigation.

Arctic Pilot Vol III - UK Hydrographic Office, 2012

Arctic Ocean Sailing Directions - Canadian Ice Service website

Ice Bears and Kotik - Peter Webb, Seafarer Books, 2008.
Two-handed circumnavigation of Svalbard (formerly Spitzbergen) by sail and oar.

Barrow's Boys - Fergus Fleming, Granta Books.
Early 19th century British government-sponsored Arctic exploration.

Rowing to Latitude - Jill Fredston, North Point Press, 2002
20,000 miles rowed in Arctic and sub-Arctic waters.

The Northwest Passage - Willy de Roos, Bodley Head, 1980.
Passage by yacht in the 1970s.

Ocean Crossing Wayfarer - Frank Dye, Adlard Coles, 2006.
To Iceland and Norway in a 16ft Open Dinghy.

Northabout - Jarlath Cunnane, The Collins Press, 2006.
Sailing the Northeast and Northwest passages in a steel yacht.

Polar Passage - Jeff MacInnis, Random House 1989, Ivy Books 1990.
Through the Northwest Passage by Hobie cat.

Sea, Ice and Rock - Chris Bonington and Robin Knox-Johnston — Hodder 1992.
The climber and the sailor tackle Greenland together.

Frozen in Time: The Fate of the Franklin Expedition - Owen Beattie and John Geiger, Bloomsbury 2004.

The Norwegian Blue Expedition - www.norwegianblue.co.uk.
The Northwest Passage in a steel, lifting-keel yacht.

ACKNOWLEDGEMENTS

We would like to thank the following people and organisations who donated funds to support the expedition and/or the charity *Toe in the Water*:

>The Gosling Foundation
>Robin Knox-Johnston and Clipper Ventures
>Caroline and Sam Farmer
>The Pavier's Society
>The Gino Watkins Fund,
>　　Scott Polar Research Institute at Cambridge University
>Royal Marines Corps Funds
>Royal Marines Sailing Club
>HMS Temeraire AT Funds
>Royal Navy Sports Lottery
>All the other individuals who donated to the expedition
>and the charity, listed on the website: www.arcticmariner.org.

We would also like to thank the following for goods and services provided free of charge:

Mountbatten BoatHouse	Binoculars, lifejackets and VHF
Watt to Wear	Shirts
Nite Watches	Watches
Terry Hudson of Hudson E Design	Website design and management
First Air	Air fares discount
Canadian Hydrographic Service	Charts
Rooster Sailing	Discounted clothing
NTCL	Container hire
Allen Services	Transfer of boat from Edmonton to Inuvik

We would also like to thank the following individuals who gave their time and friendship to assist us:

Lieutenant Colonel Dan Bailey RM	Rear Link 2009
Major Rich Hopkins RM	Rear Link 2010
Northwood METOCs	Weather and ice forecasts
Northwood Duty Fleet Controller Staff	Emergency Rear Link
Tom Livingstone	Organisation, hospitality - Cambridge Bay
Kevin Jeffrey	Boat builder and modifications
Brigadier Simon Knapper	DA Ottawa - Weapon sponsor, SAR coord
Major Clarence Rainey	Canadian Search and Rescue
Dr Lara Herbert	Medical supplies and advice
Mark Cox	Rowing trials and boat modifications in his workshop
Jeff Schofield	Trials
Quantico Marina	Storage and movement of boat during trials
Paul Steer - Loan Pools Bicester	Loan of stores and purchase of PLBs
Corporal Sanders RM - The Camber	Loan of stores and advice
CTCRM	Loan of Satphone and pulleys
Olaf - The Arctic Chalet, Inuvik	Loan of a truck and trailer
Kim McClement and Doug Alpen	Inuvik Coastguard
Pete and Jean Hamilton	Hospitality - Cambridge Bay
Don le Blanc	Hospitality - Gjoa Haven
Alan Johnson	Hospitality - Gjoa Haven
The Storries	Hospitality - Yellowknife

We are also indebted to those who wrote articles about us to publicise the expedition and the charity.

Most of all we would like to thank Amber and Lara, who have let us conduct our adventures and realise our dreams.